W9-BYO-799

S E C O N D · R O U N D

TEA-TIME AT THE MASTERS®
A GALLERY OF CLASSIC RECIPES

The word "Masters®" is registered in
the U.S. Patent and Trademark Office
as a trademark and service mark of
Augusta National, Inc., Augusta, Georgia.

PUBLISHED BY
THE JUNIOR LEAGUE OF AUGUSTA, GEORGIA, INC.

SECOND ROUND
TEA-TIME AT THE MASTERS®

ANOTHER CLASSIC COOKBOOK FROM
THE JUNIOR LEAGUE OF AUGUSTA, GEORGIA, INC.
CREATORS OF **TEA-TIME AT THE MASTERS**®

Copyright© by the Junior League of Augusta, Georgia, Inc. 1988
Library of Congress Card Number 88-081259
ISBN 0-9621062-0-8

Additional copies of *Second Round, Tea-Time at the Masters*® may be obtained by sending $16.95 per book plus $2.50 per book for postage and handling. (Georgia residents add $1.02 per book for sales tax.)

Junior League of Augusta, Georgia, Inc.
P.O. Box 3232
Augusta, Georgia 30904

First Printing	September, 1988	20,000 copies
Second Printing	March, 1989	20,000 copies
Third Printing	June, 1991	15,000 copies
Fourth Printing	July, 1995	5,000 copies
Fifth Printing	July, 1996	10,000 copies

Printed By
Favorite Recipes® Press
P.O. Box 305142
Nashville, Tennessee 37230

The Junior League is an organization of women committed to promoting voluntarism and to improving the community through the effective action and leadership of trained volunteers. Its purpose is exclusively educational and charitable.

Foreword

Augusta is divided into two groups of people: those who rent their houses during Masters® week and go someplace else, and those who think there *isn't* anyplace else. When you step off too-busy Washington Road onto the deep green and peaceful course, it is almost as if you've intruded on a gathering of pantomime artists. Lips are moving and hands gesturing, but what you hear is grass growing, impossibly tall pines breathing, azaleas blazing.

Here Augusta—and by now thousands of lucky visitors—again divides itself. Half the people seem to be watching something, something they can't usually see against the dazzling blue sky, and the other half seem *not* to be watching something. One reads about such tableaux in the eighteenth century (when Oglethorpe founded Augusta), in those places where couples and dandies strolled about, seeing, being seen.

Over the years one sees astonishing things. A girl in hot pants, high heels competing with the pines, misery already reddening the backs of her legs. A king, wistful and small, in corduroy pants, the throne he gave up distant in his faded blue eyes. A famous football coach wondering how to apply to his game the principles of the game Bobby Jones said was played on "a small course between the ears." A Midwestern mayor wondering how a city—and the Masters® is that—operates without pollution, muggings, visible garbage.

These fairways tend to democratize. Check the confetti of a *Sports Illustrated* double-page spread of the Sunday crowd around the eighteenth green: see how many celebrities you can spot. The Augusta National, founded partly so the great Robert T. Jones could play a round without collecting a gallery, goes along with this democratization for Masters® week. The spectator is an honored guest. There are no special "enclosures" (as, for example, at Royal Ascot) for "special" patrons, around the tees or greens. There is no attempt to gouge spectators. The only unfairness is in the number of tickets sold compared to the number of people who want them.

The site of the Augusta National was a plant nursery in the nineteenth century. Here a Belgian baron, Louis Edouard Berckmans early introduced privet and wisteria from China to American gardeners. The main building, now the clubhouse, was built in 1854, and sits at the end of an extraordinary double lane of magnolia trees, probably planted at about the same time. Bobby Jones wrote:

"I shall never forget my first visit to the property. The old manor house with its cupola and walls of masonry 2 feet thick was charming. The rare trees and shrubs of the old nursery were enchanting. But when I walked out on the green terrace under the big trees behind the house and looked down over the property, the experience was unforgettable. It seemed that this land had been lying here for years waiting for someone to lay a golf course upon it. Indeed, it even looked as though it already were a golf course, and I am sure that one standing today where I stood on this first visit, on the terrace overlooking the practice putting green, sees the property almost exactly as I saw it then. The grass of the fairways and greens is greener, of course, and some of the pines are a bit larger, but the broad expanse of the main body of the property lay at my feet just as it does now."

"Then just as...now" is an expression more and more remote in our world. How fortunate for Augusta—for golf—that this site was saved.

This book's predecessor, *Tea-Time at the Masters®*, published in 1977, has run through nine printings, selling 190,000 copies and helping to pour over $200,000 into the Augusta community. Like its forerunner, *Second-Round, Tea-Time at the Masters®* is more than a book of recipes, it is a book about how people live, a book like the Masters®: of native talent, of hard work, of practice, testing, concentration, and of real pleasure given, received.

The Junior League of Augusta has never been short of hard work, or of controversy. Long before child abuse, drug abuse and battered wives had become national political issues, the League was working on these problems, setting up shelters and clinics in dangerous peripheries. The League has worked with the elderly and the handicapped, has established clinics for speech therapy and for family planning (this in the 1930's when the League was roundly condemned from local pulpits).

The Junior League has elevated the aesthetic and architectural prospects of Augusta, too, supporting historical preservation, the beautiful old Gertrude Herbert Art Institute, and in the 1960's, the Old Government House on Telfair Street.

Turn a forlorn plant nursery, once an indigo plantation, into one of the world's great golf courses. Mobilize a group of young women whose hands are already full with children, homes and jobs, into a volunteer army to put health and excitement into the quality of life in their community. And base it all on a kind of tradition and history that helps stabilize our world. Great golf. Great food.

Starkey Flythe, Jr.

Design and Illustration: David Wesko, Wesko Design, Dallas, Texas
Agency: McBride, Dealey & Associates, Dallas, Texas
Client: Lincoln Property Company

THE MASTERS®

Each spring, champions of the game of golf gather at the Augusta National Golf Club to compete in the first of America's major tournaments, the Masters®.

Born of the dreams of legendary golfer Bobby Jones and of devoted organizer Clifford Roberts, the Augusta National Golf Club began in 1932 as an exclusive club specializing in winter play. From its inception the club was national in scope, drawing its members from across the country. They hired Dr. Alister Mackenzie of Scotland to fashion the famous eighteen holes on nearly three hundred acres of rolling hills surrounding a nineteenth century plantation house.

Two years later the founders planted the modest seed of a major golf tournament, which they called the Augusta National Invitation Tournament. Nurtured by its founders for forty years and by others since, it became the Masters® Tournament, one that has emerged as a principal event of competitive golf and the only major tournament played annually on the same course.

Year after year, the flowers of spring burst forth to adorn the course and grounds for contender and spectator alike. As if in honor of its beautiful setting, the tournament has remained dedicated to sportsmanship, a reflection of the ideals of its founders who believed in a gentlemanly game.

COOKBOOK COMMITTEE

CHAIRMAN: Julie Textor Badger
CO-CHAIRMAN: Rosemary Duvall Speer
RECIPE EDITOR AND PAST CHAIRMAN: Anne Dennis Trotter
RECIPE EDITOR: Betty Mayton Powell
PROOFING EDITOR: Lee Gostin Robertson
INDEX EDITOR: Donna Schleicher Martin
EXECUTIVE COMMITTEE LIAISON: Martha Mason Gibson
SUSTAINING ADVISORS: Marian Carter Clark
　　　　　　　　　　　　　Carolyn Watkins Magruder
　　　　　　　　　　　　　Ann Bentley Mitchell

RECIPE STAFF

Robin Reeve Allen
Mary Donna McCorvey Beman
Ginger Bond Browning
Shirley Freeman Day
Gayle Ivey Durst
Libby McKnight Engler
Nancy Futrelle Fletcher

Martha Saul Giles
Kay Weatherwax Hicks
Dale Miller Nalley
Carol Hull Palmer
Beth Russell Trotter
Avis Brown Yount

PAST COMMITTEE MEMBERS

Martha Barrett Banick
Susie Swett Bell
Ann Land Ellis
Anne Hester Devoe
Hope Hayes Maxwell

Marcia Sisterhen McIntosh
Kate Hudson Paine
Peggy Brown Roberts
Patricia McKinney Shelton
Mary Alice Green Way

Masterful Menus

Cocktail Parties

Menu 1
Artichokes "Iced" with Caviar, p. 9
Curried Chutney Dip, p. 11
Shrimp Snack, p. 31
Chicken Niçoise, p. 21
Marinated Broccoli, p. 36
Fran's Cream Cheese Brownies, p. 306
Madeleines, p. 310

Menu 2
Spinach Dipping Sauce, p. 12
Smoked Oyster Roll, p. 34
Buck's Scrumptious Marinated Shrimp, p. 31
Sherried Drumettes, p. 20
Amaretto Brownies, p. 307

Menu 3
Mexican Caviar, p. 15
Baked Brie, p. 19
Cocktail Roast with Horseradish Sauce, p. 25
Old-Fashioned Southern Rolls, p. 47
Simply Terrific Crab, p. 33
Party Vegetable Platter, p. 37
Kahlúa Dip, p. 13
Chocolate Sherry Cream Bars, p. 308

Tee-riffic Tail-Gate Menus
Menu 1
Marinated Broccoli, p. 36
Curried Tomato Soup, p. 74
or
Tomato Dill Soup, p. 75
Steak Supper Salad, p. 113
Whole Wheat Butterhorns, p. 48
Ginger Puff Cookies, p. 313

Menu 2
Buck's Scrumptious Marinated Shimp, p. 31
Toni's Rice Salad, p. 114
Spicy Carrots, p. 36
Ruth's Orange Crisps, p. 309

Menu 3
Hip's Green Beans, p. 91
Spicy Carrots, p. 36
Mustard Glazed Corned Beef, p. 164
(Served sliced on rye sandwich rolls)
Dr. Bennett's Favorite Hot Mustard, p. 22
Coconut Pound Cake, p. 245

Family Suppers
Mixed Greens with Tee-Off Dressing for Two, p. 118
Pepper Steak, p. 154
Banana Muffins, p. 64
Carrots Fettucine, p. 212
Ice Cream with Praline Sundae Sauce, p. 304

Lemon Glazed Chicken, p. 124
Spinach and Brown Rice, Greek Style, p. 228
Whole Wheat Muffins, p. 65
Pineapple Pie, p. 259

Celebration Tossed Salad, p. 104
Quick Chicken Jambalaya, p. 127
Noonie's Zucchini, p. 231
Whipped Cream Pie, p. 268

• • •

Grand Gourmet Supper Club
Garlic Soup, p. 77
Spinach Roulade with Shrimp Sauce, p. 178
Whole Wheat Butterhorns, p. 48
Poussin Roti à L'ail Au Citron, p. 139
Broccoli Mold with Lemon Velouté Sauce, p. 208
Gratin Dauphinois, p. 220
Praline Cookie Cups with Raspberry Sauce, p. 289
or
Frozen Chocolate Elegance, p. 290

• • •

Elegant Entertaining
Curried Zucchini Soup, p. 78
Artichoke Salad, p. 93
Butternut Rolls, p. 46
Pork Loin with Bourbon, p. 173
Rice-a-Rosie, p. 224
Baked Tomatoes with Asparagus Spears, p. 234
Steamed Orange Marmalade Pudding, p. 285

Graduation Dinner
Smoked Oyster Roll, p. 34
Indian Spinach Salad, p. 101
Cinnamon Muffins, p. 65
Sadie's Chicken, p. 121
White Rice
Cherry Tomato Sauté, p. 234
Surprise Delicious, p. 271

• • •

Valentine's Day Dinner
Baked Brie, p. 19
Three Lettuce Soup, p. 75
Whole Wheat Honey Bread, p. 56
Tenderloin Filets, p. 153
Sara Ann's Wild Rice Casserole, p. 225
Coeur à la Crème, p. 279

• • •

Mardi Gras Party
New Oysters Rockefeller, p. 193
Sausage En Croûte, p. 23
Brandy Slush, p. 40
Artichoke Salad, p. 93
Whole Wheat Butterhorns, p. 48
James River Shrimp Creole, p. 187
or
Jambalaya, p. 188
Fat Tuesday Cake, p. 254
After Dinner Ice Cream Shake, p. 44

Prom Dinner
Sensational Salad, p. 102
Pop-Up Bread, p. 53
Tarragon Chicken, p. 122
Swiss Potatoes, p. 221
Baked Tomatoes with Asparagus Spears, p. 234
Chocolate Mousse Cake, p. 294

• • •

Covered-Dish Hits
Angel Hair Pasta Salad, p. 98
Sour Cream Potato Salad, p. 100
Curried Chicken-Rice Salad, p. 106
Lambert's Taco Salad, p. 112
Chicken Broccoli Supper, p. 129
Marinated Turkey Breast, p. 133
Mexican Spaghetti, p. 159
Shrimp and Rice Casserole, p. 179
Shrimp and Asparagus Casserole, p. 185
Best-in-the-West Baked Beans, p. 204
Spicy Broccoli, p. 209
Mexican Macaroni, p. 219
Sour Cream Potatoes, p. 221
Better Than Hoppin' John, p. 224
Tempting Tomato Pie, p. 235
Granny's Pound Cake, p. 243
Chocolate Pound Cake, p. 244
Banana Nut Cake, p. 249
Pineapple Pie, p. 259
Pecan-Cheese Pie, p. 266
Frosted Cream Cheese Brownies, p. 305
Praline Bars, p. 309

Pasta Pleasers

Kitchen Pasta, p. 133
Chicken Primavera, p. 134
Spaghettini Bolognese, p. 159
Mexican Spaghetti, p. 159
Manicotti, p. 160
Fettucine Milano, p. 162
Veal Scallopine, p. 164
Shrimp Feta, p. 177
Simply Elegant Shrimp, p. 180
Red Bell Pepper Shrimp, p. 181
Shrimp and Sausage Verandah, p. 183
Shrimp and Asparagus Casserole, p. 185
Linguini with White Clam Sauce, p. 194
Seafood Vermouth with Pasta, p. 195
Pasta with Red Seafood Sauce, p. 196
Fettucine Alfredo, p. 219
Pasta with Artichokes and Mushrooms, p. 220

•••

Bridge Club Luncheon

Livia's Coffee Cake, p. 61
French Mint Tea, p. 41
Angel Hair Pasta Salad, p. 98
or
Gulf Coast Salad, p. 111
Orange-Kiwi Salad, p. 91
Old-Fashioned Southern Rolls, p. 47
Orange Alaska Pie, p. 269

Bridal Luncheon
Sparkling Cranberry Punch, p. 42
Carole's Easy Caesar Salad, p. 106
Chicken Primavera, p. 134
Potato Yeast Rolls, p. 45
Cold Lemon Soufflé, p. 284

• • •

The Best Brunches
(Mix and match an assortment of these
suggested recipes for a spectacular menu!)
Bellini, p. 38
Livia's Coffee Cake, p. 61
Pineapple-Nut Bran Muffins, p. 66
Jim's Biscuits, p. 49
Miss Gussie's Cinnamon Rolls, p. 58
Nannie's Waffles, p. 62
Sausage Ring, p. 61
Brunch Egg Casserole, p. 68
Overnight Egg Soufflé, p. 68
Oven Omelet, p. 69
Best-Ever Grits, p. 216
Tempting Tomato Pie, p. 235

Holiday Goodies
Microwave Peanut Brittle, p. 320
Toffee, p. 320
Bourbon Soaked Chocolate Truffles, p. 321
Peanut Butter Candy, p. 322
Crunchy Krispies, p. 311
Christmas Cookies, p. 313
Ginger Puff Cookies, p. 313
Caramel Popcorn, p. 318

• • •

Great Gifts
Cranberry Chutney, p. 17
Dr. Bennett's Favorite Hot Mustard, p. 22
Champagne Mustard, p. 23
Old South Barbeque Sauce, p. 132
Augusta's Best Strawberry Bread, p. 51
Fruited Rice Curry, p. 226
Toffee Sauce for Ice Cream, p. 303

• • •

Second Round Revision Committee:

1995/96 Tea-Time Publications Chairman:
Karin Gage Calloway

1995/96 Tea-Time Publications Vice Chairman:
Muriam Johnson Davison

1995/96 Sustaining Advisors:
Betty Mayton Powell
Lee Gostin Robertson

Committee Members:
Marian Carter Clark
Bunny Seckinger Garcia
Carolyn Watkins Magruder
Ann Bentley Mitchell
Anne Dennis Trotter

CONTENTS

The golfing history excerpts highlighted throughout this book were taken, with permission, from *The Masters® Annuals* which are published by Augusta National Golf Club.

NOTES ON NUTRITION

When choosing fruits, remember that those with edible skin and/or seeds are highest in fiber.

To get fiber from vegetables, it is not necessary to eat them raw. Cooking may reduce volume, but it does not affect fiber.

Beans and legumes (dried peas, lentils) are not only excellent sources of fiber, but are great protein sources without all the cholesterol of meat.

For excellent sources of iron in the diet, eat raisins, chili with beans, clams, oysters, liver, beans (navy, kidney, lima), spinach, dried peaches, prune juice or a bran cereal.

If you want to counteract those cancer-causing nitrates in salted or smoked meats such as salami, hot dogs and corned beef, make sure to eat something with vitamin C in it such as oranges, tomatoes, grapefruits and lemons.

Researchers say increasing the amount of Omega 3-Fatty Acids in your diet helps prevent heart disease. Good choices for Omega 3-Fatty Acids are salmon, mackerel, herring, and trout.

For those watching their weight or cholesterol level, try substituting yogurt for sour cream or Neufchâtel cheese for cream cheese in recipes.

Skim milk has half the calories of whole milk and only ⅙ the cholesterol.

If looking for a vegetable oil high in polyunsaturated fat, try 100% safflower, sunflower, or corn oil.

When milk is not a favorite, think of sardines, cheese, yogurt, oatmeal, salmon or greens to get the calcium needed in your diet.

Substitute two egg whites for one whole egg to get the same benefit without the cholesterol.

For the cholesterol conscious, margarine can be substituted for butter in most recipes.

Brown rice in place of white rice is a great way to increase fiber consumption.

Diet drinks make great substitutes in a punch or beverage recipe to cut down on calories.

Bouillon cubes are a wonderful way to season vegetables without any extra calories.

Removing the skin from chicken or cutting off the excess fat from meat before cooking can save a lot of calories.

When watching sodium consumption, try other herbs and spices in place of salt. For a saltless mixture try: 2 teaspoons garlic powder, 1 teaspoon basil, 1 teaspoon anise seed, 1 teaspoon oregano, 1 teaspoon powdered lemon rind or dry lemon juice.

Garlic powder has no salt and all the flavor of garlic salt.

APPETIZERS AND BEVERAGES

♪ ARTICHOKES "ICED" WITH CAVIAR

Yield: 8-10 servings

2   8½-ounce (drained weight) cans artichoke hearts, well drained
1   8-ounce package cream cheese, softened
1-2 tablespoons mayonnaise

2   tablespoons sour cream
½   cup finely chopped onion
2   2-ounce jars black caviar, drained
    Fresh parsley to garnish

• Cut artichokes into small pieces. Drain again.
• Mound artichokes in center of large serving platter.
• Combine cream cheese, mayonnaise, sour cream and onion. Beat until smooth.
• "Ice" artichokes with cream cheese mixture.
• Sprinkle caviar on top.
• Garnish with parsley.
• Serve with butter-flavored crackers.

This spectacular hors d'oeuvre is a Cookbook Committee favorite.

SMOKED SALMON DIP

Yield: 2 cups

1   4-ounce package smoked salmon
¼   cup chopped onion
1   8-ounce package cream cheese, softened
½   teaspoon fresh lemon juice

¼   teaspoon pepper
1   tablespoon milk
1   teaspoon sliced scallion
3   teaspoons red caviar, drained and divided
    Scallion greens to garnish

• Combine salmon, onion, cream cheese, lemon juice, pepper, milk and scallion in blender or food processor. Process until smooth.
• Gently fold in 2 teaspoons caviar.
• Cover. Refrigerate at least 2 hours. (May be prepared 2 days before serving.) Garnish with remaining 1 teaspoon caviar and scallion greens.
• Serve with crackers.

An elegant appetizer to begin an evening.

KAREN'S DIP

Yield: 12-14 servings

2 8-ounce packages cream
cheese, room temperature
½ cup mayonnaise
⅓ cup grated Parmesan cheese
¼ cup chopped green onion

10 slices bacon, cooked and
crumbled
1 5-ounce jar green olives,
drained and chopped
2-3 drops Tabasco

• Combine all ingredients. Blend well. Chill.
• Serve as a dip or form into a ball.
• Serve with wheat crackers.

DILL SAUCE

Yield: 1 quart

1 pint mayonnaise
1 pint sour cream
3 tablespoons minced fresh onion
3 tablespoons McCormick's Bon
Appetit Seasoning

3 tablespoons dill weed
3 tablespoons chopped fresh
parsley
Fresh vegetables

• Combine all ingredients and blend well.
• Refrigerate until ready to serve.
• Serve with assorted fresh vegetables.

Also delicious as a spread with smoked salmon on crackers.

SHRIMP DIP

Yield: 2 cups

1 3-ounce package cream
cheese, softened
1 cup sour cream
2 teaspoons fresh lemon juice
1 0.7-ounce package Italian salad
dressing mix

½ cup finely chopped cooked
shrimp or 1 4¼-ounce can
shrimp, drained and chopped

• Combine cream cheese and sour cream. Beat well.
• Add remaining ingredients. Blend well.
• Cover and chill at least one hour before serving.
• Serve with wheat crackers.

CURRIED CHUTNEY DIP

Yield: 30-40 servings

3 8-ounce packages cream
   cheese, softened
1 10-ounce jar Bengal hot
   chutney, chopped
1 10-ounce jar mango chutney,
   chopped
1 5¼-ounce can crushed
   pineapple, drained
½ 4-ounce box crystallized ginger,
   finely chopped (may be softened
   in pineapple juice)

3 tablespoons curry powder
1 tablespoon garlic powder
1 11½-ounce can cashew nuts,
   chopped
1 8-ounce carton sour cream
   King-size Fritos or crackers

• Beat cream cheese until smooth.
• Add chutneys, pineapple, ginger, curry powder and garlic powder. Mix well.
• Just before serving, stir in nuts and sour cream.
• Serve with king-size Fritos or crackers.

A delightful and unique dip.

LIBBY'S SURPRISE

Yield: 2 cups

1 2-ounce jar black caviar, drained
4 hard-cooked eggs, chopped
1 6-ounce jar marinated artichoke
   hearts, drained and chopped
1 bunch green onions, chopped

6 tablespoons mayonnaise
Parsley and carrot flowers to
garnish
Melba rounds

• Pour caviar into a sieve and allow to drain. (This eliminates bleeding.)
• Layer ½ the eggs, artichokes, caviar, onions and mayonnaise in a small
  glass bowl.
• Repeat layers.
• Cover with plastic wrap.
• Chill 24 hours.
• Unmold onto tray. Garnish with parsley and carrot flowers.
• Serve with melba rounds.

Appealing to the eye, as well as to the palate.

SPINACH DIPPING SAUCE

Yield: 10 servings

2-3 jalapeño peppers, chopped, reserving some seeds
1 medium onion, chopped
2 tablespoons vegetable oil
1 4-ounce can chopped green chilies or 2 hot green chilies, seeded and chopped
2 tomatoes, peeled, seeded and chopped
1 10-ounce package frozen chopped spinach, thawed and squeezed dry
1½ tablespoons red wine vinegar
1 8-ounce package cream cheese, softened
2½ cups grated Monterey Jack cheese
1 cup half and half
Salt and pepper to taste
Paprika

- In a small skillet, sauté jalapeño peppers, seeds, and onion in oil 4 minutes or until soft.
- Add green chilies and tomatoes. Cook, stirring constantly, for 2 minutes. Remove from heat. Transfer to mixing bowl.
- Stir in spinach, vinegar, cream cheese, Monterey Jack cheese, half and half, salt and pepper.
- Pour into a buttered 10-inch round baking dish. Sprinkle with paprika.
- Bake at 400° for 20-25 minutes, or until hot and bubbly.
- Serve with tortilla chips.

Guests will love this pungent dip.

CHILE CON QUESO

Yield: 20 servings

1 pound Velveeta cheese
1 8-ounce package grated Cheddar or Mozzarella cheese
1 10-ounce can Ro-Tel diced tomatoes and green chilies
4 tablespoons Pace® picante sauce (mild or hot)

- Melt cheeses with other ingredients in double boiler or crock pot and heat thoroughly.
- Transfer to serving bowl.
- Serve warm with tortilla chips.

A great hit with men.

KAHLÚA DIP

Yield: 1 cup

1 8-ounce package cream cheese, softened	2 tablespoons chopped almonds, toasted
¼ cup Kahlúa	Fresh strawberries, pineapple
2 tablespoons evaporated milk	spears or apple wedges
2 tablespoons sugar	

• Beat cream cheese until smooth.
• Slowly add Kahlúa, milk and sugar, beating well.
• Refrigerate until ready to serve.
• Top with almonds. Serve with fresh strawberries, pineapple spears, or apple wedges.

Thin, sweet cookies provide a delicious alternative to fruit.

For a quick dip for strawberries, combine 1 7-ounce jar marshmallow cream and 1 8-ounce package softened cream cheese. Whip well and serve.

SPICY FIESTA DIP

Yield: 20-25 servings

½ pound ground beef	1 cup green chilies, chopped
½ pound Velveeta cheese	1 tomato, chopped
½ pound sharp Cheddar cheese	3 dashes Tabasco
1 roll garlic cheese	Tortilla chips
1 egg, beaten	

• Crumble ground beef in large heavy skillet. Brown. Drain well.
• Lower temperature. Add all cheeses.
• Cook slowly and stir until cheeses are melted.
• Remove from heat.
• Add egg. Stir well. (Recipe may be frozen at this point.)
• Bake at 275° until bubbly.
• Stir in chilies, tomato and Tabasco.
• Serve hot in a chafing dish with tortilla chips.

PARTY SANDWICH FILLING

Yield: 20 servings

1 carrot	2 tablespoons water
1 medium green pepper	¾ cup mayonnaise
1 cucumber, peeled and seeded	1 teaspoon seasoned salt
1 small onion	Pepper to taste
2 tomatoes, peeled and seeded	Very thinly sliced bread with
1 envelope unflavored gelatin	crust removed

- In food processor, coarsely chop vegetables with several on/off motions. Be careful not to overprocess.
- Drain vegetables well, reserving ¼ cup liquid. (Vegetables may be chopped by hand and ¼ cup water used in place of vegetable liquid.) May be necessary to squeeze vegetables with a towel to ensure that all liquid is removed.
- Dissolve gelatin in ¼ cup vegetable liquid and water. Heat to dissolve.
- Combine gelatin mixture with vegetables.
- Add mayonnaise, seasoned salt and pepper.
- Refrigerate several hours or until set.
- Cut bread into bite-size pieces. Spread with filling.

PITA PIZZAS

Yield: 72 appetizers

1 pound Italian sausage, mild or hot	1 pound Mozzarella cheese, shredded
1 package (6 rounds) Pita bread	1 2-ounce package thinly sliced pepperoni
1 cup butter, softened	
1 6-ounce can tomato paste	
1 6-ounce can sliced mushrooms, finely chopped	

- Crumble sausage in skillet and brown. Drain.
- Cut Pita bread with scissors to form two complete rounds.
- Spread inner side of each round with butter.
- Spread layer of tomato paste.
- Cut into 6 triangles.
- Cover each triangle with sausage, chopped mushrooms and cheese.
- Top with a slice of pepperoni.
- Bake at 350° for 10 minutes or until crisp. Pizzas may be frozen after preparation and baked when ready to serve.

MEXICAN CAVIAR

Yield: 4-6 servings

2   4-ounce cans chopped black olives, drained
1   4-ounce can chopped green chilies, drained
3   tablespoons vegetable oil
2   tablespoons red wine vinegar
1   green onion, chopped
2-3 fresh tomatoes, chopped
¼   teaspoon garlic powder, or to taste
Salt to taste
⅛   teaspoon Tabasco, or to taste

• Combine all ingredients.
• Serve with tortilla chips.

Canned tomato wedges may be substituted when fresh tomatoes are not available.

CHUTNEY ROLL

Yield: 10-12 servings

1   8-ounce package cream cheese, softened
½   cup chutney, finely chopped
½   cup chopped almonds, toasted
1   tablespoon curry powder
½   teaspoon dry mustard
½   cup sliced almonds

• Beat cream cheese until smooth.
• Add chutney, chopped almonds, curry powder and mustard. Beat well.
• Shape cheese mixture into a log.
• Wrap in waxed paper and chill at least 1 hour.
• Roll log in sliced almonds. Chill several hours or overnight.
• Serve with assorted crackers.

Makes a nice dessert cheese when served with thin ginger snaps.

VIDALIA ONION SPREAD

Yield: 6-8 servings

1 cup coarsely chopped Vidalia onions
1 cup Hellmann's mayonnaise
1 cup grated Cheddar cheese
Paprika

• Combine onions, mayonnaise and cheese.
• Pour into 1-quart baking dish.
• Sprinkle with paprika.
• Bake at 350° for 25 minutes. Blot with paper towel to remove excess oil.
• Serve hot with Triscuits.

CHEESE TRIANGLES

Yield: 7½ dozen

16 ounces Phyllo pastry
½ cup butter, melted
2 cups grated Muenster cheese
2 3-ounce packages cream cheese, softened

¼ cup cottage cheese
1 egg
½ teaspoon minced onion

- Allow Phyllo to thaw in refrigerator 24 hours.
- Brush 2 layers of Phyllo with butter. Stack. Cut into 2-inch strips.
- Combine cheese, cream cheese, cottage cheese, egg and onion.
- Place 2 teaspoons cheese mixture on each strip. Roll in triangular shape, like a flag.
- Continue with remaining pastry and cheese mixture.
- Brush each triangle with butter.
- Bake on ungreased cookie sheet at 400° for 15-20 minutes or until golden brown.

This flaky appetizer melts in your mouth.

FAN'S CHEESE STRAWS

Yield: 11-12 dozen

2 scant cups sifted all-purpose flour
1 teaspoon salt
1 teaspoon baking soda

1-2 teaspoons cayenne pepper
1 pound extra sharp Cheddar cheese, grated
½ cup butter, softened

- Sift together flour, salt, baking soda and cayenne pepper. Add to grated cheese. Stir.
- Add butter. Blend well.
- Cover tightly with plastic wrap. Allow to sit on counter 24 hours.
- Knead well. Cover tightly again and allow to sit another 24 hours.
- Press dough through a cookie press into desired shape onto greased baking sheet.
- Bake at 400° for 8-10 minutes. Store in airtight container.

The cheese straw that EVERYBODY loves.

CURRIED CHEESE WITH CRANBERRY CHUTNEY

Yield: 6-8 servings

1 8-ounce package cream cheese	¼ teaspoon salt
1½ cups grated sharp Cheddar cheese	1 cup CRANBERRY CHUTNEY, or enough to cover top
2 tablespoons dry sherry	Green onions, thinly sliced
¾ teaspoon curry powder	

• Blend together cream cheese, Cheddar cheese, sherry, curry powder and salt.
• Shape into a ½-inch thick circle on serving platter.
• Spread chutney over entire surface.
• Sprinkle with onions.
• Serve with crackers.

An unusual combination of flavors with a beautiful red color.

CRANBERRY CHUTNEY

Nelson Danish
Augusta, Georgia
Yield: 3½ cups

2 cups fresh cranberries	⅛ teaspoon salt
½ cup water	1 8-ounce can crushed pineapple (in its own juice)
½ cup raisins	
1 small onion, chopped	¼ cup chopped celery
1 scant cup sugar	¼ cup chopped pecans or walnuts
¼ teaspoon ginger	½ cup peeled and chopped apple
¼ teaspoon cinnamon	1-2 tablespoons lemon juice
⅛ teaspoon ground allspice	

• Combine cranberries, water, raisins, onion, sugar, ginger, cinnamon, allspice and salt in Dutch oven.
• Cook, uncovered, over medium heat 15 minutes or until cranberry skins pop.
• Stir in pineapple and juice, celery, pecans and apples which have been sprinkled with lemon juice.
• Reduce heat to low. Cook, uncovered, 30 minutes, stirring frequently.
• Serve warm or chilled.

Excellent served with poultry, game or our CURRIED SHRIMP.

BRANDY CHEDDAR MOLD

Yield: 18 servings

1 8-ounce package cream cheese	1 teaspoon Tabasco
8 ounces New York extra sharp Cheddar cheese, grated	¼ teaspoon salt
	¼ teaspoon white pepper
3 tablespoons finely chopped green onion	¼ teaspoon black pepper
	¼ cup brandy
1 tablespoon Worcestershire sauce	½ cup chopped pecans
	¼ cup chopped fresh parsley

- Cream cheeses together.
- Mix in onion, Worcestershire sauce, Tabasco, salt, peppers and brandy.
- Pour into a 2-cup mold lined with plastic wrap. Refrigerate until firm.
- Turn out onto serving plate. Top with pecans and parsley.
- Serve with wheat crackers.

A zippy rendition of the too-tired cheese ball.

HOT CHEESE PUFFS

Yield: 8-10 servings

1 8-ounce package cream cheese, softened	2 tablespoons chopped chives
	¼ teaspoon cayenne pepper
1½ teaspoons grated onion	¼ cup grated Parmesan cheese
½ cup mayonnaise	1 small loaf thinly sliced bread

- In food processor or bowl, combine all ingredients except bread. Blend well. (This mixture may be prepared several days ahead and refrigerated.)
- Cut bread into 1½-inch rounds with a small biscuit cutter.
- Spread each round with cheese mixture. (Rounds may be frozen on a baking sheet at this point and stored in an airtight container. They may be baked directly from freezer without thawing.)
- Bake at 350° for 15 minutes. Serve hot from oven.

An excellent quick or do-ahead appetizer.

BAKED BRIE

Yield: 8-10 servings

½ cup coarsely chopped pecans 1 1-pound wheel baby Brie cheese
1 tablespoon butter or margarine, ¼ cup dark brown sugar
  melted

• Toast pecans in butter at 300° for 10 minutes, stirring occasionally.
• Place Brie in small quiche or pie pan.
• Cover top of Brie with brown sugar.
• Sprinkle with toasted pecans.
• Increase oven temperature to 325°. Bake Brie for 15 minutes.
• Serve with bland wafers or crackers.

An excellent hot cheese.

BAKED BRIE 'N CRUST

Betty Gaines
Augusta, Georgia
Yield: 20-25 servings

1 2-pound round sourdough bread ¾ cup butter, softened
1 1-pound wheel baby Brie with 1 2-ounce package slivered
  mushrooms   almonds

• Scoop out center of bread so that Brie will fit inside. Reserve top of bread.
• Spread inside of bread with butter.
• Place Brie in bread.
• Sprinkle almonds on Brie.
• Cover with bread top.
• Cover with aluminum foil.
• Bake at 375° for 30-45 minutes, or until cheese has melted.
• Uncover. Remove top.
• Continue cooking until almonds are toasted.

Bread top can be cubed, brushed with melted butter and baked at 250° until crisp. Spread cubes with Baked Brie.

PECAN CHICKEN STRIPS

Yield: 8-10 servings

¾-1 pound chicken breasts,
    skinned and boned
1 egg white, lightly beaten
2 tablespoons sherry or white wine

1 teaspoon salt
2 tablespoons cornstarch
¼ pound pecans, finely chopped
  Oil

- Cut chicken into strips.
- Combine egg white, sherry, salt and cornstarch.
- Add chicken. Soak at least 15 minutes.
- Coat chicken with pecans.
- Sauté in oil until golden brown. Do not overcook.

Serve hot with our APRICOT DIPPING SAUCE or a honey mustard.

SHERRIED DRUMETTES

Yield: 10 servings

2 pounds chicken wings,
    disjointed and tips discarded
¼ cup vinegar
½ cup soy sauce

½ cup sherry
3 teaspoons Tabasco
½ teaspoon seasoned salt
  Pepper to taste

- Arrange drumettes in 9x13-inch baking dish.
- Combine vinegar, soy sauce, sherry and Tabasco. Pour over chicken.
  Marinate several hours.
- Remove from marinade.
- Bake chicken in baking dish at 300° for 1 hour. Turn, bake 1 additional
  hour.
- Sprinkle both sides of drumettes with seasoned salt and pepper.
- Serve warm or at room temperature with Apricot Dipping Sauce.

Apricot Dipping Sauce:
8 ounces apricot jam

2 tablespoons cider vinegar

- In saucepan, slowly warm jam.
- Stir in vinegar.

The Apricot Sauce gives an unusual flavor to this old favorite.

FIVE SPICE WINGS

Yield: 20-30 servings

⅔ cup soy sauce
½ cup honey
2 tablespoons vegetable oil
2 cloves garlic, minced

2 teaspoons Chinese Five Spice powder
2½ pounds chicken wings, disjointed and tips discarded

• Combine soy sauce, honey, oil, garlic and Five Spice powder.
• Pour over chicken. Marinate 4 hours, turning occasionally.
• Remove wings to broiler rack.
• Bake at 375° for 45 minutes, turning and basting every 15 minutes.

An easy chicken appetizer with a pungent flavor.

CHICKEN NIÇOISE

Yield: 10-12 servings

4 chicken breast halves, cooked, boned and skinned
1 5¾-ounce (drained weight) can pitted black olives, drained
1 8½-ounce (drained weight) can artichoke hearts, drained and halved
1 pound fresh mushrooms, sliced

⅓ cup red wine vinegar
⅓ cup Dijon mustard
Dash salt
Dash cracked pepper
½ teaspoon tarragon
½ teaspoon oregano
¾ cup virgin olive oil

• Cut chicken into large chunks. Combine with olives, artichoke hearts and mushrooms. Set aside.
• Combine vinegar, mustard, salt, pepper, tarragon and oregano. Whisk in olive oil until well blended.
• Pour dressing over chicken mixture. Stir gently to coat well.
• Chill several hours. Serve with toothpicks.

1½ pounds medium cooked and cleaned shrimp may be substituted for chicken. May also use a combination of chicken and shrimp.

DIDDY'S SUMMER SAUSAGE

Yield: 5 pounds

5   pounds lean ground beef
9   tablespoons Morton's Tender Quick Salt
2½ teaspoons mustard seed
2½ teaspoons coarsely ground pepper
1   teaspoon Lawry's seasoned salt
2   tablespoons Liquid Smoke
2   teaspoons garlic powder
2   teaspoons onion salt

• Sprinkle meat with all seasonings. Knead well. Refrigerate overnight.
• The next day, knead again. Refrigerate overnight.
• The next day, knead again. Shape into four rolls.
• Place on rack of broiler pan. Bake at 150° for 10 hours, turning after 5 hours.
• Serve with DR. BENNETT'S FAVORITE HOT MUSTARD and wedges of cheese.

Will keep in refrigerator for several weeks.

DR. BENNETT'S FAVORITE HOT MUSTARD

Yield: 3 pints

6   ounces Colman's dry mustard
⅛   teaspoon cayenne pepper
¼   teaspoon white pepper
¼   teaspoon black pepper
2   cups sugar
1½ cups vinegar
1   teaspoon salt
3   eggs
½   cup butter, cut into pieces

• Combine mustard and peppers. Add enough water to make a thick paste. Set aside.
• In double boiler, combine sugar, vinegar and salt. Heat over simmering water until sugar is dissolved.
• Remove from heat. Slowly add mustard paste one tablespoon at a time.
• In separate bowl, beat eggs well.
• Add mustard sauce, one tablespoon at a time, to eggs.
• Return mixture to double boiler. Bring to a boil.
• Remove from heat. Add butter, stirring until melted and smooth.
• Cool completely. Refrigerate.

*Excellent hot mustard. Will keep for months in the refrigerator—
if it lasts that long.*

CHAMPAGNE MUSTARD

Yield: 1 quart

15 tablespoons Colman's dry mustard	1 ½ teaspoons pepper
1 ½ cups sugar	6 eggs, beaten
3 tablespoons all-purpose flour	¾ cup vinegar
1 ½ teaspoons salt	¾ cup champagne
	3 tablespoons butter

• Combine mustard, sugar, flour, salt and pepper in double boiler.
• Add eggs, vinegar and champagne.
• Blend together thoroughly with a wire whisk.
• Cook over simmering water, stirring occasionally, until mixture is thickened.
• Add butter and stir until melted.
• Refrigerate until ready to serve. Keeps indefinitely.

This makes a wonderful accompaniment for cocktail meats.
Pour a generous amount of champagne mustard over a wedge of Saga cheese. Serve with bland crackers.

SAUSAGE EN CROÛTE

Yield: 8-10 servings

1 sheet frozen puff pastry	1 large tomato, diced
1 pound sausage	1 cup shredded Swiss cheese
½ cup chopped onion	3 tablespoons chopped parsley
⅓ cup chopped green pepper	

• Thaw puff pastry 20 minutes.
• Brown sausage.
• Add onion and green pepper. Cook until tender.
• Remove from heat and drain.
• Add tomato, cheese and parsley.
• Unfold and roll pastry on lightly floured board to a 14x10-inch rectangle.
• Spread sausage mixture on pastry. Roll up lengthwise, jelly-roll fashion. Pinch edges to seal.
• Form into circle and pinch ends together.
• Transfer to broiler pan.
• Cut ⅔ way through roll at 1 ½-inch intervals and turn pieces with cut side showing.
• Bake at 425° for 20 minutes or until golden brown.

A winner every time!

LIVER PATÉ

Yield: 1 loaf

½	pound sweet Italian sausage, skinned	½	teaspoon pepper
1	pound chicken livers	¼	teaspoon nutmeg
1	small onion, chopped	11-12	ounces cream cheese, softened
2	tablespoons bourbon	2	tablespoons butter, softened
⅓	cup whipping cream		Chopped fresh parsley to
1	teaspoon salt		garnish

- Grease an 8x4x2-inch loaf pan or mold. Line with waxed paper or plastic wrap.
- Cook sausage, but do not brown. Remove from pan. Drain and reserve drippings.
- Sauté chicken livers in sausage drippings until livers are no longer pink. Do not allow to overcook. Remove from pan.
- Combine onion and bourbon in blender or food processor. Purée until smooth.
- Add livers and sausage, alternating with cream. Purée until smooth.
- Add salt, pepper and nutmeg.
- Pour mixture into prepared mold. Cover and chill overnight.
- Before serving, unmold paté onto serving tray. Peel away waxed paper or plastic wrap.
- Combine cream cheese and butter. Beat until smooth.
- Spread cream cheese frosting on top and sides of paté.
- Garnish with parsley. Refrigerate until ready to serve.
- Serve with saltine crackers.

POOR MAN'S LIVER PATÉ

Yield: 10-20 servings

1	8-ounce roll liverwurst, room temperature	1	tablespoon butter, melted
1	3-ounce package cream cheese, room temperature	¼	teaspoon salt
		¼	teaspoon pepper
4	teaspoons mayonnaise		Pinch cayenne pepper
⅓	cup whipping cream		Pinch nutmeg
1	tablespoon Worcestershire sauce	1	tablespoon dry vermouth
		½	teaspoon curry powder

- Combine all ingredients. Mix well.
- Serve at room temperature with butter-flavored crackers.

COCKTAIL ROAST WITH HORSERADISH SAUCE

Yield: 50 servings

1 10-12 pound sirloin tip or bottom round roast

1 4-ounce jar Jane's Krazy Mixed-Up Salt

• Trim all fat from meat.
• Rub roast with salt.
• Place in shallow roasting pan.
• Cook at 500° for 5 minutes per pound, not to exceed 55 minutes total cooking time.
• Turn oven off and allow roast to stand in oven 2 hours.
• Cool before slicing.
• Serve with assorted breads and rolls and Horseradish Sauce.

Horseradish Sauce:
1 8-ounce package cream cheese, softened

4 tablespoons horseradish
2 tablespoons vinegar

• Combine all ingredients and beat until smooth.
• Refrigerate until ready to serve.

Roast may be cooked several days in advance. Allow it to return to room temperature before slicing.

SUGARED BACON STRIPS

Winnie and Arnold Palmer
4 time Masters' Champion
Yield: 15-20 servings

½-1 pound bacon, room temperature

1 cup brown sugar

• Roll, pat or shake raw bacon in brown sugar.
• Place bacon strips in a flat pan with sides.
• Bake at 300° until bacon is well done, about 30-40 minutes. Remove with tongs and drain on brown paper bags.
• As it cools, bacon will get hard and can be broken into smaller pieces or served whole.

25

ARTICHOKE TACO DIP

Yield: 20-25 appetizers

1 8½-ounce (drained weight) can artichoke hearts, drained and chopped
1 6½-ounce jar marinated artichoke hearts, drained and chopped

1 4-ounce can chopped green chilies, drained
2 cups shredded sharp Cheddar cheese
Mayonnaise

• Combine artichoke hearts. Place in 2-quart baking dish.
• Sprinkle with chilies.
• Cover with cheese.
• Spoon teaspoons of mayonnaise on top.
• Bake, uncovered, at 350° for 10-15 minutes or until cheese is melted.
• Serve with corn chips.

A snap to fix for unexpected company.

TEX-MEX TASTER

Yield: 15-20 servings

3 ripe avocados
2 tablespoons lemon juice
1 bunch green onions, finely chopped
1 16-ounce carton sour cream
1 8-ounce jar picante sauce, hot or mild

2 ripe tomatoes, peeled and chopped
2 small green peppers, chopped
8 ounces Monterey Jack cheese, grated
Tortilla chips

• Peel and mash avocados.
• Add lemon juice. Mix well.
• Layer all ingredients in following order: avocado, onions, sour cream, picante sauce, tomatoes, peppers and cheese.
• Chill and serve with tortilla chips.

This light, delicious appetizer will be a hit at the 19th hole.

NACHOS CASSEROLE

Maria Floyd
wife of Raymond Floyd,
1976 Masters® Champion
Yield: 18-20 servings

½ pound lean ground beef
½ pound Chorizo (Mexican sausage) or hot Italian sausage
1 large onion, finely chopped
½ teaspoon Tabasco
Salt
2 1-pound cans refried beans
1 4-ounce can whole green chilies, rinsed, seeded, deveined and chopped, or 6 ounces fresh Anaheim or poblano chilies, roasted, peeled, seeded, deveined and chopped

6 ounces Monterey Jack cheese, shredded
6 ounces sharp Cheddar cheese, shredded
2 cups mild taco sauce
½ cup chopped scallions
¾ cup sliced pitted ripe olives
2 cups Guacamole
1 cup sour cream
Tortilla chips, preferably homemade

- In large skillet, crumble ground beef and sausage.
- Add onion and cook, stirring, until meat is lightly browned and onion is softened, about 5 minutes. Pour off any fat and season with Tabasco and salt to taste. Set aside to cool.
- Spread refried beans in large (4 quart) shallow baking dish. Spread meat on top. Sprinkle chilies over meat.
- Toss together cheeses and arrange on top. Drizzle taco sauce over all, in a decorative pattern. (The recipe may be made ahead to this point. Cover and refrigerate up to 24 hours. Let return to room temperature before baking.)
- Bake at 350° for 20-30 minutes or until hot and bubbly.
- Remove from oven and immediately sprinkle with the chopped scallions and sliced olives. Mound the Guacamole in the center.
- Top with sour cream, leaving some Guacamole showing around the edges. Serve with tortilla chips for dipping.

Guacamole:
Yield: 2 cups

2 ripe avocados, coarsely mashed
1 medium tomato, peeled, seeded and coarsely chopped

1 tablespoon finely chopped onion
1 4-ounce can whole green chilies, rinsed and finely chopped

- Combine all ingredients in a bowl. Stir to blend well.

Serve with MARVELOUS MARGARITAS as the prelude to a Mexican dinner.

HENRI'S SEAFOOD SAUCE

Yield: 1½ cups

1 tablespoon Creole mustard	½ teaspoon salt
1 cup mayonnaise	2 tablespoons cider vinegar
1 tablespoon olive oil	Dash Tabasco
1 clove garlic, minced	Pepper to taste
2 tablespoons grated onion	

• Combine all sauce ingredients. Chill overnight.

A delicious seafood sauce. May be served with shrimp,
oysters, crab or lobster.

SHRIMP SOUFFLÉ

Yield: 8 cups

3 8-ounce packages cream cheese, softened	1 large tomato, finely chopped
1 16-ounce carton small-curd cottage cheese	1 large onion, finely chopped
2 7-ounce cans shrimp, drained and mashed	2-3 jalapeños, finely chopped
2½-3 pounds shrimp, cooked and cut into chunks	1½ teaspoons salt
	Tabasco to taste
	Tortilla or corn chips

• Combine cream cheese and cottage cheese. Blend until smooth.
• Add shrimp, tomato, onion, jalapeños, salt and Tabasco.
• Heat in double boiler, stirring frequently. Be careful not to overheat or
  mixture will get too soft.
• Serve in chafing dish with chips for dipping.

A marvelous hors d'oeuvre for a crowd.

DEVILED SHRIMP

Vera Stewart
Vera Stewart Occasions
Augusta, Georgia
Yield: 1 5-cup mold

3 pounds medium shrimp,
  cooked, peeled and deveined
2 8-ounce packages cream
  cheese, softened
1 medium onion, grated
1 tablespoon Tabasco
1 tablespoon Durkee Famous
  Sauce

4 teaspoons pickle relish,
  finely chopped
¼ cup cocktail sauce with
  horseradish
1 teaspoon salt, or to taste
  Pepper to taste

• Cut each shrimp into thirds. Set aside.
• Combine cream cheese, onion, Tabasco, Durkee Sauce, relish and cocktail
  sauce. Mix well.
• Fold in shrimp. Add salt and pepper.
• Pour into a 5-cup fish mold. Refrigerate until firm.
• Unmold onto platter lined with red-leaf lettuce.
• Serve with crackers.

Watch this disappear at a cocktail party!

SAUTÉED SHRIMP

Yield: 8-10 servings

2 tablespoons butter
2 pounds shrimp, peeled and
  deveined
1 tablespoon Greek seasoning

1 teaspoon garlic powder
1 teaspoon oregano
6 tablespoons fresh lemon juice

• Melt butter over medium-high heat in heavy skillet. Add shrimp.
• Sprinkle shrimp with seasonings and stir. Add lemon juice.
• Sauté 5-6 minutes. Drain.
• Serve immediately.

An easy, spicy beginning to a summer supper.

MARINATED SHRIMP

Yield: 25 servings

5	pounds shrimp, cooked, peeled and deveined	2	cups vegetable oil
4	medium onions, thinly sliced	1	10-ounce bottle Durkee Famous Sauce
2-3	bay leaves	1	tablespoon sugar
1	cup tarragon vinegar	1	teaspoon salt

• Layer shrimp, onions and bay leaves in large glass dish.
• Combine vinegar, oil, Durkee Sauce, sugar and salt.
• Pour over shrimp, stirring gently to coat.
• Chill 24 hours or up to 2 days.
• To serve, drain marinade from shrimp and remove bay leaves.
• Transfer shrimp to serving bowl.

SHRIMP-STUFFED CELERY

Yield: 2 cups

	Celery	½	teaspoon salt
1	8-ounce package cream cheese, softened	2	teaspoons mayonnaise
1	teaspoon Worcestershire sauce	½	pound shrimp, cooked, peeled and deveined
1	small onion, grated		

• Clean celery and chill in ice water until crisp.
• Combine cream cheese, Worcestershire sauce, onion, salt and mayonnaise. Blend well.
• Mash shrimp. Add to cream cheese mixture.
• Cut celery into 4-inch lengths. Stuff with shrimp mixture.
• Refrigerate until ready to serve.

Take this on your next outing at the river.

SHRIMP SNACK

Betty Gaines
Augusta, Georgia
Yield: 40 servings

10 pounds medium or large
   shrimp, cooked, peeled and
   deveined
1 10-ounce bottle Durkee
   Famous Sauce
½ cup ketchup
2 cups mayonnaise
1 8-ounce jar Grey Poupon or
   other Dijon mustard

1 3½-ounce bottle capers,
   drained
2 cups chopped celery
1 cup chopped green onions
8 teaspoons Worcestershire
   sauce
   Juice of 6 lemons or more, if
   desired

- Combine all ingredients.
- Refrigerate 24 hours.
- Serve with toothpicks.

An Augusta favorite!

BUCK'S SCRUMPTIOUS MARINATED SHRIMP

Yield: 30 servings

2 cups vegetable oil
1 cup olive oil
2 cups vinegar
1 teaspoon pepper
2 tablespoons salt

3 teaspoons garlic powder
1½ tablespoons paprika
1 large onion, thinly sliced
5 pounds fresh shrimp, cooked
   peeled and deveined

- Combine vegetable and olive oil, vinegar, pepper, salt, garlic powder and
  paprika.
- Add onion and shrimp. Toss well.
- Refrigerate 24 hours.
- Drain just before serving. Serve with toothpicks.

The name says it all.

HOT CRABMEAT

Yield: 30 servings

3 8-ounce packages Philadelphia cream cheese
2 6½-ounce cans white crabmeat
2 cloves garlic, minced
½ cup mayonnaise
2 tablespoons Pommery mustard

¼ cup sherry
1 tablespoon grated onion
1 teaspoon Lawry's seasoned salt
1 teaspoon Tabasco
2 tablespoons chives

• Heat all ingredients together in double boiler until well blended and cheese is melted.
• Serve in chafing dish with melba rounds. (To enhance flavor, refrigerate overnight before serving.)

HOT CRABMEAT CANAPÉS

Yield: 3 dozen rounds

½ pound crabmeat
6 tablespoons mayonnaise
½ teaspoon salt
½ teaspoon MSG
1 tablespoon grated onion

1 teaspoon fresh lemon juice
½ cup freshly grated Parmesan cheese
Small rounds of white bread
Paprika

• Combine crabmeat, mayonnaise, salt, MSG, onion, lemon juice and cheese. Mix well.
• Spread on bread rounds. Sprinkle with paprika.
• Broil until bubbly and lightly browned.

These are wonderful when served piping hot.

SIMPLY TERRIFIC CRAB

Yield: 16-20 servings

1 medium onion, finely chopped
1 cup chopped celery
1 cup chopped green pepper
½ cup margarine
2 pounds fresh crabmeat
2 cups Hellmann's mayonnaise

2 cups soft bread crumbs
2 teaspoons fresh lemon juice
2 teaspoons Worcestershire sauce
1 teaspoon salt
¼ teaspoon pepper
2 cups toasted bread crumbs

• Sauté onion, celery and green pepper in margarine.
• Combine with crab, mayonnaise, soft bread crumbs, lemon juice, Worcestershire sauce, salt and pepper.
• Pour into 1-quart baking dish and top with toasted bread crumbs.
• Bake, uncovered, at 375° for 30 minutes.

Serve with toasted pita triangles or round buttery crackers.

BACON-WRAPPED SCALLOPS

Yield: 36 appetizers

1 cup all-purpose flour
1 tablespoon salt
1 tablespoon paprika
1 teaspoon white pepper
1¼ teaspoons garlic powder

1 egg
1 cup milk
1¼ cups bread crumbs
36 sea scallops
12 bacon strips, cut into thirds

• Combine flour, salt, paprika, pepper and garlic powder.
• Beat together egg and milk.
• Roll each scallop in flour mixture. Shake off excess.
• Dip in egg mixture. Coat with bread crumbs.
• Wrap each scallop with bacon and secure with toothpick.
• Place in greased 9x13-inch baking dish. Bake at 400° for 20-25 minutes or until bacon is crisp.
• Drain and serve hot.

Great when served with our own HENRI'S SEAFOOD SAUCE.

OYSTERS MARIAN

Marian Clark and Ann Mitchell
Catering to You
Augusta, Georgia
Yield: 15 servings

1 pound bacon, partially frozen	1 teaspoon pepper
1 cup finely chopped green pepper	½ teaspoon cayenne pepper
1 4-ounce jar pimentos, drained and chopped, or ½ cup chopped red pepper	1 tablespoon paprika
	1 quart select oysters, well drained
	Saltine crackers
1 teaspoon salt	

- Process bacon in food processor in small chunks until finely chopped. Remove to mixing bowl.
- Add green pepper, pimentos or chopped red pepper, salt, pepper, cayenne pepper and paprika to chopped bacon. Blend well.
- In 2-quart rectangular baking dish, place oysters singly in rows without touching.
- Top with bacon mixture.
- Bake at 350° for 30 minutes, or until bacon is done.
- Serve with saltine crackers.

These make an elegant appetizer when served in shells.

SMOKED OYSTER ROLL

Yield: 1 roll

2-3 tablespoons mayonnaise	½ small onion, grated
1 8-ounce package cream cheese, softened	2 cloves garlic, pressed
2 teaspoons Worcestershire sauce	1 3¾-ounce can smoked oysters, drained and finely chopped
⅛ teaspoon salt	

- Combine mayonnaise and cream cheese. Blend until smooth.
- Add Worcestershire sauce, salt, onion and garlic.
- Spread into ½-inch thick rectangle on waxed paper.
- Spread oysters on top of cream cheese mixture.
- Place in freezer a few minutes, until just firm.
- Remove from freezer.
- Roll jelly-roll fashion.
- Chill 24 hours.
- Serve with crackers.

SMOKED OYSTER CHEESE BALL

Nelson Danish
Augusta, Georgia
Yield: 1 cheese ball

8-9 ounces Camembert cheese, softened
1 8-ounce package cream cheese, softened
¼ cup unsalted butter, softened
1 tablespoon brandy

1 3¾-ounce tin smoked oysters, drained, rinsed and chopped
1 cup chopped pecans
Smoked oysters, optional, to garnish

• Cream together cheeses and butter
• Add brandy and oysters. Blend well.
• Chill several hours.
• Shape mixture into 1 large ball or 2 smaller balls.
• Wrap in plastic wrap. Store in refrigerator.
• When ready to serve, bring to room temperature. Garnish with additional smoked oysters, if desired. Serve with crackers.

Brie may be substituted for Camembert.

MARINATED MUSHROOMS AND ONIONS

Yield: 10 servings

1 pound fresh mushrooms
2 tablespoons butter
1 cup tarragon vinegar
¾ cup vegetable oil
2 cloves garlic, minced
1 teaspoon sugar

3 tablespoons water
1½ teaspoons salt
3 dashes Tabasco
⅛ teaspoon pepper
1 large onion, thinly sliced

• Sauté mushrooms in butter.
• Combine vinegar, oil, garlic, sugar, water, salt, Tabasco and pepper.
• Combine mushrooms and butter with onion. Add to vinegar mixture.
• Store in airtight container overnight. Refrigerate, turning several times.
• Partially drain before serving.

MARINATED BROCCOLI

Yield: 8-10 servings

1 bunch fresh broccoli
2 5¾-ounce (drained weight) cans
  pitted black olives, drained

3 ounces Blue cheese, crumbled
1 8-ounce bottle Italian dressing
1 pint cherry tomatoes

• Blanch broccoli in boiling water 2 minutes. Drain. Plunge in ice water. Drain.
• Combine broccoli, olives and cheese. Toss with dressing.
• Refrigerate overnight.
• Just before serving, cut tomatoes in half and toss with other ingredients.

SPICY CARROTS

Yield: 8-10 servings

1 pound carrots, peeled
1 cup white vinegar
½ cup sugar
¼ cup chopped onion
1 teaspoon pickling spices

½ teaspoon salt
¼ teaspoon dry mustard
2. cloves garlic, pressed
½ teaspoon pepper

• Cut carrots into 3-inch julienne slices. Set aside.
• Combine remaining ingredients. Bring to a boil.
• Add carrots.
• Cover and simmer 5 minutes. Cool.
• Place in covered container and refrigerate until ready to serve.
• Drain and remove pickling spices before serving. (This can be prepared up to 1 week ahead.)

A most refreshing, low-calorie snack any time. Especially nice on a hot day.

PARTY VEGETABLE PLATTER

Yield: 20 servings

1 bunch fresh broccoli	1 green pepper, sliced
1 head cauliflower	2 cups sliced zucchini, cut into
2 cups sliced carrots, cut into	½-inch slices
½-inch slices	¼ cup margarine

- Break broccoli and cauliflower into florets.
- Arrange prepared vegetables on a 10-inch glass platter: broccoli around outside edge, then cauliflower, carrots, and green pepper in concentric circles with zucchini in center.
- Dot vegetables with margarine.
- Cover with plastic wrap.
- Microwave on HIGH 5-7 minutes.
- Serve with Zesty Sauce.

Zesty Sauce:

¼ cup grated onion	¼ cup horseradish
1 tablespoon butter	½ teaspoon salt
1 cup mayonnaise	¼ teaspoon pepper

- Place onion and butter in a 1-quart baking dish.
- Microwave on HIGH 3 minutes.
- Add mayonnaise, horseradish, salt and pepper. Mix well.

HOT OLIVE BITES

Yield: 72 wedges

2 4-ounce cans chopped black	3 green onions, chopped
olives, drained	¼ teaspoon curry powder
2 cups grated Cheddar cheese	⅛ teaspoon pepper
1 cup mayonnaise	6 English muffins, split

- Combine olives, cheese, mayonnaise, onions, curry powder and pepper.
- Spread olive mixture on all muffin halves.
- Cut each half into 6 wedges.
- Place on cookie sheet.
- Bake at 375° for 8-10 minutes, or until hot and bubbly.
- Serve warm.

The wedges may be frozen on a cookie sheet before baking. Store in airtight containers or freezer bags until ready to use.

BELLINI

Yield: 5-6 servings

6 ripe peaches, peeled and
   quartered
1 cup sugar

Juice of 1 lemon
3 cups water
Sparkling wine

• In food processor, combine peaches, sugar, lemon juice and water.
• Purée to make a peach nectar. Pour into tall wine glasses, filling ¼ full.
• Add sparkling wine to fill. Stir and serve.

For a delicate touch, float a peach slice in each glass.

SHRUG

Yield: 6-8 servings

1 fifth cream sherry or white port
1 12-ounce can frozen limeade
   concentrate

Juice of one lemon
1 cup water

• Combine sherry, limeade concentrate and lemon juice.
• Stir in water.
• Place in freezer overnight.
• Serve.

MARVELOUS MARGARITAS

Yield: 4 servings

1 6-ounce can frozen limeade
   concentrate, thawed
¾ cup tequila
¼ cup Triple Sec

Ice
Lime wedges
Salt

• Combine limeade concentrate, tequila and Triple Sec in blender.
• Add enough ice to fill blender ¾ full. Blend well.
• Rub rims of 4 glasses with lime. Dip rims in salt.
• Pour mixture into prepared glasses and serve.

The perfect beginning to a "south of the border" supper.

SANGRIA BLANC

Yield: 8 servings

3½ cups dry white wine, chilled
½ cup Triple Sec
¼ cup sugar

1 10-ounce bottle club soda, chilled
Orange, lemon and lime slices
to garnish

• Combine wine, Triple Sec and sugar.
• When ready to serve, add club soda and garnish.

A cool, refreshing summertime drink.

COFFEE LIQUEUR

Yield: 2 quarts

4 cups strong coffee, freshly
  brewed
4 cups sugar

1 fifth vodka
1 vanilla bean, split lengthwise

• Combine coffee and sugar in a stainless steel pot.
• Bring mixture to a boil. Simmer 5 minutes.
• Allow to cool. Stir in vodka.
• Place split vanilla bean in glass jar. Add cooled liquid. Seal.
• Allow to age at least 1 month.

FROZEN MARGARITAS

Yield: 1 gallon

1 fifth light tequila
1¼ cups Triple Sec
6 6-ounce cans frozen limeade
  concentrate, thawed

9 cups water
Salt
Lime wedges to garnish

• Combine tequila, Triple Sec, limeade concentrate and water in large freezer
  container. Stir well.
• Freeze approximately 2 days, stirring vigorously every 8-12 hours.
• Remove from freezer before serving. Let stand 15-20 minutes.
• Stir vigorously.
• Serve with lime wedges in glasses with salted rims.

A must for any Mexican gathering. Olé!

BRANDY SLUSH

Yield: 3 quarts

9 cups water, divided
2 cups sugar
4 family size tea bags
1 12-ounce can frozen orange
  juice concentrate

1 12-ounce can frozen lemonade
  concentrate
2 cups brandy, apricot or peach
7 Up or Sprite

- Combine 7 cups water and sugar. Bring to a boil. Remove from heat and set aside.
- Bring remaining 2 cups water to a boil. Add tea bags. Remove from heat and steep 20 minutes.
- Remove tea bags and boil tea until darkened.
- Add orange juice and lemonade concentrates and brandy.
- Combine with sugar water and mix well. Freeze.
- To serve, place 2 scoops of mixture in glass. Fill with 7 Up or Sprite.

Keeps indefinitely in freezer.

DALE'S PARTY PUNCH

Yield: 50-60 servings

6 cups sugar
2 quarts boiling water
2 ounces citric acid
1 46-ounce can unsweetened
  pineapple juice

1 46-ounce can unsweetened
  orange juice
4 quarts cold water
2 28-ounce bottles ginger ale

- Dissolve sugar in boiling water.
- Add citric acid, pineapple juice, orange juice and water.
- Place in large freezer container. Freeze until solid.
- Five hours before serving, remove from freezer.
- Crack with ice pick. Stir in ginger ale.
- Serve slushy.

For a colorful punch, food coloring may be added before freezing. Citric acid may be found at the pharmacy.

FRENCH MINT TEA

Yield: 8 servings

13 individual tea bags
¼ cup fresh mint leaves, lightly
   packed
1 quart water

1 6-ounce can frozen orange juice
   concentrate
1 cup sugar
   Juice of 2 lemons

• Combine tea bags and mint leaves with water.
• Cover and bring to a boil.
• Remove from heat. Steep 30 minutes. Remove tea bags.
• Add orange juice concentrate, sugar, lemon juice and additional water to
  make 2 quarts of liquid.
• Strain and chill.

BOLD LOUISVILLE PUNCH

Yield: 1 ½ gallons

1 46-ounce can unsweetened
   orange juice
1 46-ounce can unsweetened
   pineapple juice
1 cup fresh lemon juice
½ cup fresh lime juice

1 teaspoon vanilla
½ teaspoon almond extract
4 cups sugar
3 quarts water
1 28-ounce bottle ginger ale,
   optional

• Combine all ingredients except ginger ale. Stir until sugar dissolves.
• Add ginger ale, if desired, just before serving.
• Serve chilled.

Children love this fruity punch.

BARBARA'S PUNCH

Yield: 50 servings

1 ounce citric acid
3 cups sugar
3 quarts water
1 6-ounce can frozen orange juice
   concentrate, thawed

1 6-ounce can frozen lemonade
   concentrate, thawed
1 46-ounce can pineapple juice

• Combine all ingredients in freezer container.
• Place in freezer and stir every hour until slushy.

MOUNT VERNON PUNCH

Yield: 1 gallon

3 cups fresh lemon juice
  Grated rind of 2 lemons
2 quarts water
1½ cups brandy

1½ cups rum
4 cups sugar
  Fresh mint leaves to garnish

- Combine all ingredients, except mint leaves. Mix thoroughly to dissolve sugar.
- Place mixture in freezer. Stir every 30 minutes until mixture is consistency of sherbet, about 3 hours.
- Garnish with fresh mint leaves. Serve.

This is a sweet punch. Amount of sugar may be reduced.

SPARKLING CRANBERRY PUNCH

Yield: 25 servings

2 quarts cranberry juice, chilled
1 6-ounce can frozen pink
  lemonade concentrate, thawed

1 2-liter bottle Sprite

- Combine cranberry juice and lemonade concentrate.
- When ready to serve, add Sprite.
- Serve chilled.

PERCOLATOR PUNCH

Yield: 16 cups

2 quarts apple juice
1 quart cranberry juice
1 cup orange juice
¾ cup lemon juice

¼ cup water
½ cup sugar
2 teaspoons whole allspice
2 teaspoons whole cloves

- Combine all juices, water and sugar in large percolator.
- Place allspice and cloves in basket. Perk and serve.

HOT SPICED TEA

Yield: 16-20 cups

2 cups boiling water	1 6-ounce can frozen orange
2 family size tea bags	juice concentrate
⅔ cup lemon juice	2 quarts water
1½ cups sugar, or to taste	1 3-inch cinnamon stick

• Pour boiling water over tea. Cool and remove tea bags.
• Add remaining ingredients and simmer at least 20 minutes.
• Remove cinnamon stick from tea and serve hot.

Add bourbon or rum for a special treat.

HOT APPLE CIDER

Yield: 12-16 servings

1 gallon apple cider	⅓ cup sugar
2 teaspoons whole cloves	⅓ cup light brown sugar
2 teaspoons whole allspice	2 oranges, sliced
2 3-inch cinnamon sticks	1 lemon, sliced

• Combine all ingredients in heavy saucepan.
• Simmer 20 minutes.
• Strain and serve hot.

Fills the house with a delicious aroma.

ANNE'S IRISH CREAM

Yield: 5 cups

4 eggs	½ pint half and half
2 tablespoons instant coffee	2 tablespoons chocolate syrup
½ cup boiling water	1 14-ounce can condensed milk
1½ cups Irish whiskey	2 tablespoons vanilla

• Whip eggs.
• Dissolve coffee in boiling water.
• Combine eggs, coffee and remaining ingredients. Blend well. Strain.
• Store in refrigerator up to 3 weeks.

Serve as a liqueur or add to coffee.

HOT BUTTERED RUM MIX

Yield: 3 cups

1 16-ounce box dark
   brown sugar
½ cup butter (no substitute)
1¼ teaspoons cinnamon
1 teaspoon nutmeg

¼ teaspoon cloves
1 teaspoon rum flavoring
   Rum
   Lemon slices to garnish

• Combine brown sugar, butter, cinnamon, nutmeg, cloves and rum
  flavoring.
• Store in refrigerator.
• When ready to serve, place 1 tablespoon of mixture in mug. Add 2 ounces
  rum.
• Fill mug with hot water. Stir.
• Garnish with lemon slices.

A great hot toddy in front of the fire.

AFTER DINNER ICE CREAM SHAKE

Yield: 6-8 servings

½ gallon vanilla ice cream,
   softened

¼ cup Amaretto
¼ cup Creme de Cacao or Kahlúa

• Fill blender ¾ full with ice cream.
• Add Amaretto and Creme de Cacao or Kahlúa.
• Blend until smooth.
• Serve in oversized wine glasses.

*For a different flavor, substitute coffee ice cream for vanilla, increase Creme
de Cacao to ½ cup and omit Amaretto.*

BREADS, CHEESE AND EGGS

BETTY'S SWEET POTATO BISCUITS

Yield: 20-24 biscuits

2	cups self-rising flour	1¾	cups cooked, mashed sweet
1	cup sugar		potatoes (about 4 medium
⅔	cup shortening		potatoes)
		⅛-¼	cup milk

- Combine flour and sugar.
- Cut in shortening until mixture resembles cornmeal.
- Add sweet potatoes.
- Add enough milk to make a workable dough. (If sweet potatoes were baked, more milk may be required; if boiled, less milk.)
- Turn dough onto well-floured board. (Handle carefully. It is delicate!) Knead several times.
- Roll dough to ½ - ¾-inch thickness. (May be helpful to use a stockinet on rolling pin.) Cut with a 2-inch biscuit cutter. Place on lightly greased baking sheet.
- Bake at 400° for 10-15 minutes or until lightly browned. Watch carefully—these burn easily.

POTATO YEAST ROLLS

Yield: 4 dozen rolls

2	cups warm water (105°-115°)	⅔	cup sugar
2	packages yeast	2	teaspoons salt
1	cup shortening	1	teaspoon baking powder
1	cup mashed potatoes	½	teaspoon baking soda
7½	cups sifted all-purpose flour		

- Warm a large mixing bowl with hot water.
- Dissolve yeast in water. Add shortening and potatoes. Mix well.
- Sift together flour, sugar, salt, baking powder and baking soda.
- Add to yeast mixture. Mix until well blended.
- Cover with a damp towel. Let rise for 1½-2 hours or until doubled in bulk.
- Punch dough down. (Dough can be refrigerated at this point for 5-6 days before proceeding.)
- For clover-leaf rolls, lightly grease muffin pans. Shape dough into 1-inch balls and place 3 dough balls in each muffin cup. Cover and let rise until doubled in bulk, about 1 hour.
- For Parker House rolls, grease baking sheet. Roll dough to ¼-inch thickness on floured board. Cut with 2-inch biscuit cutter. Brush with melted butter and fold in half. Place on baking sheet. Cover and let rise for 1-1½ hours or until doubled in bulk.
- Bake at 400° for 15-20 minutes.

BUTTERNUT ROLLS

Yield: 24 large or 48 small rolls

¼ cup lukewarm water (105°-115°)
1 teaspoon sugar
2 packages yeast
1 cup milk
1 cup raisins
1 cup Butternut Squash Purée
⅓ cup firmly packed light brown sugar
¼ cup unsalted butter, melted and cooled

1 whole egg plus 1 egg yolk, lightly beaten
1 tablespoon grated lemon rind
2 teaspoons salt
1 teaspoon cinnamon
6-7 cups all-purpose flour
1 egg
Pinch salt

• In large bowl, combine warm water and sugar. Dissolve yeast in this water 15 minutes or until it is foamy.
• In saucepan, scald milk. Add raisins and let mixture cool to 105°-115°.
• Combine milk mixture, Squash Purée, brown sugar, butter, eggs, lemon rind, salt and cinnamon. Add to yeast mixture.
• Stir in 6 cups flour with a wooden spatula.
• Knead dough on floured surface 8-10 minutes, or until smooth. More flour may be added if dough is too sticky.
• Place dough in greased bowl, turning once.
• Cover dough loosely. Let rise in warm place until doubled in bulk, about 1½ hours.
• Punch down dough, divide in half, and roll each half into a 24-inch log.
• Cut each log into 12 pieces. Form each piece into a smooth ball and arrange balls on lightly greased baking sheets. (For smaller rolls, cut logs into 24 pieces.)
• Cover rolls loosely. Let rise in warm place 45-60 minutes, or until almost doubled in bulk.
• Brush rolls with 1 egg which has been beaten lightly with a pinch of salt.
• Bake at 375° for 15 minutes, or until they sound hollow when bottoms are tapped.
• Allow to cool on rack. (Rolls may be frozen at this point.)

(continued)

Butternut Squash Purée:
1 2½-pound butternut squash

• On a lightly greased baking sheet, bake squash 35-40 minutes or until tender.
• Allow squash to cool. Peel and seed. Cut into small pieces and purée.
• Squash purée may be refrigerated or frozen until ready to use.

These rolls are a favorite of our Cookbook Committee. They are well worth the effort and make an appealing addition to any holiday meal. THE BEST!

OLD-FASHIONED SOUTHERN ROLLS

Yield: 3 dozen rolls

2	cups milk	6-7	cups White Lily flour, sifted
½	scant cup sugar		and divided
1½	teaspoons salt	½	teaspoon baking soda
6	tablespoons shortening	½	teaspoon baking powder
1	package yeast		

• Scald milk with sugar, salt and shortening.
• Cool to lukewarm (105°-115°) and add yeast.
• Add 3½ cups flour, mixing well.
• Cover. Let rise in warm place until doubled in bulk, about 1 hour.
• Sift together 1 cup flour, baking soda and baking powder and add to dough.
• Then add enough flour, about 1½ cups, to make dough stiff enough to handle.
• Turn onto well-floured surface and knead 5 minutes.
• Place in greased bowl, turning to grease top.
• Cover with plastic wrap and place in refrigerator. (Dough will keep 8-10 days.)
• When ready to bake, take out desired amount of dough.
• Roll dough on floured surface to ½-inch thickness. Cut with 2½-inch biscuit cutter and place on greased baking sheet.
• Cover and let rise about 1-2 hours, or until doubled in bulk.
• Brush tops of rolls with melted margarine.
• Bake at 400° for 10-12 minutes.

WHOLE WHEAT BUTTERHORNS

Yield: 36 rolls

2½-3	cups all-purpose flour, divided	2	teaspoons salt
2	packages yeast	2	cups whole wheat flour
1¾	cups water	6	tablespoons butter, softened
⅓	cup light brown sugar	½	cup chopped walnuts or pecans
3	tablespoons shortening		Melted butter
2	tablespoons honey		

- In mixing bowl combine 1½ cups all-purpose flour and yeast. Set aside.
- In saucepan, heat water, brown sugar, shortening, honey and salt, stirring constantly, until liquid is warm (115°-120°) and shortening is almost melted.
- Add liquid to flour mixture. Mix at low speed for 30 seconds, scraping sides of bowl constantly. Beat 3 minutes at high speed.
- Stir in whole wheat flour and as much remaining all-purpose flour as can be mixed with a spoon.
- Turn onto lightly floured surface and add all-purpose flour to make a moderately stiff dough that is smooth and elastic. Knead 6-8 minutes.
- Shape into ball and place dough in lightly greased bowl, turning once to grease top.
- Cover and let rise in warm place until doubled in bulk, about 1½ hours.
- Punch down and turn onto lightly floured surface. Divide dough into 3 equal portions and shape each into a ball.
- Cover and let rise 10 minutes.
- On lightly floured surface, roll each ball of dough into a 12-inch circle.
- Spread circle with 2 tablespoons butter and sprinkle with about 3 tablespoons nuts.
- Cut circle into 12 wedges. To shape butterhorns, begin at wide end of wedge and roll toward point.
- Place point-side down 2-3 inches apart on greased baking sheet.
- Repeat procedure with remaining dough.
- Cover rolls and let rise in warm place until almost doubled in bulk, about 20-30 minutes.
- Brush with melted butter.
- Bake at 400° for 10-12 minutes or until done. (May be frozen after baking and reheated as needed.)
- Brush with butter to serve.

A unique dinner roll.

JIM'S BISCUITS

Yield: 24 biscuits

5-7 tablespoons shortening   ⅔ cup buttermilk
2   cups White Lily self-rising flour

- Cut shortening into flour until mixture resembles cornmeal.
- Add buttermilk. Mix well.
- Place batter on floured board; knead 4-6 times or until dough is smooth.
- Roll to desired thickness. Cut with a 2-inch biscuit cutter.
- Place on lightly greased baking sheet.
- Bake at 425° for 15-18 minutes.

ROSA'S CORNBREAD

Yield: 10-12 servings

1½	cups self-rising white cornmeal	1	egg
		1¼-1½ cups milk	
2	tablespoons all-purpose flour	1	tablespoon vegetable oil
2	tablespoons sugar		

- Combine cornmeal, flour and sugar. Blend well.
- Beat together egg, milk and oil. Add to dry ingredients.
- Pour into greased 8x8-inch baking dish or iron skillet.
- Bake at 400° for 20 minutes, or until golden brown.

Delicious! A true Southern cornbread.

SOUR CREAM CORNBREAD

Yield: 10-12 servings

½ cup vegetable oil, divided   1 cup self-rising yellow cornmeal
1 cup sour cream   2 eggs, beaten
1 8½-ounce can cream style corn   ½ teaspoon salt

- Pour ¼ cup oil into an 8x8-inch pan or large iron skillet. Place in 400° oven.
- Combine remaining oil, sour cream, corn, cornmeal, eggs and salt. Mix well.
- Remove pan from oven.
- Pour batter into hot pan.
- Bake 30 minutes.

A unique taste for an old favorite.

JALAPEÑO CORNBREAD

Yield: 15 servings

2 eggs
1 cup cottage cheese
1 cup cream style corn
1 small onion, grated
½ cup bacon drippings, melted
1 cup yellow cornmeal
1½ teaspoons salt

3 teaspoons baking powder
1 tablespoon sugar
1 cup grated Cheddar cheese
2-4 jalapeño peppers, chopped and partially seeded
⅓ cup butter, melted

- Combine eggs, cottage cheese, corn, onion, bacon drippings, cornmeal, salt, baking powder, sugar, cheese and jalapeños. Blend until smooth.
- Pour mixture into greased 9x13-inch baking dish.
- Bake at 350° for 30-45 minutes.
- Remove from oven. Immediately pour butter over cornbread in pan.
- When all butter is absorbed, cut into squares. Serve hot.

Hot and spicy.

SUNDAY CORNBREAD

Yield: 8 servings

1 cup all-purpose flour
1 cup yellow cornmeal
½ teaspoon salt
⅓ cup sugar

4 teaspoons baking powder
2 eggs
⅓ cup margarine, melted
1 cup milk

- Combine flour, cornmeal, salt, sugar and baking powder.
- Stir in eggs, margarine and milk. Mix well.
- Pour into greased 10-inch iron skillet.
- Bake at 425° for 25-30 minutes. Serve warm with butter.

A wonderfully sweet cornbread.

AUGUSTA'S BEST STRAWBERRY BREAD

Yield: 2 loaves

3 cups all-purpose flour	1¼ cups vegetable oil
2 cups sugar	2 10-ounce packages frozen
1 teaspoon baking soda	strawberries, thawed and
1 teaspoon salt	chopped
1 teaspoon cinnamon	1 cup chopped pecans
4 eggs, beaten	

- Sift flour, sugar, baking soda, salt and cinnamon into large mixing bowl. Make well in center.
- Combine eggs, oil, strawberries and pecans.
- Add to sifted ingredients, stirring until well combined.
- Spoon batter into 2 greased and floured 9x5-inch loaf pans.
- Bake at 350° for 1 hour.
- Cool bread in pans 10 minutes.
- Remove bread from pans. Cool completely on wire racks.

CRANBERRY LOAF

Yield: 2 loaves

½ cup shortening	¼ teaspoon salt
1 cup sugar	1 teaspoon baking soda
1 egg, beaten	1 teaspoon baking powder
1 cup raisins	1 teaspoon cinnamon
½ cup chopped nuts	1 16-ounce can jellied cranberry
1¾ cups sifted all-purpose flour	sauce or whole cranberry sauce

- Cream shortening and sugar. Add egg.
- Stir in raisins and nuts.
- Sift together flour, salt, baking soda, baking powder and cinnamon. Add to creamed mixture.
- Stir in cranberry sauce.
- Spoon into 2 greased and floured 9x5-inch loaf pans.
- Bake at 350° for 40-50 minutes.
- Remove from pans and cool on wire rack.

JULIE'S NUT BREAD

Yield: 1 loaf

1 cup firmly packed brown sugar
1 cup sour cream
1 egg, beaten
2 cups all-purpose flour

1½ teaspoons baking powder
1 teaspoon baking soda
1 cup chopped pecans

• Blend brown sugar and sour cream.
• Add egg, flour, baking powder and soda. Mix well.
• Fold in pecans.
• Spoon into a 9x5-inch greased loaf pan.
• Bake at 350° for 30-45 minutes or until tester inserted in middle comes
out clean.

*We dare you to try this quick and easy bread! Tastes so good
straight out of the oven.*

LEMON TEA BREAD

Yield: 3 loaves

2 cups butter, softened
2 cups sugar
6 eggs
5 cups all-purpose flour, sifted
3 ounces lemon extract

1 teaspoon baking soda, dissolved
in 1 tablespoon boiling water
1 cup chopped pecans
2 cups golden raisins

• Cream together butter and sugar.
• Add eggs one at a time, beating well after each addition.
• Mix in flour, lemon extract and baking soda.
• Fold in pecans and raisins.
• Spoon into 3 greased 8x4-inch loaf pans.
• **Bake at 350° for 1 hour and 15 minutes.**

Perfect for a coffee, a morning meeting or an afternoon tea.

PIZZA BREAD

Yield: 2 loaves

3 eggs
1 tablespoon oregano
3 tablespoons grated Parmesan
  cheese

2 loaves frozen dough, thawed
8 ounces pepperoni
8 ounces Provolone cheese

• Beat together eggs, oregano and Parmesan cheese.
• Roll dough into two 8x14-inch rectangles.
• Spread egg mixture on dough, reserving 3 tablespoons.
• Layer pepperoni and Provolone cheese on top of egg mixture.
• Roll dough jelly-roll style.
• Place seam-side down on greased baking sheet and seal ends.
• Brush with reserved egg mixture.
• Bake at 350° for 35-40 minutes.
• Can be frozen after baking. Reheat in foil.

This makes a great appetizer or a fun meal for children.

POP-UP BREAD

Yield: 2 loaves

3-3¼ cups all-purpose flour,
     divided
1   package yeast
½   cup milk
½   cup water

½   cup vegetable oil
¼   cup sugar
1   teaspoon salt
2   eggs, beaten

• Grease 2 1-pound coffee cans with vegetable shortening.
• Combine ½ cup flour and yeast.
• Heat milk, water, oil, sugar and salt over low heat (110°). Stir well.
• Add liquid ingredients to flour mixture. Beat until smooth, about 2 minutes.
• Blend in eggs.
• Stir in remaining flour to make a stiff dough. Beat at medium speed until
  smooth and elastic, about 1 minute.
• Divide dough into coffee cans. Cover cans with lids or plastic wrap. Let rise
  in warm place until light and bubbly, about one hour. (Dough should rise to
  within ½ inch of top of cans.) Remove covers.
• Bake at 375° for 30-35 minutes.
• Allow bread to cool in cans 15 minutes, then remove to wire rack.

Wonderful served with butter and jam. Will become a family favorite.

SALLY LUNN BREAD

Yield: 1 10-inch Bundt

1 cup milk
½ cup shortening
¼ cup water
4 cups sifted all-purpose flour, divided

⅓ cup sugar
2 teaspoons salt
2 packages yeast
3 eggs

- Heat milk, shortening and water until warm (120°). (Shortening does not need to melt.)
- Combine 1⅓ cups flour, sugar, salt and yeast in large mixing bowl.
- Add warm liquid to dry ingredients. Beat at medium speed 2 minutes.
- Gradually add ⅔ cup flour and eggs. Beat at high speed for 2 minutes.
- Add remaining flour. Mix well.
- Transfer to greased bowl, turning to grease top. Let rise in warm place until doubled in bulk, about 1 hour and 15 minutes.
- Punch dough down with spatula and turn into greased 10-inch Bundt pan.
- Cover and let rise in warm place 30 minutes, increasing bulk by ⅓-½.
- Bake at 350° for 40-50 minutes.
- Run knife around center and outer edges of bread. Turn onto serving platter.

This old favorite is good served warm on a cold day with vegetable soup. Serve any leftovers for breakfast with our STRAWBERRY BUTTER.

MISS KITTY'S RAISIN BREAD

Yield: 2 loaves

1½ packages yeast
½ cup warm water
1 tablespoon vegetable oil
½ teaspoon salt
1 cup sugar

1¾ cups water
¼ cup evaporated milk
6½ cups all-purpose flour, divided
1½ cups raisins
Butter, melted

- Dissolve yeast in warm water.
- Combine oil, salt, sugar, water, evaporated milk and 4½ cups flour.
- Add yeast mixture.
- Place in greased bowl, turning once to grease top.
- Cover and let rise in warm place 2 hours.
- Stir in 2 cups flour and raisins.
- Divide into two parts and put into two greased loaf pans. Brush with butter.
- Cover and let rise 45 minutes.
- Bake at 325° for 30-45 minutes or until browned.

BOSTON BROWN BREAD

Yield: 4-5 loaves

2	cups white cornmeal	1	cup molasses
2	cups whole wheat flour	2	cups buttermilk
½	cup medium or coarse rye flour	1½	cups water
1	cup all-purpose flour	3	rounded teaspoons baking
2	teaspoons salt		soda

• Sift together cornmeal, flours and salt.
• Combine molasses, buttermilk, water and baking soda. Add to dry ingredients.
• Pour into 4 or 5 greased 20-ounce cans filling only ⅔ full. Cover with 2 thicknesses of greased heavy-duty aluminum foil. Secure tightly with string.
• Place cans in broiler pan. Add about 1 inch hot water to pan.
• Bake at 400° for 1 hour.
• Remove cans from water. Reduce heat to 350° and continue baking 30 minutes.
• Reduce heat to 300° and bake 15 minutes.
• Remove bread from cans. Cool on wire rack.

Complicated but well worth the trouble.

WHITE BREAD

Yield: 2 loaves

2	cups milk	1	teaspoon salt
3	tablespoons butter	5½-6	cups all-purpose flour,
½	cup sugar		divided
1	package Rapid Rise yeast		

• Heat milk and butter to 125°-130°.
• While milk mixture is heating, combine sugar, yeast, salt and 5 cups flour in large mixing bowl.
• Add milk mixture to flour mixture.
• Knead 4 minutes, adding flour if needed.
• Place dough in greased bowl, turning to grease top. Cover with plastic wrap.
• Let rise 30-40 minutes, or until dough is doubled in bulk.
• Punch dough down and knead on floured board 5-10 times.
• Divide and shape into 2 loaves.
• Place in 2 greased 9x5-inch loaf pans.
• Cover and let rise 30-40 minutes, or until almost doubled in bulk.
• Bake at 375° for 30 minutes. If bread browns too quickly, cover with foil.

WHOLE WHEAT HONEY BREAD

Yield: 1 loaf

1¾ cups all-purpose flour, divided
1½ cups whole wheat flour
1 teaspoon salt
1 package Rapid Rise yeast
½ cup milk

½ cup water
¼ cup honey
2 tablespoons margarine
1 egg white
1 tablespoon cold water

- In large bowl, combine ¾ cup all-purpose flour, whole wheat flour, salt and yeast.
- Heat milk, water, honey and margarine to 125°-130°.
- Stir milk mixture into flour mixture.
- Add enough remaining flour to make a soft dough.
- Knead 4 minutes on floured surface.
- Roll dough into 8x15-inch rectangle.
- Roll up from long side into loaf. Seal seams and ends.
- Place on greased baking sheet. Cover.
- Place baking sheet on shallow pan filled ½ full with boiling water.
- Let rise 20 minutes.
- Cut 4 slashes ½-inch deep in top of loaf.
- Brush loaf with egg white mixed with cold water.
- Bake at 400° for 20 minutes.
- Remove to wire rack and cool.

A quick and easy bread that only takes about an hour from start to finish.

STRAWBERRY BUTTER

½ cup butter, softened

Juice from 1 10-ounce carton frozen strawberries, thawed

- Combine butter and juice.
- Beat until smooth and well blended.

CINNAMON ROLLS

Yield: 36 rolls

Dough:

1 package yeast
¼ cup warm water (105°-115°)
4 cups sifted all-purpose flour
1 teaspoon salt
¾ teaspoon grated lemon peel

¼ cup sugar
1 cup butter, cut into small pieces
2 eggs, beaten
1 cup milk, scalded and cooled to lukewarm (105°-115°)

Filling:

1 cup sugar
2 tablespoons cinnamon

1 cup raisins, divided
1 cup chopped pecans, divided

Glaze:

2 cups sifted powdered sugar
2 tablespoons milk

1 teaspoon vanilla

• Dissolve yeast in warm water.
• Combine flour, salt, lemon peel and sugar. Cut in butter.
• Combine eggs, milk and yeast. Add to flour mixture. Blend.
• Cover tightly and refrigerate overnight.
• When ready to use, divide dough in half. Refrigerate one half until ready to use.
• On floured board, roll dough into an 8x12-inch rectangle.
• Combine sugar and cinnamon for Filling.
• Sprinkle half the sugar mixture, half the raisins, and half the pecans on dough.
• Roll tightly jelly-roll fashion.
• Slice each roll into 18 1-inch slices.
• Place cut-side up on greased baking sheet.
• Repeat with remaining dough and Filling.
• Cover and let rise about 1 hour.
• Bake at 400° for 12-15 minutes or until golden brown.
• Beat together Glaze ingredients. Spread on warm rolls.

MISS GUSSIE'S CINNAMON ROLLS

Yield: 5 dozen

Dough:

4	cups milk	1	cup margarine
4	packages yeast	1	heaping tablespoon
1½	teaspoons salt		shortening
1	cup sugar	13-15	cups all-purpose flour
5	eggs, beaten		

- Warm milk to 105°-115°.
- Remove from heat. Pour into large bowl and add yeast, salt and sugar, mixing well.
- Let yeast mixture sit until it bubbles, about 5-10 minutes.
- Add eggs, margarine and shortening. Mix until margarine and shortening become soft.
- Add flour, 1 cup at a time (about 14 cups) until dough is no longer sticky.
- Divide dough in half. Place in 2 large greased bowls, turning once to grease top. Cover and let rise 1 hour or until doubled in bulk. Punch down.
- Sprinkle board with 3 tablespoons flour and knead dough a few times.
- Roll each half into a 15x23-inch rectangle. (For smaller rolls, divide dough into 3 or 4 pieces and make smaller rectangles.)

Filling:

3	cups margarine	4	tablespoons cinnamon
3	cups sugar		

- Combine all ingredients.

Glaze:

1	16-ounce box powdered sugar, sifted	5-6	tablespoons milk
2	tablespoons margarine, melted		

- Combine all ingredients.

(continued)

Assembly:
- Spread half the Filling on each rectangle.
- Roll each rectangle, lengthwise, jelly-roll fashion. Seal seam.
- Cut into 1-1½-inch pieces.
- Touch bottom of roll in flour and place floured-side down on greased baking sheet.
- Cover and let rise 1-1½ hours, or until almost doubled in bulk.
- Bake at 350° for 18-20 minutes or until browned.
- Spread Glaze on hot rolls.

Miss Gussie is a life-long resident of St. Simons Island, Georgia. Anyone from the St. Simons area would recognize Miss Gussie's name and reputation for cinnamon rolls.

WHOLE WHEAT ENGLISH MUFFIN BREAD

Yield: 2 loaves

3 cups all-purpose flour	2 packages Rapid Rise yeast
3 cups whole wheat flour	2 cups milk
1 tablespoon sugar	½ cup water
2 teaspoons salt	Cornmeal
¼ teaspoon baking soda	

- Mix all-purpose and whole wheat flour.
- In large bowl, combine 5 cups flour mixture, sugar, salt, baking soda, and yeast.
- Heat milk and water to 125°-130°. Add to dry ingredients. Mix well.
- Stir in remaining flour to make a stiff batter.
- Sprinkle two greased 9x5-inch loaf pans with cornmeal. Spoon batter into pans. Sprinkle top with cornmeal.
- Cover and let rise 40 minutes in warm place.
- Bake at 400° for 25 minutes.
- Remove from pan immediately and cool on wire rack.
- To serve, toast slices, then spread with butter and homemade preserves.

Equally as good when only all-purpose flour is used.

BLUEBERRY BREAKFAST CAKE

Yield: 1 cake

Cake:

¼ cup butter, softened
¾ cup sugar
1 egg
2 cups all-purpose flour

2 teaspoons baking powder
½ teaspoon salt
½ cup milk
2 cups blueberries

• Cream together butter and sugar. Add egg.
• Sift together flour, baking powder and salt.
• Add sifted ingredients alternately with milk to creamed mixture.
• Fold in blueberries. (Batter will be very thick.)
• Spread into greased 9x13-inch baking pan.
• Sprinkle Topping over batter.
• Bake at 375° for 30-35 minutes.

Topping:

½ teaspoon cinnamon
½ cup firmly packed light brown
   sugar

¼ cup all-purpose flour
¼ cup butter, cut into small pieces

• Combine cinnamon, brown sugar and flour in bowl.
• Cut in butter until mixture is crumbly.

OLD-FASHIONED CRUMB CAKE

Yield: 16-20 squares

2½ cups all-purpose flour
¾ cup butter, softened
1½ teaspoons cinnamon
1 cup sugar
1 teaspoon nutmeg
½ teaspoon salt

1 egg, beaten
1 cup sour milk (to make, add
   1 teaspoon white vinegar to
   1 cup milk)
1 teaspoon baking soda

• Blend flour, butter and cinnamon until mixture resembles cornmeal.
• Reserve 1 cup flour mixture for top.
• Add sugar, nutmeg, salt, egg, sour milk and baking soda. Blend slowly.
• Pour into greased 9-inch square baking dish.
• Sprinkle reserved crumb mixture on top.
• Bake at 350° for 30 minutes, or until straw inserted in center comes out
  clean.

A light, spicy snack cake.

LIVIA'S COFFEE CAKE

Yield: 1 10-inch cake

½ cup butter, softened
¾ cup sugar
1 teaspoon vanilla
3 eggs
2 cups all-purpose flour, sifted
1 teaspoon baking powder
1 teaspoon baking soda

1 cup sour cream
6 tablespoons butter, softened
1 cup firmly packed light
   brown sugar
2 teaspoons cinnamon
1 cup chopped pecans

• Cream together butter, sugar and vanilla until light and fluffy.
• Add eggs one at at time, beating well after each addition.
• Sift together flour, baking powder and baking soda.
• Add sifted ingredients to creamed mixture alternately with sour cream, blending well after each addition.
• Spread slightly less than half the batter in greased 10-inch tube pan lined with waxed paper.
• Cream together 6 tablespoons butter, brown sugar and cinnamon.
• Add pecans and mix well.
• Sprinkle half the pecan mixture over batter in pan.
• Cover with remaining batter.
• Sprinkle with remaining pecan mixture.
• Bake at 350° for 50 minutes.

The perfect bread to satisfy that early morning sweet tooth.

SAUSAGE RING

Yield: 10 servings

1 loaf frozen bread dough,
   thawed
1 pound bulk sausage, cooked
   and drained

1¾ cups grated Mozzarella cheese
1 teaspoon oregano
½ teaspoon basil
1 egg white, beaten

• Roll bread dough into a 6x16-inch rectangle.
• Spread sausage on dough.
• Sprinkle with cheese, oregano and basil.
• Roll dough lengthwise, jelly-roll fashion. Pinch seams. Place on greased baking sheet.
• Curve dough into a circle, pinching ends together.
• Make slits in top about every 1½-2 inches.
• Cover. Let rise until doubled in bulk, about 1-1½ hours.
• Brush with egg white.
• Bake at 350° for 20-25 minutes.

DOUGHNUTS

Yield: 2 dozen

4¼ cups all-purpose flour
4   teaspoons baking powder
1¼ teaspoons nutmeg
½   teaspoon salt
2   eggs
1   cup sugar

2   tablespoons margarine, softened
1   cup milk
1¼ teaspoons vanilla
    Vegetable oil
    Powdered sugar, optional

• Sift together flour, baking powder, nutmeg and salt. Set aside.
• Cream eggs and sugar until light and fluffy.
• Add margarine, milk and vanilla. Blend well.
• Add dry ingredients all at once, stirring until just smooth. Dough will be very soft.
• Knead lightly on floured surface. Roll to ⅜-inch thickness. Cut with floured doughnut cutter.
• Heat oil to 375° in electric frying pan.
• Fry doughnuts, a few at a time, in hot oil until golden brown, turning once.
• Drain on paper towels.
• Sprinkle with powdered sugar, if desired.

Fry the doughnut holes, too! Children will make them disappear.

NANNIE'S WAFFLES

Yield: 6-8 waffles

1 cup milk
2 eggs, separated
2 tablespoons vegetable oil

1 cup all-purpose flour
1 teaspoon baking powder
  Pinch salt

• Preheat waffle iron.
• Combine milk, egg yolks, and oil in medium-size bowl.
• Sift together flour, baking powder and salt.
• Add dry ingredients to milk mixture. Blend well.
• Beat egg whites until dry. Fold into batter.
• Cook until golden brown.
• Serve with melted butter and syrup or honey.

Light and fluffy.

GERMAN PANCAKES

Yield: 1 pancake

2 tablespoons all-purpose flour
2 tablespoons milk
1 egg, slightly beaten

1 tablespoon butter
Powdered sugar
Lemon juice

- In small bowl combine flour, milk and egg, leaving batter slightly lumpy.
- Melt butter in an 8 or 9-inch round baking dish in oven.
- Pour batter into baking dish, making sure entire pan is covered.
- Bake at 425° for 15-18 minutes.
- Sprinkle with powdered sugar and lemon juice.

Great Saturday morning breakfast!!! Especially good topped with fresh fruit.

WHOLE WHEAT PANCAKES

Yield: 12-14 pancakes

1 cup whole wheat pancake mix
½ cup wheat germ
2 tablespoons nonfat dry milk
2 teaspoons baking powder

½ teaspoon salt
2 eggs, beaten
1½ cups milk
1 cup mashed bananas, optional

- Combine pancake mix, wheat germ, milk powder, baking powder and salt.
- Beat together eggs and milk. Add to flour mixture until just moistened.
- Fold in bananas, if desired.
- Use ¼ cup batter for each pancake. Bake until bubbles break on surface and edges are dry.
- Turn and bake until golden. Serve with butter or margarine and syrup.

A light, delicious pancake that's nutritious, too!

FREEZER FRENCH TOAST

Yield: 16 slices

8 eggs
2 cups milk
4 tablespoons sugar
2 teaspoons vanilla
½ teaspoon nutmeg

16 slices day-old French bread, or
1 16-ounce loaf, cut into ¾-inch
thick slices
Melted butter

• Beat together eggs, milk, sugar, vanilla and nutmeg in a large bowl.
• Place bread slices on rimmed baking sheet.
• Pour egg mixture over bread and let stand 5 minutes.
• Turn slices and let stand until all egg mixture is absorbed.
• Freeze, uncovered, until firm. Transfer frozen slices to airtight container.
  Store in freezer until ready to bake.

To Serve:
• Place desired number of frozen slices on greased baking sheet.
• Brush each with butter.
• Bake at 450° for 8 minutes.
• Turn slices and brush with butter.
• Bake 10 minutes, or until lightly browned.
• Serve with powdered sugar, honey or syrup.

Wonderful to have on hand for overnight guests!

BANANA MUFFINS

Yield: 12-16 muffins

⅓ cup sugar
¼ cup vegetable oil
1 egg
2 cups all-purpose flour
2 teaspoons baking powder

1 teaspoon salt
½ cup milk
1 cup mashed bananas
1 teaspoon grated lemon rind

• Combine sugar, oil and egg. Beat well.
• Combine flour, baking powder and salt. Blend well.
• Add dry ingredients to sugar mixture alternately with milk. Stir well after
  each addition.
• Stir in bananas and lemon rind. Do not beat. (Batter will be very stiff.)
• Spoon into prepared muffin pans.
• Bake at 400° for 20-25 minutes.

WHOLE WHEAT MUFFINS

Yield: 12 muffins

2 cups whole wheat flour
¾ cup sugar
½ teaspoon salt
¼ cup butter or margarine

1 teaspoon baking soda
1 cup buttermilk
1 egg

• Combine flour, sugar and salt. Cut in butter.
• Add baking soda to buttermilk and mix until foamy. Stir in egg.
• Add buttermilk mixture to dry ingredients. Mix until just moistened.
• Spoon into greased muffin pans. Bake at 350° for 20 minutes.

These are also good as mini-muffins. Even children love them.

CINNAMON MUFFINS

Yield: 20 muffins

¾ cup butter, softened
1½ cups sugar
3 eggs
2¼ cups all-purpose flour
1 tablespoon baking powder

Pinch salt
1 tablespoon cinnamon
¾ cup milk
¾ cup raisins, optional

• Cream butter and sugar.
• Beat in eggs, one at a time.
• Sift together flour, baking powder, salt and cinnamon.
• Add dry ingredients alternately with milk, mixing well after each addition.
• Add raisins, if desired.
• Spoon into greased muffin pans.
• Bake at 350° for 20-25 minutes.

The smell of cinnamon brings everyone to the kitchen.

PINEAPPLE-NUT BRAN MUFFINS

Yield: 5-6 dozen muffins

1   15-ounce box Post Raisin
     Bran cereal
2½ cups sugar
5   cups all-purpose flour
5   teaspoons baking soda
1   teaspoon salt
1   cup vegetable oil

1   quart buttermilk
4   eggs, slightly beaten
2   cups raisins
2½ cups chopped pecans or
     walnuts
2   20-ounce cans crushed
     pineapple, drained

• Combine cereal and sugar in large bowl.
• Sift together flour, baking soda and salt. Add to cereal mixture.
• Add oil, buttermilk and eggs. Mix well.
• Stir in raisins, nuts and pineapple.
• Spoon mixture into greased muffin pans, filling ½-⅔ full.
• Bake at 350° for 20-25 minutes. (If using mini-muffin pans, bake only
  15 minutes.)
• Batter will keep in refrigerator 4-6 weeks.

A delicate bran muffin.

BEST-EVER SHERRIED BRAN MUFFINS

Yield: 12-14 muffins

½ cup golden raisins
   Cream sherry
¼ cup sugar
½ cup butter
½ cup shortening
1   teaspoon baking soda

1   cup buttermilk
½ cup all-purpose flour
   Pinch salt
2   cups All-Bran cereal
1   egg, well beaten

• Soak raisins overnight in sherry to cover. Drain.
• Cream together sugar, butter and shortening.
• Dissolve baking soda in buttermilk. Add to creamed mixture.
• Sift flour. Add salt. Sift again. Add to creamed mixture.
• Stir in raisins, cereal and egg.
• Grease muffin pans and place in 400° oven until hot.
• Spoon mixture into hot muffin pans filling ⅔ full.
• Bake at 400° for 15 minutes.
• Let stand in pans 5 minutes. Remove carefully.

A morning or luncheon delight!

BUTTERMILK BRAN MUFFINS

Yield: 2 dozen

½ cup butter	3 cups all-purpose flour
1¼ cups sugar	2 teaspoons baking soda
2 cups buttermilk	1 teaspoon salt
2 eggs	½ cup raisins
3 cups 100% Bran cereal	

- Cream butter and sugar until light and fluffy.
- Add buttermilk and eggs. Blend well.
- Add cereal. Mix well. Let stand 5 minutes.
- Sift together flour, baking soda and salt.
- Add dry ingredients to cereal mixture, blending well.
- Stir in raisins.
- Spoon mixture into greased muffin pans.
- Bake at 350° for 25-30 minutes.
- Serve warm with butter.

Try these versatile muffins substituting ½ cup chopped pecans or ½ cup coconut for raisins.

EGG NESTS

Yield: 5 servings

4 ounces cream cheese	Grated Parmesan cheese
1 4¼-ounce can deviled ham	5 eggs, separated
5 slices whole wheat bread, crusts removed	

- Combine cream cheese and deviled ham. Blend well.
- Spread on bread slices. Place on lightly greased baking sheet.
- Sprinkle Parmesan cheese on top of cream cheese mixture.
- Beat egg whites until stiff.
- Mound equal amounts of egg whites on top of prepared slices.
- Using the back of a spoon, make an indentation in center of each egg white to resemble a nest.
- Drop an unbroken egg yolk into center of each egg nest.
- Bake at 375° for 10-15 minutes depending on desired consistency of egg yolks.

This different dish is fun and an attractive way to make breakfast exciting.

BRUNCH EGG CASSEROLE

Yield: 8-12 servings

4 cups seasoned croutons
2 cups grated Cheddar cheese
8 eggs, slightly beaten
4 cups milk
1 teaspoon salt

½ teaspoon pepper
8 slices bacon, cooked and crumbled or 1 pound bulk sausage, cooked, drained and crumbled

• Combine croutons and cheese.
• Place in greased 3-quart baking dish.
• Combine eggs, milk, salt and pepper. Mix until well blended.
• Pour over crouton mixture.
• Sprinkle crumbled bacon or sausage on top.
• Bake at 325° for 1 hour.

A delightfully different brunch casserole.

OVERNIGHT EGG SOUFFLÉ

Yield: 8-12 servings

2 cups torn bread pieces, crusts removed
1¾ cups milk
12 eggs, slightly beaten
1 teaspoon salt
¼ teaspoon pepper

4 tablespoons butter or margarine
8 slices Swiss cheese
1 pound bacon, cooked and crumbled

• Soak bread in milk. Drain, reserving milk.
• Combine milk, eggs, salt and pepper.
• Melt butter in large skillet over medium-high heat. Add eggs and cook until scrambled. Carefully stir in soaked bread.
• Pour into greased 2-quart rectangular baking dish. Layer cheese over eggs.
• Sprinkle crumbled bacon on top.
• Bake at 400° for 15 minutes.
• Refrigerate overnight.
• When ready to serve, bake at 325° for 30-45 minutes.

Serve with fruit and sweet muffins. A great way to have bacon and eggs without the last minute preparation!

CRABMEAT BRUNCH CASSEROLE

Yield: 10-12 servings

¼	cup butter	2	cups sour cream
3	tablespoons all-purpose flour	12	eggs, hard-cooked and sliced
1½	cups half and half	1	pound bacon, cooked and crumbled
1	teaspoon fine herbs	½	pound mushrooms, sautéed
2	teaspoons dried parsley	12-16	ounces fresh backfin lump crabmeat
2	teaspoons dried chives		
1½	teaspoons salt	1½	cups grated Cheddar cheese
½-1	teaspoon white pepper		

- Make a white sauce with butter, flour and half and half.
- Add herbs, parsley, chives, salt and pepper. Stir until thickened.
- Adjust seasonings and remove from heat.
- Add sour cream. Blend well.
- In greased 13x9x2-inch baking dish, layer half the eggs, bacon, mushrooms, crabmeat and sauce. Repeat layers.
- Sprinkle with cheese.
- Cook at 350° for 30-35 minutes. Be careful not to overcook.

Omit crabmeat for a different but tasty version of this recipe.

OVEN OMELET

Yield: 6 servings

8 eggs	½ cup chopped ham, optional
½ cup sour cream	2 tablespoons butter, melted
½ teaspoon salt	
1 cup grated Cheddar cheese or ½ cup Cheddar and ½ cup Swiss cheese	

- Blend together eggs, sour cream and salt.
- Stir in cheese.
- Add ham, if desired.
- Pour egg mixture into greased 1½-quart baking dish.
- Drizzle butter over top.
- Bake at 350° for 18-20 minutes, or until set.
- Tilt dish to distribute butter over top.

This dish has a soft texture and is easy to prepare.

BREAKFAST/BRUNCH CASSEROLE

Yield: 18-24 servings

3 dozen eggs
½ cup milk
½ cup butter
2 10¾-ounce cans cream of
mushroom soup
2 cups grated sharp Cheddar
cheese, divided

½ cup sherry
2 pounds sausage, cooked and
drained, or chopped ham
1 pound mushrooms, sliced and
sautéed

- Combine eggs and milk, blending well.
- Scramble egg mixture in butter until soft.
- Combine soup, 1½ cups cheese and sherry in medium saucepan. Heat until cheese melts.
- In each of two greased rectangular baking dishes, layer scrambled eggs, sausage or ham, and mushrooms.
- Pour soup mixture over mushrooms.
- Top with remaining ½ cup cheese.
- Cover with aluminum foil and refrigerate overnight.
- Bake, uncovered, at 275° for 50 minutes.

This wonderful brunch or luncheon dish is great for a crowd.

BOURSIN CHEESE QUICHE

Yield: 4-6 servings

1 9-inch deep-dish pie crust,
unbaked
1 cup grated Swiss cheese,
divided
¼ cup chopped green onions
¼ cup chopped ripe olives

⅔ cup cherry tomatoes, halved
3 eggs
½ cup whipping cream
5 ounces Boursin cheese,
softened

- Sprinkle ¾ cup Swiss cheese on bottom of pie crust.
- Sprinkle onions, olives and tomatoes over cheese.
- Beat together eggs, whipping cream and Boursin cheese in medium bowl, processor or blender.
- Pour mixture into pie crust.
- Sprinkle with remaining Swiss cheese.
- Bake at 375° for 40-50 minutes.
- Let stand 5 minutes before cutting.

This different quiche adds zip to any brunch.

SUNDAY MORNING QUICHE

Yield: 6-8 servings

1 10-inch deep-dish pie crust, unbaked
2 cups grated Cheddar cheese, divided
2 cups grated Swiss cheese, divided
4 slices bacon, chopped
½ pound hot bulk sausage
1 small onion, chopped
½ green pepper, chopped
1 4-ounce can sliced mushrooms, drained
4 eggs
¼ cup milk

• Cover bottom of pie crust with 1 cup Cheddar cheese and 1 cup Swiss cheese.
• Cook together bacon, sausage, onion and green pepper. Drain well.
• Spread sausage mixture in pie crust. Sprinkle with mushrooms.
• Top with remaining cheese.
• Beat eggs with milk. Pour over other ingredients.
• Bake at 375° for 45-55 minutes.

This quiche can be made a day ahead and baked the next morning. Great to have for overnight guests or on Christmas morning.

TUNA QUICHE

Yield: 6 servings

1 10-inch deep-dish pie crust, unbaked
1 6½-ounce can tuna, drained
1½ cups grated Swiss cheese
½ cup finely chopped onion
2 eggs, beaten
1 5-ounce can evaporated milk
1 tablespoon fresh lemon juice
1 teaspoon chopped fresh chives
1 teaspoon white wine Worcestershire sauce
¾ teaspoon garlic salt
½ teaspoon salt
⅛ teaspoon dry mustard

• Prick bottom and sides of pie crust with a fork. Bake at 400° for 5 minutes. Remove from oven.
• Spread tuna in pie crust.
• Sprinkle with cheese and onion.
• Beat together eggs, milk, lemon juice, chives, Worcestershire sauce, garlic salt, salt and mustard. Pour over tuna, cheese and onions.
• Bake at 400° for 15 minutes. Reduce heat to 350° and bake 20 minutes or until done.

May be frozen before baking. Then just thaw and bake.

71

SHRIMP QUICHE

Yield: 6 servings

½ pound cooked, chopped shrimp
2 tablespoons butter or margarine
¼ cup dry white wine
1 10-inch deep-dish pie crust, unbaked
3 eggs, beaten

1 cup half and half
½ teaspoon salt
¼ teaspoon pepper
¼ cup grated Swiss cheese
1 tablespoon fresh, chopped parsley

• Sauté shrimp in butter 1 minute.
• Add wine. Bring mixture to a boil. Boil 30-45 seconds. Drain.
• Place shrimp in pie crust.
• Combine eggs and enough half and half to make 1½ cups of liquid.
• Add salt and pepper.
• Pour egg mixture over shrimp.
• Sprinkle cheese and parsley on top.
• Bake at 375° for 30-35 minutes.

ZESTY PIMENTO CHEESE

Yield: 4 cups

1½ pounds grated sharp Cheddar cheese, room temperature
½ cup Kraft horseradish sauce
½ cup mayonnaise

1 tablespoon prepared mustard
1 7-ounce jar chopped pimentos, drained

• Combine cheese, horseradish sauce, mayonnaise and mustard in large bowl. Beat until desired spreading consistency is reached. (Beat just until well blended for a chunkier spread.)
• Add pimentos. Blend well.
• Store in refrigerator.

SOUPS AND SALADS

STRAWBERRY SOUP

Yield: 6-8 servings

2 pints fresh strawberries	¾ cup white wine
4 cups water	5 lemon slices
1½ cups sugar	1 cup whipping cream, whipped
½ teaspoon salt	Sliced fresh strawberries to
1½ cups sour cream, divided	garnish

- Purée strawberries with water in blender. Pour into saucepan.
- Add sugar, salt, 1 cup sour cream, wine and lemon slices. Heat, stirring constantly.
- Remove lemon slices.
- Fold remaining sour cream into whipped cream.
- Serve in individual bowls. Garnish with whipped cream mixture and sliced strawberries.

CHILLED CARROT SOUP WITH DILL

Yield: 6-8 servings

1 medium onion, chopped	Dash cayenne pepper
2 tablespoons butter	1 teaspoon fresh lemon juice
1 pound carrots, sliced	1 teaspoon salt
2 cups chicken broth	1 tablespoon dill weed
1 cup half and half	

- In Dutch oven, sauté onion in butter.
- Add carrots and broth. Cook until carrots are tender.
- Purée in blender or food processor, in small amounts, until smooth.
- Add half and half, cayenne pepper, lemon juice, salt and dill weed. Chill.

CHILLED CANTALOUPE SOUP

Yield: 6 servings

3 medium cantaloupes, halved	1½ cups orange juice
¾ cup dry sherry	Fresh mint leaves to garnish
¾ cup sugar	

- Scoop pulp from cantaloupes, leaving shells ½-inch thick.
- Combine pulp, sherry, sugar and orange juice in blender. Blend until smooth.
- Chill thoroughly.
- Serve in cantaloupe shells. Garnish with mint.

CUCUMBER SOUP

Yield: 4-6 servings

2 large cucumbers, peeled,
seeded and sliced
2 tablespoons butter
1 green onion, chopped
1 bay leaf
1 tablespoon all-purpose flour
3 cups chicken broth

1 teaspoon salt
Pepper to taste
Juice of ½ lemon
1 cup half and half
1 teaspoon dill weed
Sour cream to garnish

• In Dutch oven, sauté cucumbers in butter until tender.
• Add green onion and bay leaf. Simmer 20 minutes.
• Stir in flour. Cook 2 minutes.
• Add chicken broth, salt and pepper. Simmer 20 minutes. Remove bay leaf.
• Purée in blender. Chill.
• Add lemon juice, half and half and dill weed. Chill until ready to serve.
• Garnish with sour cream.

CURRIED TOMATO SOUP

Yield: 4 servings

2　medium onions, sliced
1-2 tablespoons curry powder
¼　cup butter
2　14½-ounce cans tomatoes
1　bay leaf
¼　teaspoon thyme

¼　teaspoon salt
⅛　teaspoon pepper
½　cup cooked rice, optional
　　Yogurt or sour cream and
　　lemon slices to garnish

• Sauté onions with curry powder in butter until onions are transparent.
• Add tomatoes, bay leaf, thyme, salt, pepper and rice, if desired.
• Simmer 30 minutes. Remove bay leaf.
• Purée in blender until smooth. Chill.
• Serve with yogurt or sour cream and a slice of lemon.

A rich, thick soup. To serve warm, add 1 cup half and half after heating.

TOMATO DILL SOUP

Yield: 6 servings

3 large tomatoes, peeled and
   chopped
1 medium onion, chopped
1 clove garlic, minced
1 teaspoon salt
¼ teaspoon pepper

2 sprigs fresh dill
1 tablespoon tomato paste
¼ cup cold water
½ cup cooked macaroni
1 cup chicken broth
¾ cup whipping cream

- Combine tomatoes, onion, garlic, salt, pepper, dill, tomato paste and water in stock pot. Cover and simmer 12-15 minutes. Cool.
- Add macaroni and purée in blender.
- Blend in chicken broth and cream.
- Chill before serving.

THREE LETTUCE SOUP

Yield: 4-6 servings

1 head Romaine lettuce
1 head Boston lettuce
1 head leaf lettuce
1 teaspoon minced onion
3 tablespoons butter

3 tablespoons all-purpose flour
2 14½-ounce cans chicken broth
   Salt and pepper to taste
1 cup half and half
   Grated Parmesan cheese

- Wash and tear lettuce, but do not dry.
- Place in Dutch oven, cover and cook over medium heat until limp, about 7-8 minutes.
- Purée in blender or food processor.
- Sauté onion in butter 3 minutes.
- Add flour. Cook 2 minutes.
- Gradually add broth and lettuce purée.
- Season with salt and pepper.
- Simmer until thickened.
- Add half and half. Heat thoroughly.
- Sprinkle with Parmesan cheese.

A favorite of our Cookbook Committee.

CURRIED SQUASH SOUP

Yield: 8 servings

1	medium onion, chopped	2½	cups chicken broth
4	tablespoons butter	1	5-ounce can evaporated milk
1	cup peeled, chopped apple	1	tablespoon fresh lemon juice
2	teaspoons curry powder	½	teaspoon salt
1½-2	cups cooked yellow squash	⅛	teaspoon pepper

- In Dutch oven, sauté onion in butter until transparent.
- Add apple and curry powder. Cook 5 minutes.
- Add squash and chicken broth. Bring to a boil. Reduce heat and cook 15 minutes. Cool.
- Process small amount of soup at a time in blender or food processor until smooth.
- Add milk, lemon juice, salt and pepper. Stir well.
- Serve warm or cold.

VEGETABLE SOUP NIVERNAIS

Yield: 8 servings

½ cup butter		1	cup sliced potatoes
1 cup sliced carrots		1	tablespoon salt
1 cup sliced turnips		4	cups water
1 cup sliced leeks		1	cup whipping cream
1 cup chopped celery			Carrot or celery curls to garnish

- Melt butter in deep, heavy pot.
- Add vegetables and salt.
- Simmer over low heat 20 minutes.
- Place mixture in blender or food processor. Process until desired consistency is reached.
- Return to pot, add water and simmer 20 minutes.
- Chill.
- Stir in cream. Serve chilled.
- Garnish with carrot or celery curls.

GARLIC SOUP

Yield: 6-8 servings

4	tablespoons butter, divided	2	pounds potatoes, peeled
2	leeks (white and light green		and cubed
	parts only) trimmed and	1	teaspoon salt
	sliced, about 2 cups	1	teaspoon chopped fresh
12-15	cloves garlic, peeled (about		parsley
	½ cup)	1	cup whipping cream
6	cups chicken broth		Croutons to garnish

- In Dutch oven, melt 2 tablespoons butter. Sauté leeks and garlic 2-3 minutes.
- Add chicken broth, potatoes, salt and parsley. Bring to a boil. Reduce heat, cover and simmer 45 minutes.
- Purée in blender or food processor until smooth.
- Add cream. Heat to a boil. Swirl in remaining butter.
- Serve hot. Garnish with croutons.

Do not be afraid to try this delightful soup. The flavor is smooth and delicious.

RED BELL PEPPER SOUP

Yield: 6 servings

4 medium red bell peppers, chopped	3 tablespoons butter, divided
2 leeks, chopped (white portion only)	2 cups chicken broth
	2 cups whipping cream
1 medium onion, chopped	Salt and white pepper to taste

- In heavy saucepan, sauté peppers, leeks and onion in 1 tablespoon butter until transparent, about 10 minutes.
- Add broth and cream. Increase heat and simmer until reduced by ⅓, about 30 minutes.
- Purée in blender. Return mixture to saucepan. Simmer 15 minutes.
- Remove from heat. Stir in remaining butter, salt and pepper.
- Serve hot.

CURRIED ZUCCHINI SOUP

Yield: 8 servings

6 medium zucchini, sliced	1 teaspoon salt
1 large onion, sliced	½ teaspoon pepper
5 carrots, sliced	½ teaspoon Morton Nature's
4 cups chicken broth	Seasons
1½-2 teaspoons curry powder	1-1½ cups half and half
1-2 cloves garlic, crushed	

• In saucepan, combine zucchini, onion, carrots, chicken broth, curry powder, and garlic.
• Simmer, covered, 30 minutes.
• Allow mixture to cool.
• Blend in food processor or blender until chunky, or until desired consistency is reached.
• Add salt, pepper, Morton Nature's Seasons, and half and half.
• Serve hot or cold.

This soup is best if some vegetables remain chunky.

SHERRIED MUSHROOM SOUP

Yield: 6-8 servings

1 pound fresh mushrooms, sliced	1 tablespoon dry sherry
½ cup finely chopped onion	1 teaspoon salt
4 tablespoons butter, divided	¼ teaspoon pepper
3 tablespoons all-purpose flour	2 cups half and half
1¼ cups chicken stock or 1	
10¾-ounce can chicken broth	

• In large skillet, sauté mushrooms and onion in 2 tablespoons butter 5-7 minutes, stirring frequently.
• In Dutch oven, melt remaining butter. Stir in flour. Cook until lightly browned.
• Remove from heat. Gradually add broth, sherry, mushrooms, onion, salt and pepper. Cook until thickened, stirring constantly. Simmer 15-20 minutes.
• Add half and half.
• Heat thoroughly, being careful not to boil.

VERZADA ASTURIANS

Yield: 8 servings

2	small ham hocks	1	15-ounce can Great Northern
½	pound slab smoked bacon		beans, drained
2-4	beef short ribs, fat removed	3	medium potatoes, peeled
1	small onion, chopped		and diced
½	green pepper, chopped	½	teaspoon sugar
1	clove garlic, minced	¾-1	teaspoon savory
1	14½-ounce can tomatoes	1-1½	teaspoons salt, or to taste
1	bay leaf		
2	16-ounce packages frozen collard greens		

- Place ham hocks, bacon and short ribs in large Dutch oven. Cover with water.
- Bring mixture to a boil. Skim fat, if necessary.
- Reduce heat. Add onion, green pepper, garlic, tomatoes and bay leaf.
- Cover. Cook over medium heat 1 hour or until meat is tender. Cool.
- Remove ham from bone and dice. Remove bacon and discard, or dice, if returning to soup. Discard bones and bay leaf.
- Refrigerate broth and meat separately overnight.
- Remove fat from broth surface. Purée broth and vegetables in blender or food processor.
- Slowly reheat broth. Add collard greens, beans, potatoes, sugar, savory, diced ham and diced bacon, if desired.
- Bring to a boil, then simmer 15 minutes.
- Stir in salt. Cover. Cook 30 minutes longer, or until greens and potatoes are tender.

Verzada Asturians translates to "Amazing way to prepare the lowly collard green".

WHITE WINE FISH FUMET

Craig Calvert
Calvert's and C-Grill
Augusta, Georgia
Yield: 8 cups

1 large onion, sliced	2 cups dry white wine
½ small carrot, sliced	8 cups water
1 tablespoon butter	Bouquet garni
½ cup mushrooms, chopped	½ teaspoon salt
4 pounds fish heads and bones, (preferably white fish)	½ teaspoon white pepper

• Sauté onion and carrot in butter.
• Add mushrooms, fish heads and fish bones. Cover and cook over low heat 15 minutes or until bones fall apart.
• Add wine and water. Bring briskly to a boil.
• Add bouquet garni and salt. Cook over medium heat 35-60 minutes to reduce stock.
• Add pepper during last 10 minutes of cooking.
• Strain

*Chef's note: Substitute chicken bones for fish bones to make an excellent chicken stock. The greater the reduction of liquid, the more intense the flavor.

▶ "He was a gentleman and there was laughter in his heart and on his lips, and he loved his friends...He was the best golf player the world has ever known...a fine, decent human being. The world is lesser, and Augusta—where he was so well known, loved and respected—the poorer, for his loss. But they are incredibly richer for having known his presence."

Comment by Paul Gallico about Bobby Jones

NEW ORLEANS CRAB AND ASPARAGUS BISQUE

Craig Calvert
C-Grill
Augusta, Georgia
Yield: 12 servings

¼ cup chopped shallots	4 cups WHITE WINE FISH
1 teaspoon minced garlic	FUMET or clam juice
1 tablespoon thyme	2¼ cups chopped fresh steamed
1½ teaspoons oregano	asparagus, divided
3 bay leaves	4 cups milk
2 teaspoons Tabasco	1¼ ounces chicken base or
1 cup plus 1 tablespoon unsalted	bouillon to taste
butter, divided	3 cups Alaskan king crabmeat
9 ounces all-purpose flour	½ cup sherry
⅓ cup chopped carrots	Dash white pepper
⅓ cup chopped celery	Sour cream
⅓ cup chopped onion	Sliced green onions

• In heavy saucepan, cook shallots, garlic, thyme, oregano, bay leaves and Tabasco in 1 cup butter.
• Bring to a low boil. Reduce heat. Cook 5 minutes.
• Remove from heat. Add flour and mix well.
• Return to heat. Cook 3-5 minutes.
• In small skillet, slowly cook carrots, celery and onion in 1 tablespoon butter until tender. (This is called a mirepoix.)
• Add FISH FUMET and mirepoix to flour mixture. Boil 5 minutes.
• Add 1½ cups asparagus, milk and chicken base. Simmer 20 minutes. Purée in blender or food processor.
• Add crabmeat, remaining asparagus, sherry and pepper.
• Adjust seasonings.
• Garnish each serving with sour cream and green onions.

An excellent luncheon dish served over angel hair pasta
with fresh steamed vegetables.

CORN CHOWDER

Jim King
The Bristol at Arrowhead
"The Country Club of the Rockies"
Yield: 12 servings

6	ounces salt pork, diced	1	pound fresh corn, cut from cob
½	pound onions, diced	1	leek, diced
4	ounces all-purpose flour	2	red peppers, roasted
½	gallon chicken stock	1	pint whipping cream
	Bay leaf	1	teaspoon salt, or to taste
	Pepper		Tabasco to taste
4	12-ounce cans creamed corn		
1	pound potatoes, diced and cooked		

• Sauté salt pork until lightly browned. Add onions. Sauté until tender.
• Add flour, blending to make a roux. Cook 5-10 minutes over low heat. Do not brown.
• Blend in chicken stock. Add bay leaf and pepper. Bring to a boil.
• Add creamed corn. Return to a boil. Reduce heat to simmer. Simmer 10 minutes.
• Add potatoes, fresh corn and leek. Simmer 10 minutes.
• Peel and dice red peppers. Add to soup.
• Stir in cream, salt and Tabasco. Heat but do not boil.

MURRELL'S INLET CLAM CHOWDER

Yield: 6-8 servings

¼	pound salt pork, finely chopped	2	cups finely diced potatoes
1	cup finely chopped onion	2-3	cups water
1	cup finely chopped celery		Salt and pepper to taste
2	cups chopped clams	1	cup half and half
1	cup clam juice		

• In Dutch oven, brown salt pork. Remove.
• Add onion and celery to drippings. Sauté until transparent.
• Add clams. Cook 10 minutes.
• Add pork and clam juice. Simmer 1 hour.
• Add potatoes and water. Simmer 45 minutes.
• Season with salt and pepper.
• Add half and half. Heat thoroughly, being careful not to boil.

CORN AND SHRIMP CHOWDER

Yield: 6-8 servings

12 ounces bacon
2 onions, chopped
2 cloves garlic, minced
1 cup finely chopped celery
3 tablespoons finely chopped green pepper
1 cup finely chopped carrots
¼ cup all-purpose flour
4 cups chicken broth
1 bay leaf
3 cups finely diced potatoes

1 teaspoon salt
½ teaspoon pepper
⅛ teaspoon cayenne pepper
⅛ teaspoon paprika
1 17-ounce can cream style corn
1 16-ounce can whole kernel corn
2 cups half and half
1 pound shrimp, cooked, peeled and deveined
Parsley to garnish

- In Dutch oven, cook bacon. Crumble and set aside. Reserve ¼ cup drippings.
- In reserved drippings, sauté onions, garlic, celery, green pepper and carrots until tender.
- Blend in flour, stirring constantly 2 minutes.
- Add broth and bay leaf, stirring occasionally, until thickened.
- Add potatoes, salt, pepper and paprika. Cook 20 minutes or until potatoes are tender.
- Add corn. Heat thoroughly.
- Stir in half and half.
- Add shrimp. Heat thoroughly but do not boil. Remove bay leaf and adjust seasonings.
- When ready to serve, sprinkle each serving with crumbled bacon and parsley.

*For a wonderful cheese-vegetable chowder, omit shrimp and add
2 cups grated sharp Cheddar cheese.*

▶ "The Masters® is the aristocrat of golf—the acme of color, refinement and fan appeal. It rises aloof and alone above the rest."
Billy Sixty, Milwaukee Journal

CHICKEN GUMBO

Yield: 2½ quarts

1	3-pound chicken	1	cup sliced fresh okra
6	tablespoons bacon drippings	5	ears fresh corn, cut from cob
1	large onion, chopped	1	cup chopped, cooked ham
3	ribs celery, chopped	1	teaspoon salt
1	large green pepper, chopped	¼	teaspoon cayenne pepper
¼	cup chopped fresh parsley	1	teaspoon thyme
1	clove garlic, minced	2-3	dashes Tabasco
3	tablespoons all-purpose flour		Cooked rice
4	cups peeled and chopped tomatoes		

- Cook chicken in salted water until tender. (To make a richer broth, add 2 cloves crushed garlic, 1 onion, quartered, 2 ribs celery and two carrots.) Cool and remove meat from bones. Reserve 1½ cups broth.
- Melt bacon drippings in Dutch oven over medium-high heat.
- Add onion, celery, green pepper, parsley and garlic. Cook 15 minutes, stirring occasionally.
- Add flour. Cook 5-10 minutes, stirring constantly.
- Add chicken, tomatoes, broth, okra, corn, ham, salt, cayenne pepper, thyme and Tabasco. Bring to a boil.
- Reduce heat and cover. Simmer 30 minutes, stirring occasionally.
- To serve, place gumbo in each bowl and spoon cooked rice on top.

A meal in itself.

LEMON CHICKEN SOUP

Yield: 8 servings

6	cups chicken broth	3	chicken breast halves, cooked and diced
½-¾	cup raw rice		Salt and pepper
3	egg yolks		
⅓	cup fresh lemon juice		

- Bring broth to a boil. Gradually add rice.
- Reduce to simmer and cover. Cook 25 minutes or until rice is tender.
- Meanwhile, whisk egg yolks and lemon juice together.
- When rice is cooked, add 2 cups broth to lemon juice and egg mixture and then whisk into remaining soup.
- Add chicken and return to medium heat. Cook until steaming. Do not boil.

BRUNSWICK STEW

Yield: 10-12 servings

1	4-5 pound hen	½	lemon, sliced
1	3-pound pork shoulder	1	14-ounce bottle ketchup
½	cup chopped onion	2½	ounces Worcestershire sauce
1	cup water	1	tablespoon vinegar
4	tablespoons chicken fat	⅛	teaspoon cayenne pepper
2	16-ounce cans cream style corn	1	teaspoon salt
2	16-ounce cans tomatoes, undrained	¼	teaspoon pepper
			Tabasco to taste
		2	slices bread, crumbled, optional

- Cook chicken and pork separately in salted water until tender.
- Remove chicken and reduce broth to 2 cups.
- Remove pork and reduce broth to 1 cup.
- Remove meat from bones and grind.
- Combine meat, onion, reduced broths, 1 cup water and chicken fat. Simmer 4 hours.
- Add corn, tomatoes, lemon, ketchup, Worcestershire sauce, vinegar, cayenne pepper, salt, pepper and Tabasco.
- Heat thoroughly. (If soup is too thin, add bread to thicken.)
- Remove lemon and serve.

CHICKEN BRUNSWICK STEW

Yield: 6-8 servings

1 2-3 pound chicken, cut into pieces	1 cup barbeque sauce
Garlic salt	1 tablespoon liquid smoke
2 16-ounce cans cream style corn	1 tablespoon seasoned salt
1 10-ounce bottle ketchup	1 teaspoon cayenne pepper, or to taste
1 16-ounce can tomatoes	

- Sprinkle chicken with garlic salt. Cover with water. Simmer until tender. Cool.
- Remove meat from bones. Reserve 2 cups broth.
- Combine chicken, corn, ketchup, tomatoes, barbeque sauce, liquid smoke, salt and cayenne pepper. Add broth as needed to reach desired consistency. Simmer 1-1½ hours.
- May be served over rice or in soup bowls.

TOMORROW'S CHILI

Yield: 12 servings

8	ounces dried pinto beans	1½	tablespoons vegetable oil
2	28-ounce cans whole tomatoes, undrained and chopped	2½	pounds ground venison
		1	pound lean ground pork
		½	cup chili powder
5	large onions, chopped	2	tablespoons salt
4	large green peppers, chopped	1½	teaspoons pepper
2	cloves garlic, minced	1½	teaspoons MSG
½	cup chopped parsley		
½	cup butter or margarine, melted		

- Place beans in 6-quart Dutch oven. Cover with water to 2 inches above beans. Soak overnight. Drain and rinse.
- Cook beans, covered, in water over medium heat 1 hour or until tender. Reduce heat, add tomatoes, and simmer 5 minutes.
- Add onions and green peppers. Continue cooking an additional 10 minutes, stirring often.
- Stir in garlic and parsley.
- Melt butter and oil in heavy skillet. Cook venison and pork until browned, stirring often to crumble. (3½ pounds ground beef may be substituted for the venison and pork.) Add to vegetables.
- Stir in chili powder, salt, pepper and MSG. Cover and simmer 1 hour. Uncover and simmer an additional 30 minutes.

▶ "I find that the corner is the most exciting series of golf holes that I've ever played. They (11-12-13) may not be the most difficult holes in golf, but they are certainly the most exciting. Under tournament conditions, when the pressure is on, the wind is blowing, and all the things that can happen are happening, those holes will give you the thrill which you really want or you might be looking for in golf or in life."
Arnold Palmer commenting on Amen Corner.

"The crowd's politeness and quietness stilled the heart of Amen Corner. As he lined up his eight foot putt against a backdrop of pine, poplar, oak, and a couple of weeping willows that abound on the edge of Rae's creek, all he could hear was the sounds of nature—the rushing waters of the creek, the mating call of a bob-white nearby and perhaps the croaking of a bullfrog in the pond behind—and the beating of his own heart.
He got the final line from his caddy, hunched his broad shoulders over his putter and rapped it home.
It was over."
Loren Smith commenting on the putt that Fuzzy Zoeller sank to become 1979 Masters® Champion

RAYMOND'S SPICY CHILI

Maria Floyd
wife of Raymond Floyd,
1976 Masters® Champion
Yield: 10-12 servings

3	pounds lean beef	3	tablespoons chili powder
¼	cup vegetable oil	¾	teaspoon ground cumin
2	cloves garlic, finely chopped	1	teaspoon paprika
1	small onion, finely chopped	1	teaspoon salt
1½	cups tomato sauce	¼	teaspoon black pepper
1	12-ounce can beer	¼	teaspoon cayenne pepper

• Have butcher cut beef into ½-inch cubes. In a heavy pot, heat oil, add meat, and cook over low heat until meat turns gray. Do not let it brown.
• Add garlic and onion. Cover and simmer 8 minutes.
• Add tomato sauce and beer. Cover and let simmer about 12 minutes. (If the consistency is too thin, thicken it as follows: Mix 2 tablespoons flour with water to make a thin paste, add to chili and cook 10 minutes.)
• Add remaining ingredients to meat sauce.
• Simmer, covered, 1½-2 hours over low heat. The meat is done when it breaks apart with a fork.

SPLIT PEA SOUP WITH BEER

Yield: 8 servings

1	tablespoon butter	7½	cups water
1	cup chopped onion	1	bay leaf
1	cup sliced carrots	¼	teaspoon thyme
½	cup chopped celery	1	tablespoon vinegar
1	ham bone	2-3	teaspoons salt
1	16-ounce package dried split peas	½	teaspoon pepper
1	12-ounce can beer	½	teaspoon Tabasco

• In large Dutch oven, melt butter.
• Add onions, carrots and celery. Cook 10 minutes.
• Add ham bone, peas, beer, water, bay leaf, thyme, vinegar, salt, pepper and Tabasco. Cover and bring to a boil.
• Reduce heat, skim off any foam, and simmer, covered, 2 hours.
• Remove bone. Chop and reserve meat.
• Purée soup in blender. Return to pan.
• Add meat and adjust seasonings.

POLISH SAUSAGE SOUP

Terry Wick
Eat-Cetera Delicatessen
Augusta, Georgia
Yield: 8-10 servings

2 quarts chicken broth
1 soup bone plus meat
1 pound Polish kielbasa
4 carrots, sliced
1 large onion, chopped
2 chicken bouillon cubes
2 beef bouillon cubes
½ teaspoon caraway seeds
¼ teaspoon onion powder
¼ teaspoon garlic powder
¼ teaspoon celery salt
½ teaspoon Italian spices
1 tablespoon chopped fresh parsley
3 medium potatoes, cubed
Salt and pepper to taste

- In large Dutch oven, combine chicken broth and soup bone. Simmer 2-3 hours, adding water as needed to maintain volume.
- Remove soup bone meat and chop. Return bone to broth.
- Slice kielbasa and cook for 10 minutes in enough water to cover. Drain. Add to broth.
- Add carrots, onion, bouillon, caraway seeds, onion and garlic powders, celery salt, Italian spices and parsley. Simmer 15 minutes.
- Add potatoes. Simmer until tender.
- Add meat, salt and pepper.

PARSLEY SOUP

Yield: 4 servings

4 medium potatoes, peeled and halved
2½ cups chicken broth
1 onion, chopped
2 tablespoons butter
2 cups chopped, fresh parsley
2 cups half and half
1 teaspoon salt, or to taste
¼ teaspoon pepper
3 slices bacon, cooked and crumbled

- Cook potatoes in chicken broth until tender.
- Sauté onion in butter. Add to potatoes. Mash.
- Place parsley in blender or food processor with half the potato mixture. Blend until smooth. Stir into remaining potato mixture.
- Add half and half and heat thoroughly.
- Add salt and pepper.
- Sprinkle with crumbled bacon.

A wonderful way to use a bountiful parsley crop. Delicious served chilled.

MARINATED ASPARAGUS

Yield: 10-12 servings

4	pounds fresh asparagus, trimmed	4	tablespoons minced parsley
1	cup vegetable oil	1	teaspoon sugar
½	cup white wine vinegar	1	teaspoon dry mustard
½	cup fresh lemon juice	¼	teaspoon freshly ground pepper
½	cup chopped green onion	½	teaspoon salt

• Steam asparagus until tender crisp.
• Combine remaining ingredients in a jar and shake.
• Pour marinade over asparagus and refrigerate 6 hours.
• Drain and serve.

A delightful addition to any summer meal.

SIRI'S SALAD

Yield: 4-6 servings

3	cups red or green seedless grapes, quartered	¾	cup Hellmann's mayonnaise
½	cup sliced green onion	3	tablespoons sour cream
½	cup chopped celery, optional	1	teaspoon sugar
		1	teaspoon fresh lemon juice

• Combine grapes, onion and celery. Toss gently.
• Blend together mayonnaise, sour cream, sugar and lemon juice.
• Stir mayonnaise mixture into grape mixture.
• Refrigerate until ready to serve.

*This most ususual salad is especially pretty served
on a bed of red leaf lettuce.*

MARINATED VEGETABLE SALAD

Yield: 10-12 servings

Marinade:

1½ cups vegetable oil
2 cloves garlic, minced
1½ teaspoons salt
½ cup vinegar

1 teaspoon sugar
1½ teaspoons Dijon mustard
⅛ teaspoon pepper

• Combine all ingredients. Blend well.

Salad:

1 pound fresh asparagus
2 14-ounce cans hearts of palm, drained
2 16-ounce cans baby carrots, drained

4-5 heads Bibb lettuce
1 4-ounce package Blue cheese, crumbled

• Remove tough ends of asparagus and cook asparagus tips in boiling water 4-5 minutes, or until tender crisp. Drain.
• Plunge into cold water. Drain.
• Combine asparagus, hearts of palm and carrots in large container.
• Pour Marinade over vegetables. Refrigerate overnight.
• When ready to serve, drain vegetables and serve on a bed of lettuce.
• Sprinkle with Blue cheese.

CUCUMBERS WITH DILL DRESSING

Yield: 4 servings

2-3 medium cucumbers, peeled and sliced
½ cup sour cream
1 teaspoon salt
1 tablespoon vinegar

1-2 drops Tabasco
2 tablespoons finely chopped chives or green onions
1 teaspoon dill weed
Dash of pepper

• Soak cucumbers in salted ice water 30 minutes. Drain well.
• Blend sour cream, salt, vinegar, Tabasco, onions, dill weed and pepper.
• When ready to serve, combine sour cream mixture with cucumbers.

Quick and cool summer fare.

ORANGE-KIWI SALAD

Yield: 8-10 servings

Salad:

1 head Romaine lettuce, torn	1 large red onion, sliced
3 kiwis, peeled and sliced	Croutons
1 11-ounce can mandarin oranges, drained	⅓ cup chopped walnuts or pecans
	3 ounces Blue cheese, crumbled

• Combine lettuce, kiwis, oranges and onion.
• Toss with Dressing.
• Top with croutons, nuts and Blue cheese.

Dressing:

½ cup extra virgin olive oil	3 tablespoons orange marmalade
⅓ cup fresh lime juice	1 teaspoon salt
3 tablespoons red wine vinegar	1 teaspoon freshly ground pepper

• Combine all ingredients. Shake well.

Introduce yourself to the fuzzy kiwi fruit. You'll become fast friends.

HIP'S GREEN BEANS

Yield: 4-6 servings

1 pound fresh green beans	2 cloves garlic, minced
¾ teaspoon Dijon mustard	1 teaspoon savory
1 teaspoon salt	1 tablespoon chopped fresh parsley
⅛ teaspoon pepper	
1½ teaspoons wine vinegar	1 2-ounce jar sliced pimentos, drained, optional
⅓ cup olive oil or vegetable oil	

• Blanch beans 3-5 minutes or until tender crisp. Plunge in ice water. Drain and dry.
• Combine mustard, salt, pepper and wine vinegar.
• Slowly beat in oil.
• Add garlic, savory and parsley.
• Toss mustard mixture with green beans. Add pimento, if desired.
• Refrigerate several hours.
• Allow salad to stand at room temperature 30 minutes before serving.

Green beans used in salads should always be tender and fresh.

BROCCOLI & CAULIFLOWER SALAD

Yield: 8-10 servings

1 bunch fresh broccoli	½ cup sliced green onion
1 medium head cauliflower	1 cup broken pecans
½ cup raisins	⅔ cup grated sharp Cheddar
8 slices bacon, cooked and crumbled	cheese

• Break broccoli and cauliflower into small florets.
• Place in large bowl and layer with remaining ingredients in order given.
• Pour Dressing over salad and refrigerate overnight.
• Toss just before serving.

Dressing:

1 cup mayonnaise	2 tablespoons vinegar
6-8 tablespoons sugar	

• Combine all dressing ingredients.

An unusual combination of flavors.

AVOCADO-MUSTARD SALAD

Yield: 4-6 servings

1 tablespoon cider vinegar	½-1 head iceberg lettuce, torn
2 tablespoons prepared mustard	Salt and coarsely ground black pepper
3 tablespoons vegetable oil	
1 large or 2 small ripe avocados, peeled	

• Combine vinegar, mustard and oil. Blend well.
• Cut avocado into 1-inch cubes.
• Combine avocado with mustard mixture.
• When ready to serve, toss lettuce and avocado mixture.
• Season with salt and pepper.

ARTICHOKE SALAD

Yield: 20 servings

Salad:

3 14-ounce cans hearts of palm, drained and sliced
3 8½-ounce cans (drained weight) artichoke hearts, drained and quartered
2 2-ounce jars chopped pimento
1 4½-ounce can chopped ripe olives
4 ounces fresh mushrooms, sliced, or 1 4-ounce can sliced mushrooms
1 pint cherry tomatoes

• Combine salad ingredients and chill.
• Just before serving, toss salad with Dressing.

Dressing:

2 teaspoons prepared mustard
1 tablespoon Worcestershire sauce
1 teaspoon salt
½ teaspoon pepper
½ cup vegetable oil
½ cup tarragon vinegar
Juice of 1 lemon
Pinch oregano
Pinch basil

• Mix and chill dressing ingredients.

BROCCOLI SALAD

Yield: 10-12 servings

2 bunches fresh broccoli, chopped
½ head fresh cauliflower, chopped
1 bunch green onions, chopped
1 3½-ounce jar stuffed green olives, drained and chopped
1 6-ounce (drained weight) can pitted, whole black olives, drained and sliced
3 hard-cooked eggs, chopped
¾ cup mayonnaise
1 tablespoon fresh lemon juice
2 teaspoons salt
1 teaspoon pepper

• Combine broccoli, cauliflower, onions, olives and eggs. Toss gently.
• Blend together mayonnaise, lemon juice, salt and pepper.
• Stir together mayonnaise mixture and broccoli mixture.
• Chill overnight.

A winter salad for a casual supper.

REFRESHING MUSHROOM SALAD

Yield: 6 servings

½ cup vegetable oil
¼ cup wine vinegar
¼ cup chopped fresh parsley
1 teaspoon salt
1 teaspoon sugar
½ teaspoon garlic powder

¼ teaspoon pepper
½ pound fresh mushrooms, sliced
2 cups sliced tomatoes
1 cup thinly sliced onion
Lettuce

- Combine oil, vinegar, parsley, salt, sugar, garlic powder and pepper. Blend well.
- Pour oil mixture over mushrooms, tossing well to coat.
- Add tomatoes and onion. Toss lightly.
- Cover. Chill 1 hour before serving.
- Serve on a bed of lettuce.

Due to their high water content, mushrooms should be cleaned with a damp paper towel, not rinsed under water.

MINCEMEAT SALAD

Yield: 8-10 servings

1 3-ounce package orange gelatin
1 cup orange juice, warmed
½ cup chopped celery
½ cup chopped pecans
1 8-ounce can crushed pineapple, undrained

Grated rind of 1 lemon
1 unpared apple, diced
1⅓ cups mincemeat
Maraschino cherries to garnish

- Dissolve gelatin in orange juice.
- Add celery, pecans, pineapple, lemon rind, apple and mincemeat. Mix well.
- Pour mixture into lightly oiled 1½-quart mold or 8-inch square pan.
- Refrigerate until firm.
- To double recipe, add one envelope of unflavored gelatin along with two packages of orange gelatin.
- When serving, garnish with cherries.

This spicy salad has a delicious, unusual flavor that is especially nice served with game or pork.

PORT WINE MOLD

Nelson Danish
Augusta, Georgia
Yield: 10-12 servings

2	3-ounce packages raspberry gelatin	1	cup chopped pecans
1¼	cups boiling water	½	cup chopped celery
1	cup port wine		Mayonnaise
1	14-ounce can crushed pineapple, undrained		

• Dissolve gelatin in boiling water.
• Add wine. Cool until gelatin mixture is consistency of egg whites.
• Add pineapple, pecans and celery. Blend well.
• Lightly grease a 1½-quart mold with mayonnaise. Spoon mixture into mold.
• Refrigerate until firm.

GRAPEFRUIT ASPIC

Yield: 8 servings

2	envelopes unflavored gelatin	¾	cup chopped celery
1	cup cold water	½	cup slivered almonds
1	cup boiling water		Lettuce
3	tablespoons fresh lemon juice		Avocado slices to garnish
¾	cup sugar		Mayonnaise
3	large grapefruit, peeled and sectioned or 3 jars grapefruit sections		

• Soak gelatin in cold water.
• Add boiling water, lemon juice and sugar. Stir until gelatin is dissolved.
• Chill until slightly congealed.
• Add grapefruit sections, celery and almonds. Blend well.
• Pour into a 2-quart mold or pan.
• Refrigerate until firm. Unmold.
• Serve on a bed of lettuce with avocado slices and mayonnaise.

95

CRANBERRY SNOW

Yield: 12-16 servings

1   pound fresh or frozen
    cranberries, ground
1   cup chopped pecans
1   20-ounce can crushed
    pineapple, drained

1½ cups sugar
1   10½-ounce bag miniature
    marshmallows
2   cups whipping cream, whipped

• Combine cranberries, pecans, pineapple and sugar in large bowl.
• Fold marshmallows into whipped cream.
• Fold whipped cream mixture into cranberry mixture.
• Chill.

A refreshing, colorful addition to any holiday meal.
Recipe can be prepared early in the day, but do not fold in whipped cream
mixture until ready to serve.

ITALIAN PASTA SALAD

Yield: 10-12 servings

1   16-ounce box multi-colored
    rotini
1   zucchini, sliced
¼   cup sliced black olives
½   pound ham, cut into julienne
    strips
1½ ounces pepperoni slices,
    halved
1½ teaspoons salt
½   red pepper, slivered
1   8½-ounce (drained weight)
    can artichoke hearts,
    quartered

1   cup chopped celery
¾   cup sliced green onion
1   teaspoon oregano
1   teaspoon thyme
1   cup prepared Good Seasons
    Italian dressing
½   cup freshly grated Parmesan
    cheese
    Freshly ground black pepper

• Prepare pasta according to package directions. Drain and rinse with
  cool water.
• Add zucchini, olives, ham, pepperoni, salt, red pepper, artichoke hearts,
  celery, green onion, oregano and thyme.
• Toss with dressing. Adjust seasonings.
• Sprinkle with Parmesan cheese and generous grinds of black pepper.

FIESTA PASTA SALAD

Yield: 10-12 servings

Dressing:

½ cup red wine vinegar   ½ cup mayonnaise
½ cup sour cream

• Combine all ingredients for Dressing. Blend well.

Salad:

1   12-ounce package twist or   2   hard-cooked eggs, chopped
    shell macaroni   1   cup grated Cheddar cheese
½ cup chopped green pepper   Salt and pepper to taste
¼ cup chopped celery   2   cups chopped, cooked shrimp,
¼ cup chopped onion   chicken, or ham, optional
½ cup sliced fresh mushrooms   Grated Parmesan cheese
1   cup chopped fresh broccoli,   Cherry tomatoes and pitted
    cooked   black olives to garnish

• Cook pasta according to package directions. Drain.
• Rinse with cool water. Drain again.
• Pour Dressing over warm pasta.
• Add green pepper, celery, onion, mushrooms, broccoli, eggs, cheese, salt
  and pepper. Toss.
• Stir in shrimp, chicken or ham, if desired.
• Chill.
• Serve on a bed of lettuce. Sprinkle with Parmesan cheese and garnish with
  tomatoes and olives.

▶   "Winning the Masters® is a dream come true. Like all other kids when I was growing up, I used to get on the practice green and practice my putting and say, 'This putt
is for the Masters®.' Well, a lot of kids do that, but I'm one kid who grew up to see his
dream come true."
                    Fuzzy Zoeller, 1979 Masters® Champion

ANGEL HAIR PASTA SALAD

Yield: 6-8 servings

Salad:
9 ounces angel hair pasta
4 tablespoons olive or vegetable oil
½ teaspoon oregano
½ teaspoon basil
1 teaspoon salt
½ teaspoon cracked pepper
4-5 medium carrots
½ pound fresh asparagus, trimmed
1½ cups fresh broccoli florets with some stem, cut on diagonal
4 green onions, sliced with some green tops
½ cup sliced pitted ripe olives
1 cup chopped ham, optional
½ pound cooked shrimp, optional
¼ cup crumbled Feta cheese
Grated Parmesan cheese, optional

- Cook pasta according to package directions. Drain.
- Rinse with cold water and separate gently. Drain again. Transfer to large salad bowl.
- Add oil, oregano, basil, salt and pepper.
- Toss gently until evenly coated.
- Adjust seasonings. Set aside.
- Slice carrots into 1-inch pieces, then slice thinly lengthwise.
- Slice asparagus diagonally into 1-inch pieces.
- Steam carrots, asparagus and broccoli 3-5 minutes, or until tender crisp.
- Drain and rinse under cold water. Drain again.
- Place vegetables, onions, olives, ham and shrimp, if desired, on top of pasta.
- Add Feta cheese.
- Cover and refrigerate.
- When ready to serve, gently toss prepared pasta salad with Dressing, by hand, until evenly coated.
- Serve with Parmesan cheese, if desired.

Dressing:
¾ cup olive or vegetable oil
6 teaspoons red wine vinegar
¼ teaspoon garlic salt
½ teaspoon salt
⅛ teaspoon cracked pepper

- Combine dressing ingredients in pint jar. Shake well. Refrigerate.

MAC-BEAN SALAD

Yield: 8-12 servings

1	16-ounce package macaroni (any shape desired)		Salt to taste
½	pound bacon, diced	2	teaspoons prepared mustard
4	tablespoons vegetable oil	1	16-ounce can green beans, drained
4-6	tablespoons vinegar	8	ounces American cheese, cubed
2	tablespoons sugar		
¾	teaspoon pepper	½	cup chopped onion

• Cook macaroni according to package directions. Drain.
• Cook bacon until crisp, reserving 3 tablespoons drippings.
• Combine bacon drippings, oil, vinegar, sugar, pepper, salt and mustard in large pot. Blend well.
• Stir in macaroni, bacon, beans, cheese and onion. Toss well.
• Cook over low heat until hot. Do not allow cheese to melt completely.

HOT AVOCADO BOAT

Yield: 2 servings

1 tablespoon red wine vinegar
1 tablespoon ketchup
1 tablespoon Worcestershire sauce
1 tablespoon sugar

1 tablespoon butter
1 ripe avocado, peeled and halved
Red leaf lettuce

• Combine vinegar, ketchup, Worcestershire sauce, sugar and butter in saucepan. Heat until almost boiling.
• When ready to serve, place each avocado half on a bed of lettuce.
• Fill avocado "boats" with hot sauce.

This recipe can easily be increased for a larger number of guests.

COLESLAW SUPREME

Yield: 10-12 servings

1 medium head cabbage, shredded	2 tablespoons cider vinegar
2 cups seedless green grapes, halved	2 tablespoons finely chopped onion
1 2-ounce package slivered almonds, toasted	1 teaspoon sugar
1 carrot, grated	1 teaspoon dry mustard
	½ teaspoon salt
	1 cup mayonnaise

- Combine cabbage, grapes, almonds and carrot. Toss and set aside.
- In separate bowl, combine vinegar, onion, sugar, mustard and salt. Blend well.
- Slowly stir in mayonnaise.
- Pour mayonnaise mixture over cabbage mixture. Toss gently.
- Chill at least 4 hours before serving.

Red seedless grapes may be substituted for green grapes to make this salad especially colorful.

SOUR CREAM POTATO SALAD

Yield: 10-12 servings

4-5 Idaho potatoes	½ teaspoon salt, or to taste
1½ cups mayonnaise	1 large onion, finely chopped
1 cup sour cream	½ cup chopped fresh parsley, divided
1½ teaspoons horseradish	
1 teaspoon celery seed	

- Boil potatoes until tender. Peel and slice.
- Combine mayonnaise, sour cream, horseradish, celery seed and salt.
- Layer ½ the potatoes in serving dish.
- Pour ½ the sour cream mixture over potatoes.
- Sprinkle with onion and ¼ cup parsley.
- Repeat layers of potatoes, sour cream and parsley.
- Cover and refrigerate overnight.

MUSHROOM-BACON SALAD

Yield: 6 servings

⅔ cup olive oil
4 tablespoons fresh lemon juice
1 teaspoon Worcestershire sauce
½ teaspoon salt
 Dash freshly ground pepper
½ teaspoon dry mustard

1 pound fresh mushrooms, sliced
 Bibb lettuce
3 green onions, sliced
12 slices bacon, cooked and
 crumbled

- Combine olive oil, lemon juice, Worcestershire sauce, salt, pepper and mustard.
- Pour over mushrooms. Marinate 4-6 hours. Drain, reserving marinade.
- On salad plate, layer lettuce and mushrooms.
- Sprinkle with green onions and bacon.
- Drizzle with marinade, if desired.

INDIAN SPINACH SALAD

Yield: 6-8 servings

Salad:
8 cups torn fresh spinach
 (approximately 10 ounces)
1½ cups chopped, unpared
 apples

½-¾ cup golden raisins
½ cup peanuts, crushed
2-3 tablespoons chopped
 green onions

- Combine all ingredients.
- Toss with Dressing.

Dressing:
¼ cup white wine vinegar
¼ cup vegetable oil
2 tablespoons chutney, chopped
½ teaspoon sugar

½ teaspoon salt
1½ teaspoons curry powder
1 teaspoon dry mustard

- Combine all ingredients in jar. Shake well.
- Chill before serving.

RED LEAF LETTUCE SALAD WITH LEMON-MUSTARD DRESSING

Yield: 4-6 servings

1 head red leaf lettuce, torn
½ cup pine nuts, lightly toasted

¼ cup freshly grated Romano cheese
Freshly ground pepper

• Combine lettuce with pine nuts in salad bowl.
• Add Romano cheese.
• Toss with Lemon-Mustard Dressing and top with pepper.

Lemon-Mustard Dressing:
Yield: 1½ cups
1 cup vegetable oil
4 tablespoons fresh lemon juice
¼ cup red wine vinegar
½ teaspoon soy sauce

1 tablespoon Colman's Hot English Mustard
1 tablespoon sugar
½ teaspoon cayenne pepper

• Combine all dressing ingredients in blender. Blend well.

A simple yet elegant salad.

SENSATIONAL SALAD

Yield: 10-12 servings

Salad:
2 large heads Romaine lettuce
1 bunch parsley, chopped
1 cup grated Romano cheese

1 4-ounce package Blue cheese, crumbled
Freshly ground pepper to taste

• When ready to serve, combine lettuce and parsley.
• Pour Dressing over lettuce mixture. Toss well.
• Sprinkle with Romano and Blue cheese. Toss again.
• Season with pepper.
• Serve immediately.

Dressing:
½ cup vegetable oil
½ cup olive oil
2½ tablespoons fresh lemon juice

1½ tablespoons vinegar
2 cloves garlic, minced
1 teaspoon salt

• Combine all dressing ingredients. Blend well.

FETA SALAD WITH WALNUT OIL DRESSING

Yield: 4 servings

Leaf lettuce, torn
Fresh spinach, torn
½ cup sliced fresh mushrooms
¼ cup pine nuts, lightly toasted

¼ cup crumbled Feta cheese
2 green onions, sliced
Freshly ground pepper

• Combine lettuce and spinach in bowl.
• Top with mushrooms, pine nuts, cheese, onions and pepper.
• Toss with Walnut Oil Dressing.

Walnut Oil Dressing:
Yield: 1 cup
¾ cup walnut oil
1 tablespoon fresh lemon juice
5 teaspoons raspberry vinegar
1 teaspoon Dijon mustard
½ teaspoon salt

¼ teaspoon basil
Cracked pepper
Pinch sugar
1 clove garlic, split

• Combine all ingredients in small jar.
• Shake just before serving.
• Store at room temperature.

GREEK-STYLE SALAD

Yield: 6-8 servings

1 cup corn oil
⅔ cup red wine vinegar
1 teaspoon oregano
1 teaspoon basil
2 teaspoons seasoned salt

½ teaspoon coarsely ground
 pepper
½ teaspoon garlic powder
Lettuce
Crumbled Feta cheese

• Combine oil, vinegar, oregano, basil, seasoned salt, pepper and garlic powder. Blend well.
• Toss with a variety of lettuce.
• Sprinkle with Feta cheese.

This dressing also makes a delicious marinade for chicken or lamb chops.

103

CELEBRATION TOSSED SALAD

Yield: 8 servings

Salad:

1 large head Romaine lettuce, torn	1 large ripe avocado, sliced
	3 ounces Blue cheese, crumbled
1 large tomato, sliced	6 slices bacon, cooked and
1 medium red onion, sliced	crumbled

- Place lettuce in bottom of large salad bowl.
- Arrange vegetables on top of lettuce. Sprinkle Blue cheese and bacon over all.
- When ready to serve, toss with Dressing.

Dressing:

¾	cup vegetable oil	1	teaspoon salt
¼	cup vinegar	4	teaspoons sugar
1	clove garlic, minced		Pepper to taste

- Combine all ingredients in jar. Shake well.

A "picture perfect" salad with minimum effort.

MY FAVORITE SPINACH SALAD

Yield: 4-5 servings

½	cup vegetable oil	1	teaspoon salt
¼	cup cider vinegar	½	teaspoon pepper
2	tablespoons sugar	10-16	ounces fresh spinach, torn
1	tablespoon Worcestershire sauce	4	strips bacon, cooked and crumbled
1	clove garlic, crushed	2	hard-cooked eggs, chopped
½	cup ketchup	3	green onions, chopped

- Combine oil, vinegar, sugar, Worcestershire sauce, garlic, ketchup, salt and pepper in a jar.
- Shake well. Refrigerate.
- Layer spinach, bacon, eggs and onion in bowl.
- Toss with dressing.

CAESAR SALAD BY CRAIG

Craig Calvert
Calvert's and C-Grill
Augusta, Georgia
Yield: 4-6 servings

1	large head Romaine lettuce	6	anchovy filets, drained and chopped
1	clove garlic, halved lengthwise		
½	cup salad oil (corn, peanut or olive)	1	egg
		¼	cup crumbled Blue cheese
1	cup French bread cubes (½-inch), crusts removed	2	tablespoons grated Parmesan cheese
¾	teaspoon salt	2	tablespoons fresh lemon juice
¼	teaspoon dry mustard	6	whole anchovy filets, optional
¼	teaspoon freshly ground black pepper		
1½	teaspoons Worcestershire sauce		

• Trim and core lettuce. Separate leaves. Wash with cold water. Drain. Dry with paper towels. Place in plastic bag and refrigerate several hours or overnight.
• Several hours before serving, crush half the garlic clove. Combine with oil in jar with tight-fitting lid. Refrigerate at least 1 hour.
• Heat 2 tablespoons oil-garlic mixture in medium skillet.
• Add bread cubes. Sauté until brown. Set aside.
• To remaining oil-garlic mixture, add salt, mustard, pepper, Worcestershire sauce and chopped anchovies. Shake vigorously. Refrigerate.
• In small saucepan, bring a 2-inch depth of water to boiling. Turn off heat. Carefully lower egg into water and let stand 1 minute. Remove. Set aside to cool.
• Just before serving, rub inside of large wooden bowl with the remaining garlic clove half. Discard clove.
• To prepare lettuce, cut out coarse rib and tear into bite-size pieces into bowl.
• Shake dressing well. Pour over lettuce.
• Sprinkle with both cheeses.
• Toss until all lettuce is coated with dressing.
• Break egg over center of salad.
• Pour lemon juice directly over egg. Toss well.
• Sprinkle with bread cubes. Toss again quickly.
• Garnish with whole anchovies, if desired. Serve at once.

The secret to the success of this salad is to thoroughly dry the Romaine leaves.

CAROLE'S EASY CAESAR SALAD

Yield: 4 servings

Salad:

1 head Romaine lettuce, torn
1 head leaf lettuce, torn

2 tablespoons grated Parmesan cheese
Croutons

• Place lettuce in salad bowl and sprinkle with Parmesan cheese and croutons.
• Pour Dressing over salad and toss.

Dressing:

¾ cup vegetable oil
¼ cup fresh lemon juice
1 tablespoon Worcestershire sauce

½ teaspoon garlic salt
1 egg, beaten
Anchovy paste, optional

• Combine dressing ingredients. Shake well.

CURRIED CHICKEN-RICE SALAD

Yield: 8 servings

2 cups cooked, diced chicken
4-5 green onions, chopped
½ cup sliced water chestnuts
⅓ cup chopped green pepper
1 cup raw rice, cooked
½ cup golden raisins

1 cup mayonnaise
½ cup chutney
1 teaspoon curry powder
½ teaspoon salt
Dijon mustard to taste
½ cup peanuts

• In large bowl, combine chicken, onions, water chestnuts and green pepper.
• Stir in rice and raisins.
• Combine mayonnaise, chutney, curry powder, salt and mustard. Blend well.
• Fold mayonnaise mixture into chicken mixture. Blend together thoroughly.
• Refrigerate until ready to serve.
• Stir in peanuts just before serving.

Enhance the flavor of this different chicken salad by cooking the rice in chicken broth.

POLYNESIAN CHICKEN SALAD

Maria Floyd
wife of Raymond Floyd,
1976 Masters® Champion
Yield: 8 servings

Salad:
6   chicken breast halves, cooked and cut into strips
½   cup slivered almonds, toasted
2-3 green onions, slivered
¼   green pepper, slivered
½   pound fresh green peas, shelled

3   ribs celery, chopped
2   papayas, cut into small squares
½   cup shredded coconut
1   cup Ming bean sprouts
3-4 fresh mushrooms, sliced
    Avocado, mushrooms, and lime slices to garnish

• Combine all ingredients. Toss together gently.
• Pour Dressing over salad. Toss lightly.
• To serve, garnish with avocado wedges, mushrooms, and twisted lime slices.

Dressing:
½-1 cup mayonnaise
1   cup chutney
1-2 teaspoons curry powder

Freshly ground black pepper
Juice of ½ lemon

• Combine dressing ingredients. Mix well.

All fresh ingredients and absolutely sensational!

"One of the unique features of the Masters® is that each year most of the former champions return to Augusta.

That doesn't happen at any other tournament and while many of the former champions are no longer active on the tour, they still are qualified to compete at the Masters®. There is a Masters® Club room reserved exclusively for those who have won the prestigious Masters® Green coat.

On Wednesday evening, they gather at the club for a dinner, hosted by the most recent champion, an idea that originated with two time winner Ben Hogan.

CHICKEN SALAD WITH AVOCADO DRESSING

Yield: 8 servings

Salad:

3 cups cooked rice
3 cups cooked, diced chicken
1 8-ounce can green peas,
    drained or 1 10-ounce package
    frozen early peas

¼-½ cup chopped onion
½   cup mayonnaise
1   teaspoon salt
1   teaspoon pepper
     Lettuce leaves

• Combine rice, chicken, peas and onion. Toss gently.
• Combine mayonnaise, salt and pepper.
• Fold mayonnaise mixture into rice mixture.
• Serve on a bed of lettuce with Avocado Dressing. Serve remaining Dressing on the side.

Avocado Dressing:

1 large avocado, peeled and
   mashed
½ cup mayonnaise
1 cup sour cream
¼ teaspoon Worcestershire sauce

⅛ teaspoon garlic salt
¼ teaspoon salt
¼ teaspoon onion salt
   Dash Tabasco

• Combine all ingredients. Blend well.

"He was always 'Mr. Roberts.'
Don't build him a monument. The monument is already there in the Augusta National Golf Course, the most majestic in the world. Don't send flowers. They adorn every one of Augusta's 18 holes—azaleas, jasmine, camellias and dogwood, shadowed by towering pines. His tombstone golf's finest spectacle.
Although the Masters® carries the thumb-print of Atlanta's immortal Bobby Jones, it was Mr. Roberts, Jones' close friend, who nurtured it in its weening years, pampered and molded and protected it until it became the model of golf tournaments everywhere.
Yet none could match it.
'The Masters®,' said author Alistair Cooke, the devotee of golf and the American heritage, 'is unique. Masters® Week is like taking a leisurely stroll in the country.' "
Will Grimsley upon the death of Clifford Roberts in 1977

ORIENTAL CHICKEN SALAD

Yield: 12-16 servings

1	5-ounce package yellow rice	2	hard-cooked eggs, chopped
4-5	cups cooked, diced chicken	½	cup chopped sweet pickle
1	8-ounce can sliced mushrooms, drained	1	small onion, finely chopped
1	5-ounce can sliced water chestnuts, drained	1	cup chopped green olives
		2½	cups chopped celery
10	ounces oriental-style vegetables, cooked and drained	¼	cup chopped green pepper
			Salt and freshly ground pepper to taste

• Cook rice according to package directions. Cool.
• Combine rice and chicken in large bowl.
• Add remaining ingredients. Toss well.
• Chill 3 hours.
• To serve, toss salad with Dressing.

Dressing:

1	8-ounce bottle creamy Italian dressing	1	tablespoon tarragon vinegar
½	cup mayonnaise	½	teaspoon curry powder
1	teaspoon sugar	½	teaspoon prepared mustard

• Combine all dressing ingredients. Blend thoroughly.

CHICKEN AND SHRIMP SALAD

Yield: 10-12 servings

4-5	cups cooked, diced chicken	½	cup mayonnaise
1-2	pounds shrimp, cooked peeled and deveined	½	cup sour cream
1	cup chopped celery	2	tablespoons Dijon mustard
2	hard-cooked eggs, chopped	1	teaspoon oregano
2	cups sweet pickle relish, rinsed and drained	1	teaspoon Tabasco
		½	teaspoon salt
½	cup chopped green onion	½	teaspoon paprika
		½	teaspoon pepper

• Combine chicken, shrimp, celery, eggs, relish and onion in large bowl.
• In separate bowl, blend together mayonnaise, sour cream, mustard, oregano, Tabasco, salt, paprika and pepper.
• Fold mayonnaise mixture into chicken mixture. Toss thoroughly.
• Refrigerate until ready to serve.

SALADE CREVETTE

Craig Calvert
Calvert's and C-Grill
Augusta, Georgia
Yield: 4 servings

Shrimp:

2 quarts water	Pinch salt
1 sprig thyme	20 large shrimp
1 sprig tarragon	

• Combine water, thyme, tarragon and salt in large saucepan. Simmer over low heat.
• Add shrimp. Cook until just pink, about 2 minutes. Drain. Cool shrimp.
• Peel and devein shrimp, leaving tails intact.
• Fold shrimp into Sauce.

Sauce:

¾ cup whipping cream	1 tablespoon minced fresh chives
2 tablespoons Dijon mustard	
1 tablespoon ketchup	1½ teaspoons Worcestershire sauce
1 tablespoon minced fresh tarragon	Juice of ½ lemon

• Combine all sauce ingredients in large bowl.

Vinaigrette:

3 tablespoons vinegar	Freshly ground pepper
2 tablespoons Dijon mustard	½ cup plus 1 tablespoon olive or walnut oil
Salt	

• Combine vinegar, mustard, salt and pepper in small bowl.
• Whisk in oil until well blended.

Salad:

4 whole artichoke hearts (canned)	16 Belgian endive leaves
32 very thin fresh green beans, blanched and halved lengthwise	16 snow peas, blanched
8 large mushroom caps, sliced	12 avocado slices
12 inner leaves of butterhead lettuce	16 apple slices

• Combine artichoke hearts and half the Vinaigrette in bowl. Mix well.
• Combine green beans and mushrooms with remaining Vinaigrette in separate bowl.

(continued)

Assembly:
• For each serving, place 3 lettuce leaves in center of plate.
• Line 5 shrimp down center of leaves, overlapping slightly with tails facing same direction.
• Place artichoke heart at top of shrimp.
• Arrange 4 endive leaves with yellow points outward at upper left of plate.
• Arrange 1 snow pea in center of each endive leaf.
• Place 3 overlapping slices of avocado at lower left of plate.
• Arrange ¼ of the green bean and mushroom mixture at lower right.
• Place 4 apple slices, overlapping at bottom of plate.

Chef's note: Any shellfish may be successfully substituted for shrimp, and vegetables and fruits may be varied in order to obtain market-fresh products.

GULF COAST SALAD

Yield: 6-8 servings

1 pound shrimp, cooked, peeled and deveined	½ teaspoon salt
	⅛ teaspoon pepper
1 cup cooked rice, cooled	½ teaspoon horseradish
¼ cup chopped green onion	½ teaspoon dry mustard
½ cup chopped celery	¼ teaspoon Tabasco
½ cup mayonnaise	1 tablespoon fresh lemon juice
2 tablespoons ketchup	

• In large mixing bowl, combine shrimp, rice, onion and celery.
• In separate bowl, combine mayonnaise, ketchup, salt, pepper, horseradish, mustard, Tabasco and lemon juice. Blend well.
• Toss mayonnaise mixture gently with shrimp mixture.
• Cover tightly and refrigerate several hours, or overnight, before serving.

LAMBERT'S TACO SALAD

Yield: 8 servings

2 pounds ground beef
1 tablespoon chili powder
1 16-ounce can New Orleans style kidney beans, drained
1 cup creamy French salad dressing, divided
1 teaspoon salt, divided
3 medium tomatoes, chopped
½ cup chopped green pepper
2 large avocados, peeled, pitted and mashed
   Juice of ½ lemon

¼ cup chopped onion
8 slices bacon, cooked and crumbled
⅛ teaspoon Tabasco
½ cup mayonnaise
   Tortilla chips
3 cups shredded lettuce
8 ounces Monterey Jack cheese, grated
   Taco sauce to taste
   Greek or jalapeño peppers to garnish

• Brown ground beef. Drain well.
• Add chili powder, kidney beans, ⅔ cup dressing and ½ teaspoon salt. Simmer 10 minutes. Set aside.
• Combine tomatoes, green pepper and remaining ⅓ cup dressing. Toss lightly. Set aside.
• Combine avocado, lemon juice, onion, bacon, ½ teaspoon salt, Tabasco and mayonnaise. Mix well.
• To assemble, layer tortilla chips, lettuce, tomato mixture, beef mixture, cheese and avocado mixture.
• Cover with taco sauce as desired.
• Garnish with Greek or jalapeño peppers.

▶ "His gift to his friends is the warmth that comes from unselfishness, superb judgement, nobility of character, and unwavering loyalty of principle."
President Dwight Eisenhower in reference to Robert Tyre Jones, Jr.

STEAK SUPPER SALAD

Yield: 6 servings

Salad:

1 1½-2 pound flank steak	1 large red pepper, cut into
¼ cup olive oil	julienne strips
½ cup red wine vinegar	½ teaspoon coarsely ground
Freshly ground black pepper	pepper
2 pounds new potatoes	Romaine and leaf lettuce
1 pound fresh asparagus	
1 pound fresh green beans, trimmed	

- Marinate steak in olive oil, vinegar and pepper 3-4 hours or overnight.
- Pan fry steak over high heat until medium rare. Cool.
- Cut steak into julienne strips.
- Boil potatoes until just tender. Do not overcook. Slice.
- Remove tough ends of asparagus and cook tips in boiling water until tender crisp. Plunge in cold water. Drain.
- Repeat cooking process with green beans.
- Cut asparagus and beans into 2-inch diagonal pieces.
- Combine beef, vegetables, pepper and Dressing. Toss well.
- Serve on a generous bed of Romaine and leaf lettuce.
- Toss just before serving.

Dressing:

1 tablespoon champagne mustard	4 tablespoons white wine vinegar
	Salt and pepper to taste
1 teaspoon Pommery mustard	½ cup olive oil

- Combine mustards, vinegar, salt and pepper. Mix well.
- Drizzle oil into mixture, whisking until well blended.

This is a sophisticated, attractive salad for a light supper. Serve with warm crusty French bread and a red wine. Perfect for a gourmet picnic.

TONI'S RICE SALAD

Yield: 6-8 servings

3½	cups cooked rice, chilled
1½-2	cups mayonnaise
3-4	teaspoons prepared mustard
½	medium onion, chopped
1½	cups sliced celery
½	teaspoon salt
½	cup cooked, crumbled bacon
1	hard-cooked egg, chopped
3	radishes, sliced
1	medium cucumber, peeled and diced
	Lettuce
	Tomato, cut into wedges

- Combine rice, mayonnaise, mustard, onion, celery and salt. Mix well. Chill.
- Just before serving, stir in bacon, egg, radishes and cucumber.
- Line platter with lettuce. Place rice mixture on top. Surround with tomato wedges.

SAUCE VINAIGRETTE FOR ASPARAGUS

Yield: 1½ cups

2	teaspoons coarse salt
1	teaspoon white pepper
½	teaspoon pepper
¼	teaspoon sugar
½	teaspoon dry mustard
1	teaspoon Dijon mustard
1	teaspoon fresh lemon juice
2	teaspoons minced garlic
5	tablespoons tarragon vinegar
2	tablespoons olive oil
1	egg
½	cup half and half

- Combine all ingredients in jar in order given. Shake well.
- Chill before using.
- Serve with fresh asparagus, cooked and chilled. (Or marinate asparagus in dressing for 8 hours.)

BLUE CHEESE DRESSING

Yield: 1 cup

¼ pound crumbled Blue cheese	1 tablespoon white vinegar
⅛ cup vegetable oil	1¼ teaspoons garlic powder
1 cup Hellmann's mayonnaise	Salt and pepper to taste
½ cup sour cream	¼ cup buttermilk

- Mix Blue cheese and oil.
- Add mayonnaise, sour cream and vinegar. Blend well.
- Stir in garlic powder, salt and pepper.
- Thin dressing to desired consistency with buttermilk.
- Store in refrigerator until ready to use. (If dressing thickens after several days, thin again with buttermilk.)

FRENCH DRESSING

Yield: 2 cups

1 rib celery, diced	2 tablespoons sugar
1 small onion, thinly sliced	Dash paprika
1 clove garlic, minced	Dash Worcestershire sauce
⅓ cup white wine vinegar	Pinch salt
⅓ cup ketchup	⅔ cup vegetable oil
2 teaspoons Dijon mustard	

- Combine all ingredients in jar. Shake well.
- Store in refrigerator. Shake well before using.

FANCY FRENCH DRESSING

Yield: 1½ pints

1 10¾-ounce can tomato soup	1 teaspoon paprika
1 cup vegetable oil	1 teaspoon pepper
¾ cup apple cider vinegar	1 teaspoon Colman's dry mustard
3 tablespoons sugar	
1½ tablespoons salt	1 small onion, grated
1 tablespoon Worcestershire sauce	1 small clove garlic, minced

- Combine all ingredients in jar in order given. Blend thoroughly.
- Store in refrigerator. Shake before serving.

115

SPINACH SALAD DRESSING

Yield: 1 pint

½   **cup vegetable oil**
¾   **cup red wine vinegar**
1   **tablespoon soy sauce**
¼-½ **cup sugar**

¾   **cup chili sauce**
1   **small onion, finely chopped,**
       optional

• Combine all ingredients in large jar. Shake well.
• Store in refrigerator until ready to use.

This dressing improves with age.

CAESAR SALAD DRESSING

Yield: 1½ cups

1   **clove garlic, minced**
       Anchovy paste to taste
1   **egg**
       Juice of 1 lemon

¾   **cup vegetable oil**
¼   **cup olive oil**
⅓   **cup white wine vinegar**
       Salt and pepper to taste

• In food processor or blender, combine garlic and anchovy paste.
• Add egg and lemon juice. Blend well.
• Combine vegetable oil, olive oil and vinegar.
• Add oil mixture to egg mixture. Mix well.
• Season with salt and pepper.

BEST "HOUSE" DRESSING

Yield: 3-4 cups

¾   **cup red wine vinegar**
1   **egg**
1   **teaspoon salt**
½   **teaspoon pepper**
1   **teaspoon seasoned salt**

½   **teaspoon garlic salt**
1   **teaspoon tarragon leaves**
½   **cup vegetable oil**
2-3 **cups mayonnaise**

• Combine vinegar, egg, salt, pepper, seasoned salt, garlic salt, tarragon
  leaves and oil in blender. Blend.
• Slowly add mayonnaise until desired consistency is reached.

MOCK CAESAR DRESSING

Yield: 2 cups

3 tablespoons wine vinegar	½ teaspoon cracked pepper
2 tablespoons finely chopped green onion	1 egg
1 teaspoon salt	½ cup grated Parmesan cheese
1 teaspoon dry mustard	1 cup vegetable oil
1 clove garlic, minced	Anchovy paste, optional

• Combine vinegar, onion, salt, mustard, garlic, pepper, egg and cheese in blender. Blend well.
• Slowly drizzle oil into blender, continuing to blend.
• Add anchovy paste, if desired. Blend again.
• Store in refrigerator in airtight container. Shake well before using.

MUSTARD-DILL DRESSING

Yield: 3½ cups

½ cup Dijon mustard	2 cups safflower or sunflower oil
½ cup cider vinegar	2 tablespoons grated Parmesan cheese
1½ teaspoons dried tarragon, crumbled	
1½ teaspoons dill weed	2 tablespoons half and half, optional

• Combine mustard, vinegar, tarragon and dill weed in medium bowl. Let stand 10 minutes.
• Slowly add oil in thin stream, whisking constantly until mixture is thickened and smooth.
• Blend in Parmesan cheese and half and half, if desired.
• Store in refrigerator in airtight jar. Shake well when ready to use.

This dressing is especially good tossed with fresh, crisp salad greens, sliced mushrooms and hearts of palm.

TEE-OFF DRESSING FOR TWO

Yield: about ⅓ cup

2 tablespoons vegetable oil
1 tablespoon red wine vinegar
1 wedge tomato, cut into small
  pieces
½ teaspoon oregano

½ teaspoon seasoned salt
½ teaspoon MSG
2 teaspoons finely chopped green
  onion
1 teaspoon chopped fresh parsley

• Combine all ingredients. Blend well.

Toss with a combination of lettuces. Add homemade pita bread croutons.
Sprinkle with grated Parmesan cheese.

TOSSED SALAD DRESSING

Yield: 1 quart

2 hard-cooked eggs
1 teaspoon salt
1 teaspoon dry mustard
½ teaspoon pepper
½ teaspoon basil
¾ cup vegetable oil

¼ cup white wine vinegar
1 teaspoon lemon juice
1 medium red onion, sliced into
  thin rings
1-3 cloves garlic, crushed, optional

• Mash eggs with fork.
• Add salt, mustard, pepper and basil. Stir to make paste. Place in 1 quart jar.
• Add oil, vinegar, lemon juice, onion and garlic, if desired. Shake well.
• Store in refrigerator. (Keeps for several weeks.)

MAC'S CHINESE SALAD DRESSING

Yield: ¼ cup

3 tablespoons vegetable oil
1 tablespoon white vinegar
1 teaspoon soy sauce

1 teaspoon sugar
¼ teaspoon dry mustard
1 clove garlic, minced

• Combine all ingredients. Mix well.
• Serve with salad greens.

For a different twist, add just enough Miracle Whip to make creamy
and serve over hearts of palm on lettuce leaves.

POULTRY AND GAME

TETO'S CURRIED CHICKEN

Yield: 10-12 servings

1 cup butter, divided	$1/4$ cup blanched almonds, finely chopped
6 pounds chicken (about 8 cups), cooked and cut into $1/2$-1-inch pieces	$1/2$ cup cream
Flour	1 large cucumber, cut into $1/2$-inch pieces
3 onions, minced	Juice of $1/2$ lemon
$1/2$ clove garlic, crushed	Rice
$1 1/4$ tablespoons curry powder	Condiments: chutney,
$4 1/4$ cups chicken broth, divided	chopped hard-cooked eggs,
2 tablespoons chutney, chopped	chopped green pepper,
$1/3$ cup raisins	chopped orange peel, chopped
2 teaspoons sugar	green onion, plumped raisins,
2 teaspoons salt	toasted cashews, toasted
8 peppercorns	grated coconut, crisp bacon
$1/2$ teaspoon ground ginger	crumbs, fried bananas

- Melt $1/2$ cup butter in large skillet or Dutch oven.
- Coat chicken with flour and brown lightly in butter in batches. Remove from skillet and set aside.
- Melt $1/4$ cup butter, and sauté onions and garlic. Remove and set aside.
- In large saucepan, cook curry powder in 2 tablespoons hot butter until smooth.
- Stir in 4 cups chicken stock. Add chicken, chutney, raisins, sugar, salt, peppercorns and ground ginger. Cover and simmer 30 minutes.
- Fry almonds in 2 tablespoons melted butter. When lightly browned, place in blender with $1/4$ cup chicken stock and blend until almonds are well ground.
- Heat cream and add almond-stock mixture, stirring constantly 5 minutes. Do not boil, and be careful not to burn.
- Add almond cream, onions and cucumber to chicken.
- Uncover and simmer until gravy is thick. (Add more chicken broth if too thick.)
- Add lemon juice. Adjust seasonings.
- Serve over rice with any, or all condiments.

A cherished Augusta recipe.

CURRIED ROASTED CHICKEN

Yield: 4 servings

1 3-4 pound chicken, cleaned and wiped dry	1 teaspoon thyme
Salt	1 teaspoon curry powder
½ cup butter, softened and divided	¼ teaspoon cayenne pepper
Juice of 1 lemon	½ teaspoon cinnamon
	¼ teaspoon nutmeg

- Sprinkle chicken with salt inside and out.
- Combine ¼ cup butter, lemon juice, thyme, curry powder, cayenne pepper, cinnamon and nutmeg. Mix into a smooth paste.
- Rub paste on chicken inside and out.
- Melt remaining butter in shallow roasting pan.
- Add chicken and return to oven.
- Bake at 450° for 10 minutes. Reduce oven temperature to 350°. Cook 20 minutes per pound, or until chicken is tender.

Variation:
If desired, add tomatoes, potatoes, onions, mushrooms and carrots during last hour of cooking time. Baste frequently.

A hearty dish for a cold winter's evening.

CHICKEN TARRAGON WITH ALMONDS

Yield: 10 servings

10 chicken breast halves, skinned and boned	½ cup slivered almonds
Salt and pepper	1 teaspoon Kitchen Bouquet
All-purpose flour	3 tablespoons all-purpose flour
6 tablespoons butter, divided	4 cups chicken broth
¼ cup brandy	½ cup dry white wine
1 tablespoon chopped onion	1 tablespoon tarragon
	Salt and pepper to taste

- Season chicken with salt and pepper. Dust lightly with flour.
- Brown chicken in 4 tablespoons butter.
- Pour brandy over chicken. Simmer 2 minutes. Remove to a 9x13-inch pan.
- Add remaining 2 tablespoons butter to pan drippings. Add onion and sauté until transparent.
- Stir in almonds and continue cooking until lightly browned.
- Blend in Kitchen Bouquet and flour. Cook 2 minutes.
- Gradually add broth, wine, tarragon, salt and pepper. Bring to a boil. (Extra chicken broth may be added during cooking, if needed.)
- Pour sauce over chicken. Bake, covered, at 325° for 1 hour.

Make, bake and freeze ahead of time for Masters® guests.

SADIE'S CHICKEN

Yield: 8 servings

1	pound fresh mushrooms, sliced	4½	cups half and half
15	tablespoons butter, divided	1	tablespoon Worcestershire
2	8½-ounce (drained weight)		sauce
	cans artichoke hearts,		Salt and pepper to taste
	drained and quartered	¾	cup dry sherry
8	chicken breast halves, skinned	½	cup grated Parmesan cheese
	and boned		Paprika
9	tablespoons all-purpose flour		

• Sauté mushrooms in 2 tablespoons butter.
• Spread mushrooms and artichoke hearts in greased 3-quart baking dish.
• Lightly brown chicken in 4 tablespoons melted butter. Layer over mushrooms and artichokes.
• Make cream sauce with 9 tablespoons butter, flour, half and half, Worcestershire sauce, salt and pepper.
• Blend sherry into sauce. Pour over chicken. Top with Parmesan cheese and paprika.
• Bake at 375° for 40 minutes.

Simplicity itself, but wonderful.

EASY GLAZED CHICKEN

Yield: 24 servings

24	chicken breast halves	2	tablespoons fresh lemon juice
	Salt and pepper	2	tablespoons Worcestershire
2	10-ounce jars currant jelly		sauce
1¼	cups water	½	cup sherry
2	tablespoons cornstarch	1	teaspoon rosemary
4	teaspoons ground allspice	1	teaspoon basil

• Sprinkle chicken with salt and pepper. Place in shallow roasting pan.
• Combine all remaining ingredients in saucepan. Bring to a boil.
• Pour sauce over chicken.
• Bake, uncovered, at 450° for 15 minutes, then at 375° for 45 minutes more. Baste occasionally.

Add sautéed onions and mushrooms to pan juices for a delicious gravy.

TARRAGON CHICKEN

Yield: 8 servings

2	tablespoons oil	1	teaspoon salt
6	tablespoons butter, divided	⅛	teaspoon pepper
8	chicken breast halves, skinned	2	cups half and half
	and boned	2	egg yolks
5	shallots, chopped	2	tablespoons all-purpose flour
2	carrots, peeled and sliced	½	pound fresh mushrooms,
1¼	cups dry white wine		thinly sliced
2	teaspoons tarragon		

• In Dutch oven, heat oil and 3 tablespoons butter. Add chicken breasts and sauté until lightly browned. Remove to platter.
• To drippings, add shallots and carrots. Sauté 5 minutes or until golden.
• Return chicken to pan. Add wine, tarragon, salt and pepper. Bring to a boil. Reduce heat to low and simmer 15 minutes.
• Remove chicken to heated platter.
• Strain drippings and return liquid to pan.
• In small bowl, combine half and half, egg yolks and flour. Blend with whisk.
• Add cream mixture to drippings and bring to a boil. If sauce becomes too thick, thin with additional white wine.
• Sauté mushrooms in remaining butter 5 minutes or until tender.
• Place mushrooms around chicken.
• Spoon sauce over chicken. Serve immediately.

An elegant dish with a delicate sauce to please the most discriminating palate.

▶ "The Masters® is definitely a distinctive golfing classic. We enjoy the environment of the club, the course and derive unusual pleasure from the mixture of hospitality with the leisurely though serious golf of this event. It is one of the few "Opens" in which we play twosomes and in which due to the system of qualification the field is limited to a number which permits unhurried play and allows every contestant a "preferred" starting time. I like the daily changing of pairings which creates an air of sociability."
Horton Smith, 1939

SUPREME CHICKEN

Yield: 12 servings

2	cups sour cream	2	cloves garlic, minced
2	tablespoons fresh lime juice	½	teaspoon pepper
4	teaspoons Worcestershire sauce	12	chicken breast halves
		1¾	cups bread crumbs
4	teaspoons celery salt	½	cup butter or margarine
2	teaspoons paprika	½	cup shortening

- Combine sour cream, lime juice, Worcestershire sauce, celery salt, paprika, garlic and pepper.
- Add chicken to sour cream mixture, stirring to coat each piece. Refrigerate overnight.
- Roll chicken in bread crumbs. Arrange in a single layer in a 9x13-inch baking dish.
- Melt butter and shortening. Spoon half the butter mixture over chicken. Bake, uncovered, at 350° for 45 minutes.
- Spoon remaining butter mixture over chicken and continue baking 10-15 minutes.

This is a tender, juicy chicken. The lime juice adds a different flavor.

POLLO CHIPOTTE

Yield: 6 servings

6	chicken breast halves, skinned and boned	1	teaspoon sugar
		¼	teaspoon paprika
2	tablespoons butter	1	4-ounce can green chilies, drained and chopped
¾	pound fresh mushrooms, sliced		
2	tablespoons chopped onion	1	12-ounce can evaporated milk
	Salt and pepper to taste	1	cup sour cream
2	tablespoons chopped fresh parsley		Egg noodles

- Cut chicken into bite-size pieces.
- Sauté chicken in butter with mushrooms, onion, salt and pepper 5 minutes.
- Add parsley, sugar, paprika and green chilies. Mix well.
- Add milk. Simmer, uncovered, 20 minutes.
- Add sour cream and heat thoroughly. (If sauce is too thin, add 1½ tablespoons cornstarch before adding sour cream.)
- Serve immediately over buttered egg noodles.

LEMON GLAZED CHICKEN

Yield: 4 servings

1	tablespoon grated lemon rind	1	teaspoon salt
¼	cup fresh lemon juice	1	teaspoon pepper
¼	cup water	1	2½-3 pound fryer, cut up
¾	cup vegetable oil, divided	1	cup all-purpose flour
1	clove garlic, minced	1½	teaspoons paprika
1	tablespoon soy sauce		Salt and pepper

• Combine lemon rind, lemon juice, water, ¼ cup oil, garlic, soy sauce, salt and pepper.
• Place chicken in marinade at least 3 hours. Drain and reserve marinade.
• Dry chicken and coat with flour which has been seasoned with paprika and salt and pepper.
• Heat remaining ½ cup oil in large, heavy skillet. Cook chicken until golden brown.
• Arrange chicken pieces in single layer in large shallow baking dish. Pour remaining marinade over chicken.
• Bake at 350° for 35-40 minutes.

A tasty chicken dish for casual company.

CHICKEN MARSALA

Yield: 4 servings

4 chicken breast halves, boned and pounded thin	Pinch thyme
Seasoned salt	1 cup sliced fresh mushrooms, sautéed
¼ cup butter	¼ cup Marsala wine
4 green onions, chopped	

• Sprinkle chicken with seasoned salt.
• Melt butter in heavy skillet over medium-high heat.
• Add onions and thyme. Cook, stirring constantly, 2-3 minutes.
• Add chicken. Cook until lightly browned.
• Turn and brown slightly on other side.
• Turn again. Do not overcook.
• Spoon mushrooms over each piece of chicken.
• Add wine and simmer until wine is almost evaporated, 3-5 minutes.
• Serve immediately!

CHICKEN BREAST MORAN

Yield: 4 servings

6 chicken breast halves, skinned
  and boned
½ cup all-purpose flour
  Salt and pepper
¾ cup unsalted butter, divided
1 cup sliced fresh mushrooms

¾ cup dry white wine or Marsala
  wine
½ cup chicken broth
  Juice of ½ lemon
½ cup grated Mozzarella cheese
¼ cup grated Parmesan cheese

• Pound chicken breasts to ⅛-inch thickness between 2 sheets of
  waxed paper.
• Season flour with salt and pepper.
• Dredge chicken in flour.
• Cook chicken, several pieces at a time, in 2 tablespoons butter over
  medium heat 6-8 minutes, turning once. Butter should be added as more
  chicken is cooked. Reserve drippings.
• Place chicken in greased 9x13-inch baking dish.
• Sauté mushrooms in ¼ cup butter.
• Sprinkle mushrooms on top of chicken.
• Add wine and chicken broth to pan drippings.
• Scrape sides and bottom of skillet and simmer 10 minutes.
• Add lemon juice.
• Pour over chicken and mushrooms.
• Sprinkle cheeses on top.
• Bake at 450° for 10-12 minutes. Serve immediately.

EASY CHICKEN ENCHILADAS

Yield: 6-8 servings

6 chicken breast halves, cooked,
  boned, and chopped
1 8-ounce package Monterey
  Jack cheese with jalapeño
  peppers, grated, divided

1 cup sour cream
½ cup sliced green onions
12 corn tortillas
½ cup vegetable oil
1 cup taco sauce

• Combine chicken, 1½ cups cheese, sour cream and green onions.
• Soften tortillas in hot oil.
• Top each tortilla with about ⅓ cup chicken mixture. Fold in half.
• Arrange tortillas in greased 9x13-inch baking dish.
• Top with taco sauce and remaining cheese.
• Bake at 350° for 30 minutes.

CHICKEN VALENCIA

Yield: 6 servings

⅔ cup raisins, divided	1 teaspoon paprika
Sherry to cover raisins	½ teaspoon garlic salt
2 tablespoons butter, softened	3-4 tablespoons shortening
¼ cup chopped, cooked ham	½ cup orange juice
1 tablespoon chopped fresh parsley	1 cup chicken broth
¼ teaspoon grated orange rind	¼ cup chopped green onion
¼ cup soft bread crumbs	Salt and pepper to taste
6 large chicken breast halves, boned	1 3-inch cinnamon stick
2 tablespoons all-purpose flour	2 tablespoons cornstarch, optional
	2 tablespoons water, optional

• Soak raisins in sherry 30 minutes. Drain, reserving liquid.
• Chop ⅓ cup raisins, reserving sherry. Combine 2 tablespoons with butter, ham, parsley, orange rind and bread crumbs to make stuffing.
• Flatten chicken breasts. Place stuffing in center of each breast. Fold chicken over and secure with toothpicks.
• Combine flour, paprika and garlic salt. Coat chicken.
• Lightly brown chicken in shortening.
• Remove excess fat from pan. Add reserved sherry, orange juice, broth, onion, salt, pepper and cinnamon stick. Simmer, covered, until chicken is tender, about 30 minutes.
• Discard cinnamon stick and skim away any fat from sauce.
• Add remaining raisins. Simmer 3-4 minutes longer.
• Sauce may be thickened with 2 tablespoons cornstarch mixed with 2 tablespoons cold water.

This makes an attractive dish when served on orange slices.

▶ "Bob was a fine man to be partnered with in a tournament....He made you feel that you were playing with a friend, and you were."
Gene Sarazen
About Robert Tyre Jones, Jr.

CHEESY CHICKEN

Yield: 6 servings

6 chicken breast halves, cooked and boned	1 teaspoon garlic salt
1 bunch fresh broccoli or 2 10-ounce packages frozen broccoli spears	¼ teaspoon salt
	⅛ teaspoon white pepper
	1 cup grated Parmesan cheese, divided
12 ounces cream cheese	½ pound mushrooms, sautéed, optional
1½ cups milk	1 2.8-ounce can onion rings

- Cut chicken into large strips.
- Cook broccoli spears until just tender.
- Melt cream cheese in milk over low heat.
- Add garlic salt, salt, pepper and ¾ cup Parmesan cheese.
- Arrange broccoli on bottom of 2-quart rectangular baking dish. Layer mushrooms on top, if desired.
- Pour 1 cup cheese mixture over broccoli.
- Lay chicken strips on top. Cover with remaining cheese mixture.
- Sprinkle with remaining ¼ cup Parmesan cheese.
- Bake, covered, at 350° for 15 minutes. Remove cover and bake an additional 15 minutes, or until thoroughly heated.
- Sprinkle with onion rings during last 5 minutes of baking.

 # QUICK CHICKEN JAMBALAYA

Yield: 4 servings

1 pound chicken breasts, skinned, boned, and cut into chunks	1 4-ounce can mushrooms
½ pound smoked sausage, cut into bite-size pieces	1 tablespoon chopped fresh parsley
1 cup raw rice	2 dashes Tabasco
1 10¾-ounce can chicken broth	½ teaspoon salt
1 10½-ounce can onion soup	⅛ teaspoon cayenne pepper
¼ cup butter or margarine, melted	1 teaspoon Tony Chachere's Creole Seasoning, optional

- Combine all ingredients. Blend well.
- Place in large baking dish.
- Bake, covered, at 350° for 1 hour and 15 minutes, stirring occasionally.

STUFFED CHICKEN BREASTS WITH WHITE GRAPE SAUCE

Yield: 12 servings

12 chicken breast halves, skinned and boned
12 slices white bread, cut into ¼-inch cubes
½ cup minced onion
½ cup finely chopped celery
¾ cup butter, melted, divided
½ teaspoon salt
¼ teaspoon pepper
¼ teaspoon sage
1 6-ounce package frozen crabmeat, thawed
1 cup all-purpose flour

- Flatten each chicken breast to ¼-inch thickness.
- Combine bread cubes, onion, celery, ¼ cup butter, salt, pepper, sage and crabmeat.
- Spoon stuffing into center of each chicken breast.
- Roll and secure with toothpick.
- Coat chicken breasts with flour. Brown in remaining ½ cup butter.
- Place chicken in 3-quart baking dish.
- Bake at 375° for 25 minutes or until tender. Serve with White Grape Sauce.

White Grape Sauce:

3 tablespoons butter
3 tablespoons all-purpose flour
1½ cups chicken broth
2 tablespoons sugar
½ teaspoon salt
2 teaspoons lemon juice
1 pound white seedless grapes

- Melt butter in heavy saucepan over low heat.
- Add flour and stir until smooth.
- Cook 1 minute, stirring constantly.
- Gradually add chicken broth.
- Cook over medium heat, stirring constantly until thickened and bubbly.
- Stir in sugar, salt and lemon juice.
- Add grapes just before serving.

CHICKEN BROCCOLI SUPPER

Yield: 6-8 servings

1 bunch green onions, chopped	½ teaspoon white pepper
2 tablespoons butter	1 8-ounce package spaghetti,
4 chicken breast halves, cooked	cooked and drained
and chopped	2½ cups grated sharp Cheddar
1 bunch broccoli, steamed and	cheese
chopped	¾ cup whipping cream
1 teaspoon salt	Paprika

• In large skillet, sauté onions in butter.
• Add chicken, broccoli, salt and pepper. Cook 5 minutes over low heat.
• Place spaghetti in greased 3-quart baking dish and cover with half the cheese.
• Pour cream over cheese.
• Add chicken mixture. Top with remaining cheese.
• Sprinkle with paprika.
• Bake at 375° for 30 minutes.

This freezes beautifully.

CHICKEN PROVENÇAL

Yield: 4 servings

1 pound chicken breasts, boned, skinned and cut into strips	6 green onions, chopped
3 tablespoons butter, divided	6 large mushrooms, sliced
3 tablespoons olive oil, divided	10 green olives, sliced
3 cloves garlic, minced	4 tablespoons chopped fresh parsley
5 sprigs fresh basil or 1 teaspoon dried basil	2 ounces sun-dried tomatoes
1 medium onion, chopped	Salt and pepper to taste

• In heavy skillet, sauté chicken in 2 tablespoons butter and 2 tablespoons olive oil 3-4 minutes, turning once.
• Add garlic. Sauté until lightly browned.
• Remove chicken. Add remaining butter and olive oil.
• Add basil, onion, green onions and mushrooms. Sauté until tender.
• Return chicken to pan. Add olives, parsley, tomatoes, salt and pepper. Sauté until all ingredients are heated thoroughly.

SESAME CHICKEN WITH CUMBERLAND SAUCE

Mary Ann Baggs
Augusta, Georgia
Yield: 6 servings

Sesame Chicken:

2 cups bread crumbs
¾ cup sesame seeds
½ cup freshly grated Parmesan
   cheese
¼ cup chopped fresh parsley
1 teaspoon freshly ground white
   pepper

6 chicken breast halves, skinned,
   boned, cut in half lengthwise,
   and pounded to ¼-inch
   thickness
2 tablespoons butter, melted

• Combine bread crumbs, sesame seeds, Parmesan cheese, parsley and
  pepper. Blend well.
• Dip chicken breasts in butter. Coat with sesame breading.
• Place on baking sheet. Bake at 425° for 20 minutes.
• Serve immediately with warm Cumberland Sauce.

Cumberland Sauce:

3 oranges
3 lemons
1 cup red currant jelly
2 tablespoons port

2 teaspoons Dijon mustard
¼ teaspoon ginger
   Dash cayenne pepper
2 teaspoons cornstarch

• Grate peel from oranges and lemons. Set aside.
• Squeeze juice from oranges and lemons.
• In saucepan combine juice, jelly, port, mustard, ginger, cayenne pepper and
  cornstarch.
• Slowly cook until well combined and simmering. Remove from heat.
• Add 2 teaspoons grated peel.

MAUI CHICKEN

Yield: 4 servings

4 chicken breast halves, skinned and boned
1 20-ounce can pineapple chunks
¼ cup soy sauce
2 tablespoons liquid from sweet pickles
2 tablespoons vegetable oil
1 small clove garlic, minced

2 teaspoons fresh ginger root or ½ teaspoon ground ginger
2 teaspoons toasted sesame seeds
2 tablespoons finely chopped green onions
4 cups crisp shredded lettuce

• Cut each breast into 4 pieces.
• Drain pineapple, reserving ¼ cup juice.
• Combine pineapple juice, soy sauce, sweet pickle liquid, oil, garlic and ginger.
• Pour marinade over chicken. Cover and refrigerate several hours.
• Drain chicken, reserving marinade.
• Arrange chicken in shallow baking dish.
• Bake at 375° for 20 minutes.
• Add sesame seeds and onions to reserved marinade.
• Spoon half the marinade over chicken. Bake 5 minutes longer.
• Add pineapple chunks to remaining marinade. Pour over chicken.
• Bake 5 minutes longer, or until chicken is tender and pineapple is heated.
• Serve on crisp shredded lettuce.
• Spoon any remaining sauce over chicken.

Good with a salad of tomatoes and cucumbers. Great for a buffet.

 # JIMBO'S BARBEQUED CHICKEN

Yield: 4-6 servings

1 chicken, cut in pieces
1 teaspoon sugar
1 onion, chopped
1 cup ketchup
½ cup fresh lemon juice

2½ tablespoons butter or margarine
1½ tablespoons Worcestershire sauce
½ teaspoon prepared mustard

• Place chicken in large Dutch oven.
• Combine sugar, onion, ketchup, lemon juice, butter, Worcestershire sauce and mustard.
• Pour over chicken. Cover and heat until simmering.
• Cook 1 hour.

UNUSUAL BARBEQUE MARINADE

Yield: 2 cups

½ cup vegetable oil
3 tablespoons vinegar
1 teaspoon poultry seasoning
1 teaspoon garlic powder

1 egg, well beaten
1 cup dry white wine
1½ teaspoons salt
¼ teaspoon pepper

• Combine all ingredients. Blend well.

BARBEQUE SAUCE

Yield: 1 quart

1 cup cider vinegar
1 cup light brown sugar
1 cup ketchup
½ cup chili sauce
½ cup Worcestershire sauce
2 tablespoons fresh lemon juice

1 teaspoon dry mustard
1 clove garlic, minced
   Dash cayenne pepper
4 tablespoons chopped onion,
   optional

• Combine all ingredients in saucepan. Simmer, uncovered, 30 minutes.
• Cool. Pour sauce into glass jars and refrigerate. Warm as needed.

OLD SOUTH BARBEQUE SAUCE

Yield: 3½ quarts

¾ cup sugar
4 14-ounce bottles Heinz ketchup
7 cups cider vinegar
1 ounce black pepper
¼ cup Tabasco

   Juice of 2 lemons
½ cup butter or margarine
1 5-ounce bottle Worcestershire
   sauce
1 6-ounce jar prepared mustard
6 tablespoons salt

• Combine all ingredients in heavy saucepan.
• Bring to a boil. Simmer 30 minutes.
• Let cool. Pour into washed and sterilized bottles. (The empty bottles may be used!)
• Let stand a few days before using. Store on pantry shelf.

Excellent over chicken or pork. The sauce for the real barbeque lover.

132

MARINATED TURKEY BREAST

Yield: 6-8 servings

1 5-7 pound turkey breast
2 teaspoons chopped fresh
 parsley
¼ cup vegetable oil

¼ cup salt
¼ cup pepper
1 cup apple cider vinegar

- Place turkey breast in browning bag and place in shallow roasting pan.
- Combine parsley, oil, salt, pepper and vinegar.
- Pour marinade over turkey breast.
- Seal bag and bake at 300° for 4-5 hours.
- Serve hot with pan drippings.

Party pleaser—disappears as fast as you can slice it.

KITCHEN PASTA

Harriet Goldsmith
Augusta, Georgia
Yield: 8 servings

1 pound rotelle or rotini pasta
1 pound chicken breasts, cooked
3 ribs celery
½ bunch broccoli
1 clove garlic, minced
5 tablespoons butter, divided
1 pound medium shrimp, cooked,
 peeled and deveined

2 tablespoons white wine
4 tablespoons all-purpose flour
2 cups milk
1 teaspoon salt
½ teaspoon white pepper
½ cup grated Parmesan cheese

- Cook pasta al dente and rinse in cold water. Set aside.
- Cut chicken and vegetables into 1-inch pieces.
- Stir-fry garlic, mashing with a fork, in 1 tablespoon butter, until light brown.
 Discard garlic.
- Stir-fry shrimp and chicken 3 minutes. Set aside.
- Stir-fry vegetables 2 minutes. Add wine. Cover and simmer 2 minutes.
 Remove lid and continue cooking 1 minute.
- Make a roux with remaining 4 tablespoons butter and flour. Slowly add milk
 and stir constantly until cream sauce has thickened.
- Add pasta, salt, pepper, chicken, shrimp and vegetables to cream sauce
 and heat.
- When thoroughly heated, add cheese.
- Serve immediately.

A colorful and tasty meal in itself. Serve with French bread and green salad.

CHICKEN PRIMAVERA

Yield: 4 servings

4 ounces linguine
2 tablespoons red wine
2 tablespoons tomato paste
1 tablespoon sugar
1 teaspoon salt
1 teaspoon dried basil, crushed
1 cup fresh or frozen cut up asparagus
1 cup sliced fresh mushrooms
1 tablespoon vegetable oil

4 chicken breast halves, skinned, boned and cubed
2 cloves garlic
1 medium tomato, peeled and chopped
¼ cup sliced pitted ripe olives
1 tablespoon chopped fresh parsley
Grated Parmesan cheese

• Cook linguine according to package directions. Drain and keep warm.
• Combine wine, tomato paste, sugar, salt and basil. Set aside.
• In large skillet, over medium heat, sauté asparagus and mushrooms in hot oil until asparagus is tender crisp. Remove from skillet.
• Add chicken and garlic to skillet. Cook about 3 minutes or until chicken is done.
• Stir in tomato and olives. Cook, stirring constantly, until mixture is heated through.
• To serve, toss chicken and vegetable mixtures with linguine.
• Top with parsley and Parmesan cheese.

SPICY STIR-FRIED CHICKEN

Yield: 4-6 servings

¼ cup vegetable oil
2 cloves garlic, minced
3 small green onions, sliced including some tops
4 chicken breast halves, boned and cut into thin strips
¼ cup soy sauce
2 tablespoons dry sherry
1 teaspoon sugar

1 teaspoon cornstarch
1 tablespoon minced ginger root or ¾ teaspoon ground ginger
½ teaspoon Tabasco
3 medium carrots, cut into julienne strips
¼ pound fresh snow peas
¼ pound fresh mushrooms, sliced

• Heat oil in wok over high heat.
• Sauté garlic and onion about 30 seconds.
• Add chicken and sauté until white.
• Combine soy sauce, sherry, sugar, cornstarch, ginger and Tabasco. Blend well.
• Add soy sauce mixture to chicken in wok. Stir in carrots, snow peas, and mushrooms.
• Stir-fry 5 minutes, or until vegetables are tender crisp.

CHICKEN ENCHILADAS

Yield: 12 enchiladas

1 10-ounce can Ro-Tel tomatoes and green chilies, chopped
1 4-ounce can green chilies, chopped
3½ ounces jalapeño relish
1 10¾-ounce can cream of chicken soup
½ teaspoon garlic salt

Pepper to taste
1 cup chicken broth
1 package of 12 corn tortillas
3-5 chicken breast halves, cooked and chopped
1 large onion, chopped
1 12-ounce package mild Cheddar cheese, grated

• Combine tomatoes, green chilies, jalapeño relish, soup, garlic salt, pepper and chicken broth. Set aside.
• Prepare tortillas according to package directions.
• Place small amount of chicken, onion and cheese on each tortilla and roll up. Place in lightly greased 9x13-inch baking dish. Reserve enough cheese to cover casserole. (Recipe may be prepared ahead up to this point.)
• Pour tomato mixture over tortillas.
• Top with remaining cheese.
• Bake, uncovered, at 350° for 25-35 minutes.

For extra zip, add more jalapeño relish.

OLD-TIME CHICKEN PIE

Yield: 6-8 servings

1 cup chopped celery
1⅓ cups chicken broth, divided
5 tablespoons all-purpose flour
¼ teaspoon pepper
½ teaspoon salt
4 tablespoons butter
½ cup milk
2 hard-cooked eggs, chopped

1 4-ounce can sliced mushrooms, drained
1 8½-ounce can English peas, drained
1 2-ounce jar chopped pimentos, drained
3 cups cooked, chopped chicken
1 unbaked pie crust

• Cook celery in ⅓ cup broth until tender. Drain.
• Combine flour, pepper and salt.
• Melt butter and stir in flour mixture.
• Stir in remaining chicken broth and milk. Cook until thickened, stirring constantly.
• Add eggs, mushrooms, peas, pimentos, chicken and celery. Mix well.
• Pour into greased 1½-quart baking dish.
• Top with pie crust.
• Bake at 350° for 40 minutes or until brown.

A hearty winter entrée.

CHICKEN PIE

Yield: 4-6 servings

2 ribs celery, chopped	1 large onion, chopped
3½ cups water	3 carrots, chopped
4-5 chicken breast halves	1 large potato, diced
1 tablespoon salt	Prepared pie crust

- Combine celery and water in large pot. Simmer 20 minutes.
- Add chicken, salt, onion, carrots and potato.
- Simmer until chicken, carrots and potato are fork tender.
- Remove chicken and allow to cool. Remove meat from bones and cut into bite-size pieces.
- Strain vegetables from stock, reserving liquid and vegetables.
- Layer chicken and vegetabes in 9x13-inch glass baking dish.
- Pour Sauce over chicken and vegetables.
- Top with pie crust.
- Make slits in crust.
- Bake at 350° for 35-40 minutes.

Sauce:

½ cup butter or margarine	1 tablespoon Worcestershire
½ cup all-purpose flour	sauce
1 cup half and half	2 tablespoons sherry or 1
2 cups reserved chicken stock	tablespoon lemon juice, optional

- Melt butter in medium saucepan.
- Stir in flour. Blend with wire whisk until smooth. Add half and half and reserved stock.
- Add Worcestershire sauce and sherry or lemon juice, if desired.
- Heat, stirring constantly, until thickened. (If sauce becomes too thick, thin with stock.)

SZECHWAN CHICKEN

Yield: 6 servings

3 tablespoons vegetable oil
2 dried whole red peppers
2 tablespoons chopped fresh
   ginger root
1 pound chicken, boned and cut
   into bite-size pieces
1 clove garlic, minced

½ cup sliced fresh mushrooms
1 green pepper, chopped
4 green onions, chopped
2 ribs celery, chopped
1 cup peanuts or cashews
   Rice

• Heat oil in wok.
• Add red peppers and cook 1 minute. Discard red peppers.
• Add ginger and cook 1 minute. Discard ginger. Add chicken and stir-fry
  5 minutes or until tender. Remove from wok and set aside.
• Stir-fry garlic and vegetables 2 minutes. Add chicken and nuts.
• Add Sauce to chicken in wok.
• Cook until thickened and well blended.
• Serve over rice.

Sauce:

2 tablespoons soy sauce
¼ cup water
1 teaspoon sherry
1 tablespoon cornstarch
1½ tablespoons sugar

1 teaspoon pepper
2 teaspoons vinegar
1 teaspoon vegetable oil
¼ teaspoon Tabasco, optional

• Combine all sauce ingredients. Blend well.

It is not surprising that the Masters® has established itself as a pattern for other tournaments to follow. The players are made to feel that they are not only invited contestants, but warmly welcomed guests. Still more important are the completely original conveniences provided for the patrons.
From a BYRON NELSON letter
Written January 1, 1946

CHICKEN-VEGETABLE STIR-FRY

Dianne Zoeller
wife of Fuzzy Zoeller,
1979 Masters® Champion
Yield: 6 servings

½ cup soy sauce
¼ cup vegetable oil
2 teaspoons sesame seeds
6 chicken breast halves, skinned
and boned
2 cups fresh broccoli florets
1 onion, thinly sliced and
separated into rings

½ pound fresh snow peas
½ cup thinly sliced celery
½ cup sliced fresh mushrooms
1 tablespoon cornstarch
½ cup water
Brown rice

• Combine soy sauce, oil and sesame seeds in large bowl.
• Cut chicken into 2-inch strips. Add to marinade. Cover and refrigerate at least 30 minutes.
• Preheat wok to medium-high (325°).
• Add chicken mixture to wok. Stir-fry 2-3 minutes.
• Remove chicken from wok and set aside.
• Add broccoli and onion rings. Stir-fry 2 minutes.
• Add snow peas, celery and mushrooms. Stir-fry 2 minutes.
• Return chicken to wok.
• Blend cornstarch and water. Add to chicken and vegetables.
• Cook, stirring constantly, until thickened.
• Serve over hot brown rice.

▶ For myself, I think the most enjoyable part of the Masters® is the way everybody in and around the Club makes me feel at home, and I know that this hospitality, in the sense of "I'm wanted at the Masters®," goes out to all players, particularly the past greats of golf. I hope I'll never be too old to want to take part in this event, and I don't think I ever will age quite that much.
From a SAM SNEAD letter
Written January 2, 1956

POUSSIN ROTI à L'AIL AU CITRON

Squab or Cornish Hens with Lemon Garlic Sauce
Yield: 6 servings

3	large cornish hens (1½ pounds or larger) or 6 squabs	½	teaspoon sugar
	Kosher salt	1	quart water
	Freshly ground pepper	1½	cups half and half
1	cup, packed, fresh garlic cloves, about 6 ounces	3	tablespoons unsalted butter, softened
3	large lemons, unpeeled, dipped in boiling water for 30 seconds and drained	¼	cup ruby or tawny port, or Madeira wine
1	teaspoon salt	2	cups unsalted chicken stock, degreased and reduced to 1 cup

- Rub hens with salt and pepper. Cover loosely and refrigerate.
- Separate garlic cloves. Blanch garlic in boiling water 2 minutes. Drain and peel.
- Peel 1½ lemons, reserving peel. Remove inner white peel and seeds. Discard. Cut peeled lemons into thin slices. Blanch reserved peel in boiling water 1 minute. Drain.
- In heavy saucepan, combine garlic cloves, lemon peel, lemon slices, salt, sugar and water. Bring to a boil. Reduce heat and simmer, uncovered, 1-2 hours or until liquid is almost evaporated and garlic is golden brown and tender. Stir occasionally to avoid burning.
- Add half and half to make garlic cream. Continue cooking, stirring frequently until mixture is reduced by one-half. Strain through a fine sieve, pushing down on solids. Discard solids. Set this sauce base aside, uncovered, until cool. Refrigerate until ready to use. (Recipe may be prepared one day in advance to this point.)
- Cut remaining 1½ lemons into quarters. Slip one quarter into the cavity of each hen. Truss birds and rub with unsalted butter.
- Arrange hens in greased roasting pan. Bake at 350° for ¾-1½ hours, depending on size. Turn hens and baste every 15 minutes to brown evenly. Place on serving platter.
- Cover loosely with foil to keep warm.
- Discard fat in roasting pan. Deglaze with wine, stirring to dissolve all particles. Add stock and reduce quickly by one half.
- Cut the hens in half. Add any juice remaining on platter to sauce. (Let juice stand a few minutes so fat will rise and can be skimmed off.) Stir in garlic cream. Reduce to 1½ cups. Adjust seasonings. Fresh lemon juice can be added here for a perfect sweet and sour balance. Serve immediately.

This is divine! A real treat for the serious cook.

CORNISH HENS VERONIQUE WITH ORANGE RICE

Yield: 12 servings

6 Cornish hens	Salt and pepper
Oil	2 cups white seedless grapes
2 tablespoons cornstarch	Orange Rice
8 tablespoons apple jelly	Avocado slices and apple
4 tablespoons orange juice	wedges to garnish
⅔ cup sauterne wine	

- Split hens in half and brown in ½ inch oil.
- Remove hens from skillet and place in shallow baking dish. Pour off oil, leaving drippings in the pan.
- Add cornstarch to drippings. Blend.
- Add jelly, orange juice, wine, salt and pepper. Heat, stirring constantly, until smooth and thickened.
- Pour mixture over browned hens.
- Bake, covered, at 350° for 1 hour.
- Add grapes and bake, uncovered, 15 minutes longer or until grapes are warm.
- To serve: place hens on mound of Orange Rice and garnish with avocado slices and apple wedges. Serve with White Grape Sauce.

Orange Rice:

3 cups water	3 tablespoons chopped onion
1 cup raw rice	¼ cup butter
½ teaspoon salt	¾ cup orange juice
1 cup diced celery with leaves	2 tablespoons grated orange rind

- In saucepan, bring water to a boil. Stir in rice and salt.
- Cook 15 minutes. Drain off any remaining water.
- While rice is cooking, sauté celery and onion in butter until onion is transparent.
- Add orange juice, rind and vegetables to cooked rice.
- Heat thoroughly.
- Remove from heat. Cover until ready to serve.

(continued)

White Grape Sauce:

1　cup butter, divided
4　egg yolks, beaten and strained
2　tablespoons fresh lemon juice

⅛ teaspoon cayenne pepper
¾ cup white seedless grapes

- Melt ½ cup butter in double boiler over hot, but not boiling, water.
- Add egg yolks. Blend well. Stir in lemon juice with whisk until smooth and thickened.
- Add remaining ½ cup butter and cayenne pepper.
- Whip until blended and smooth. (If mixture separates while cooking, add a little cream and whip smooth.)
- Stir in grapes.

CORNISH HENS WITH OYSTER STUFFING

Yield: 4 servings

½　cup chopped onion
2　tablespoons butter
2　cups crumbled cornbread
1　cup fresh bread crumbs
2　eggs, beaten
1　tablespoon Worcestershire sauce
1-2 teaspoons poultry seasoning
¼　teaspoon pepper
⅔　cup chicken broth

1　8-ounce can oysters, drained and quartered (12 large oysters)
4　1¼-pound Cornish hens
½　cup butter or margarine, melted
1　tablespoon fresh lemon juice
½　teaspoon salt
⅛　teaspoon pepper

- Sauté onion in 2 tablespoons butter until transparent.
- Combine onion, cornbread, bread crumbs, eggs, Worcestershire sauce, poultry seasoning, ¼ teaspoon pepper and broth. Mix well. Gently stir in oysters.
- Stuff hens with oyster dressing. Truss securely.
- Combine ½ cup butter, lemon juice, salt and ⅛ teaspoon pepper. Rub mixture over surface of hens. Wrap each hen in aluminum foil and place, breast side up, in deep roasting pan. Add water in roasting pan to depth of 2 inches.
- Bake at 350° for 1½ hours.
- Open foil and gently fold down around hens to form a bed. Bake an additional 20-30 minutes or until golden brown.

DOVE PIE

Yield: 6-8 servings

Pie:

20 dove breasts
    Salt and pepper
    All-purpose flour
1¼ cups butter, divided
2 cups beef broth
¾ cup vermouth

2 tablespoons Worcestershire sauce
1 cup chopped celery
½ cup chopped onion
3 hard-cooked eggs, finely chopped

• Dust dove breasts with salt, pepper and flour.
• Melt ¾ cup butter in large, heavy skillet over medium heat. Add doves. Cook until browned.
• Add beef broth, vermouth and Worcestershire sauce.
• Simmer, covered, about 3 hours or until tender, adding water if needed.
• Remove meat from bones. Reserve stock.
• Melt remaining ½ cup butter in heavy skillet. Add celery and onion. Cook over medium heat until vegetables are transparent.
• Add dove meat, eggs and stock.
• Heat thoroughly.

Crust:

1 cup butter, softened
6 ounces cream cheese, softened

2½ cups all-purpose flour

• Cream butter and cream cheese in medium bowl.
• Add flour. Blend well.
• Divide dough in half. Refrigerate until ready to use.
• When ready to assemble pie, roll each half on floured board into desired shape.

Assembly:

• Line a 9x9-inch pan with prepared crust or divide into 8 individual oven-proof ramekins. Prick crusts.
• Fill with dove mixture.
• Top pie with prepared crust.
• Bake at 400° for 30 minutes, or until golden brown.

COUNTRY STYLE DOVE

Yield: 6-8 servings

15-18 dove breasts
1 onion, coarsely chopped
2 celery ribs with leaves, coarsely chopped
1 carrot, peeled and chopped
3 beef bouillon cubes
1 chicken bouillon cube
1 bay leaf
¼ teaspoon pepper
2 tablespoons Worcestershire sauce
2 tablespoons all-purpose flour, or more, for thickening

- Combine dove, onion, celery, carrot, bouillon cubes, bay leaf, pepper and Worcestershire sauce in Dutch oven. Add enough water to cover doves.
- Bake, covered, at 350°, adding water as needed, for 3-3½ hours, or until meat is falling off bone.
- Allow to cool slightly. Remove doves from cooking liquid. Remove meat from bones. Strain liquid and return to heat.
- Slowly add flour to liquid, stirring until mixture boils and thickens.
- Add meat and heat thoroughly.

These are especially good served over grits, rice or pasta.

DOVES by CHARLES

Yield: 4-6 servings

12 dove breasts
Salt and pepper
Poultry seasoning
6 strips bacon, halved
4 tablespoons butter
½ cup water
1 pint half and half
3 tablespoons red currant jelly

- Rinse birds and wipe dry.
- Sprinkle with salt, pepper and poultry seasoning.
- Wrap ½ strip of bacon around each breast and secure with toothpick.
- Melt butter in large heavy skillet. Add doves and cook until browned. Add water. Cover and simmer about 1 hour over low heat.
- Just before serving, stir in half and half and jelly.
- Heat until gravy thickens.

DOVE MIGNON

Yield: 4 servings

8 dove breasts
1 cup prepared Good Seasons®
Italian Dressing

8 strips thick, smoked bacon

- Marinate dove breasts at least 1 hour in dressing.
- Drain dove. Wrap a strip of bacon around each dove, securing with a toothpick.
- Cook dove on grill 3 minutes per side for small breasts and 5 minutes per side for larger breasts.
- Serve immediately.

Quick, tasty, and no "mess or fuss" in the kitchen.

SWAN AND WILD RICE CASSEROLE

Yield: 6-8 servings

1 swan or Canadian goose	1 6-ounce package wild rice
2 onions, halved	½ cup chopped onion
10 peppercorns	½ pound fresh mushrooms, sliced
2 ribs celery, cut into 2-inch pieces	½ cup butter or margarine, melted
1 carrot, cut into 1-inch pieces	¼ cup all-purpose flour
1½ teaspoons salt	1½ cups half and half
¼ teaspoon pepper	1 tablespoon chopped fresh parsley
5 whole allspice	½ cup slivered almonds

- Combine swan, onions, peppercorns, celery, carrot, salt, pepper and allspice in large stock pot. Cover with water.
- Bring to a boil. Reduce heat and simmer 1 hour or until swan is tender.
- Remove bird from stock and cool. Remove meat from bone.
- Strain stock and reserve 1½ cups.
- Cook rice according to package directions.
- Sauté onion and mushrooms in butter until tender.
- Add flour. Blend until smooth, stirring constantly.
- Stir in reserved stock. Cook, stirring constantly, until thickened.
- Stir in meat, rice, half and half and parsley.
- Spoon into greased 2-quart baking dish. (May be prepared to this point a day in advance. Store in refrigerator until ready to bake.)
- Cover and bake at 350° for 15-20 minutes.
- Uncover. Sprinkle with almonds. Bake an additional 5-10 minutes.

CRAIG'S SOUR CREAM SWAN

Yield: 6-8 servings

1	swan	4	tablespoons all-purpose flour, divided
2	tablespoons salt		
1	bay leaf	1¼	cups chicken broth
1½	cups white vinegar	½	teaspoon rosemary
	Paprika	¼	teaspoon thyme
	Garlic salt	1	teaspoon salt
3	ribs celery, thinly sliced diagonally	¼	teaspoon pepper
		1½	cups sour cream
2	carrots, thinly sliced diagonally	1	pint fresh mushrooms, sliced
1	medium onion, chopped	2	tablespoons butter

- Combine swan, salt, bay leaf, vinegar and enough water to cover bird. Marinate overnight.
- Dry swan and prick skin several times with fork. Rub cavity and outside with paprika and garlic salt.
- Place swan, breast side down, on rack in shallow roasting pan. Roast at 325° for 1-1½ hours or until skin is browned.
- Spoon 2 tablespoons fat from roasting pan into heavy skillet. Add celery, carrots and onion. Cook until soft and golden.
- Stir in 2 tablespoons flour and cook, stirring constantly, 2 minutes.
- Add broth, rosemary, thyme, salt and pepper. Cook until thickened.
- Stir remaining 2 tablespoons flour into sour cream. Blend into vegetable mixture.
- Sauté mushrooms in butter.
- Remove swan to deep roasting pan, breast side down.
- Pour vegetable mixture and mushrooms over bird.
- Cover and roast 2-2½ hours or until tender.
- Spoon any excess fat from sauce. Serve sauce with sliced meat.

If swan is not available, a Canadian goose is delicious prepared this way.
Beware the spent shot!

> ▶ "Indeed, the player who stands on the plateau first tee of the Augusta National beholds no overt peril, nothing ominous or dire. And yet, by universal agreement, this is one of the most terrifying teeshots in golf."

WILD GOOSE WITH ORANGE SAUCE

Yield: 4 servings

1 5-pound goose
  Salt and pepper
1 small apple, cored and quartered
1 small onion, quartered
1 small orange, quartered

¼ cup butter
1 cup sauterne
½ cup consommé
½ pound bacon

- Wash goose and pat dry.
- Salt and pepper to taste.
- Stuff goose with apple, onion and orange. Truss legs.
- Cover goose breast with butter and place in roasting pan.
- Add sauterne and consommé.
- Bake, covered, at 275° for 1 hour. Increase temperature to 350° and bake 1 hour longer. Baste frequently with pan juices.
- Uncover and brown 15 minutes.
- Serve with Orange Sauce.

Orange Sauce:

1 cup light brown sugar
2½ tablespoons sugar
1 tablespoon cornstarch
1 tablespoon grated orange rind

1 cup orange juice
2 drops Tabasco
1 ounce Cointreau, optional

- Combine all ingredients in saucepan.
- Cook over low heat until thickened and clear.
- Add 1 ounce Cointreau, if desired, after removing from heat.

GRILLED DUCK BREASTS

Yield: 6 servings

8 ounces Italian dressing
2 ounces soy sauce
1 tablespoon Worcestershire
  sauce

12 whole duck breasts
  Salt and pepper
12 strips bacon

- Combine dressing, soy sauce and Worcestershire sauce. Marinate breasts about 4 hours, turning at least twice.
- Remove from marinade. Sprinkle with salt and pepper.
- To cook, lay bacon strips in bottom of wire grilling basket. Lay duck breasts on top of bacon. Cover duck with remaining bacon.
- Grill over hot fire, covered, 8-10 minutes on each side.

DUCK GUMBO

Yield: 6-8 servings

2-3 mallard or black ducks or 5 wood ducks
3-4 quarts water
2 bunches celery, chopped
1 bunch parsley, chopped
1-2 tablespoons salt
2 teaspoons pepper
1-2 cups butter, divided
6-10 tablespoons bacon grease, divided
1 bunch spring onions with tops, chopped
2 green peppers, chopped
3 cups chopped okra
1 clove garlic, minced
8-10 tablespoons all-purpose flour, divided

½ pound hot link sausage, cooked, optional
1 28-ounce can tomatoes
2 6-ounce cans tomato paste
4-5 bay leaves
3-4 tablespoons Worcestershire sauce
8 dashes Tabasco
1 tablespoon paprika
1 tablespoon sugar
1½ teaspoons tarragon
1½ teaspoons thyme
1½ teaspoons rosemary
1½ teaspoons filé powder

• Halve ducks and bring to boil in stock pot with water.
• Add celery, parsley, salt and pepper.
• Simmer, uncovered, 40-50 minutes or until meat begins to fall away from bone.
• Melt 1 cup butter in large heavy skillet.
• Add 3-5 tablespoons bacon grease and increase heat.
• Sauté onions, green peppers, okra and garlic.
• Remove ducks. Bone and cut into small chunks.
• Keep stock on low heat. Add onions, green pepper and okra, and simmer while roux is prepared.
• In same skillet, put 3-5 tablespoons bacon grease and enough butter to cover bottom.
• Increase heat and add flour, 1 tablespoon at a time, stirring vigorously until roux turns light brown.
• Add duck meat and brown.
• Add cooked sausage, if desired.
• Increase heat under stock while adding meat and sauce of roux.
• Bring mixture to a low boil and add tomatoes, tomato paste, bay leaves, Worcestershire sauce, Tabasco, paprika, sugar, tarragon, thyme, rosemary and filé.
• Simmer, uncovered, 4-6 hours.

STUFFED WILD DUCKS AND ORANGE SAUCE

Yield: 4 servings

4 wild ducks	½ teaspoon salt
½ pound fresh mushrooms, sliced	¼ teaspoon thyme
3 tablespoons finely chopped onions	⅛ teaspoon pepper
	2 cups wild rice, cooked
¾ cup thinly sliced celery	1 cup orange juice
¼ cup butter	Apples, oranges and parsley
2 teaspoons grated orange rind	to garnish

• Wash ducks and pat dry.
• Sauté mushrooms, onions and celery in butter about 5 minutes.
• Add orange rind, salt, thyme and pepper. Blend well.
• Pour mushroom mixture over rice and toss gently.
• Fill duck cavities with rice mixture.
• Tie legs and wings.
• Place ducks on rack in roasting pan.
• Bake at 325° for 2 hours, basting every 15 minutes with orange juice.
• Garnish with apple wedges, orange slices and parsley.
• Serve with Orange Sauce.

Orange Sauce:

½ cup hot water	1 teaspoon grated orange rind
2 tablespoons all-purpose flour	1 teaspoon grated lemon rind
⅔ cup orange juice	

• Pour off fat from roasting pan, reserving drippings.
• Add hot water to pan. Stir to incorporate pan drippings.
• Blend in flour, stirring constantly, until thickened and smooth.
• Blend in orange juice and heat thoroughly.
• Sprinkle with orange and lemon rind.

ROAST WILD DUCK FLAMBÉ

Yield: 4 servings

4	whole ducks	4	ribs celery
	Salt and pepper	2	green apples, halved and cored
	Poultry seasoning	¾	cup water
1	large onion, quartered	4	tablespoons Cognac

- Wash ducks and pat dry.
- Season cavity and outside of duck with salt, pepper and poultry seasoning.
- Place an onion quarter, a celery rib and an apple half in the cavity of each duck.
- Place ducks, breast side down, in roasting pan.
- Add ¾ cup of water.
- Bake at 325° for 1½-2 hours.
- Before serving, brown under broiler.
- To serve, place ducks on large platter and spoon Orange Sauce over ducks.
- Flame Cognac and pour over ducks and sauce.

Orange Sauce:

1	6-ounce can orange juice concentrate	1	teaspoon grated orange rind
		1	teaspoon grated lemon rind
2½	cups water	2	tablespoons cornstarch
1	cup powdered sugar	1	teaspoon thyme
½	teaspoon salt	1	teaspoon fresh lemon juice
½	teaspoon pepper	1	apple, cored and cut into wedges
½	teaspoon ground ginger		

- Combine concentrate, water, sugar, salt, pepper and ginger in a bowl.
- Add rinds, cornstarch, thyme and lemon juice. Blend well.
- Transfer to saucepan. Add apples.
- Bring to a boil over medium heat.
- Turn off heat.

GLAZED DUCKLINGS

Yield: 6 servings

3   wild ducks or 2 domestic
     ducks
     Salt and pepper
¾   teaspoon dried rosemary
     or sage
¼   cup maple syrup
1¼ cups orange juice, divided

1   cup black currant jelly
1   cup chicken broth
1   tablespoon grated fresh
     ginger root or ½ teaspoon
     ground ginger
¼   teaspoon nutmeg
¼   teaspoon curry powder

• Sprinkle cavity and outside of each duck with salt and pepper.
• Rub ¼ teaspoon rosemary or sage inside each duck.
• Place on rack in roasting pan. For domestic ducks, roast at 400° for 30 minutes per pound. For wild ducks, total cooking time at 400° will vary from 30-60 minutes. (Birds are cooked when drumstick moves easily in its socket.)
• Pierce duck skins randomly once during cooking time to allow fat to drain off.
• Thirty minutes before ducks are done, pour off fat from pan.
• Combine maple syrup and ¼ cup orange juice. Baste ducks.
• Continue cooking until ducks are tender and glazed.
• Remove from roasting pan and keep warm.
• To pan juices, add remaining orange juice, jelly, broth, ginger, nutmeg and curry powder.
• Bring to a boil, stirring until sauce is reduced and thickened slightly.
• Carve ducks or cut into individual portions.
• Serve with sauce.

This recipe is equally good with wild goose.

SAUCE FOR VENISON

Yield: 1 cup

⅓ cup red currant jelly
⅓ cup Worcestershire sauce

⅓ cup butter

• Combine all ingredients. Heat well. Serve over venison steaks.

DUCK FOR DUCK HATERS

Yield: 4 servings

2 mallard ducks, cut in half
  Salt and pepper
2 tablespoons butter
1 medium onion, finely chopped

1 apple, peeled and grated
1 teaspoon grated orange peel
4 tablespoons currant jelly
5 tablespoons sherry or port

- Season ducks with salt and pepper. Set aside.
- Melt butter in heavy skillet over medium heat. Add onion. Cook until transparent.
- Add apple and orange peel. Cook several minutes.
- Stir in jelly and wine. Cook until mixture is reduced to consistency of molasses. Remove from heat.
- Place ducks, cavity side down, about 3 inches above medium-hot fire.
- Cook 5 minutes, or until well browned.
- Turn ducks. Pierce each half 15-20 times.
- Spoon one tablespoon onion mixture into cavity of each half.
- Cook 5-10 minutes, or until done. Do not overcook.
- Serve on platter, meaty side up, with remaining sauce.

BETSY'S VENISON TERIYAKI

Yield: 4 servings

4 venison steaks, cut into strips
  or chunks
1 tablespoon vegetable oil
1 envelope onion soup mix
2 cups water, divided
2 tablespoons soy sauce
1 cup chopped green pepper

½ cup celery, sliced diagonally
1 4-ounce can mushrooms,
  drained and sliced
2 tablespoons cornstarch
1 10-ounce package frozen
  snow peas
  Rice

- Brown meat in oil.
- Add soup mix, 1½ cups water and soy sauce. Cover and cook over low heat 30 minutes.
- Add green pepper and celery. Cook 30 minutes more, stirring occasionally.
- Add mushrooms.
- Blend cornstarch and ½ cup water.
- Add to meat and stir until thickened.
- Add snow peas and cook 1 minute.
- Serve over rice.

VENISON WITH SAUCE CATALAN

Yield: 8 servings

1 venison tenderloin
2 cups milk
¼ cup all-purpose flour
½ cup butter

1 cup white seedless grapes
3 tomatoes, peeled and cut
   into wedges
3 tablespoons port

• Soak tenderloin in milk overnight.
• Cut into 4-ounce filets.
• Dredge filets in flour. Melt butter in heavy skillet. Cook filets until medium-rare.
• Add grapes and tomatoes.
• Stir in port and flame.
• Add Sauce Catalan and serve.

Sauce Catalan:
Yield: 1½ cups

1½ pounds fresh mushrooms,
   quartered
3 tablespoons butter
1 tablespoon all-purpose flour
1 cup game stock

¼ cup whipping cream
½ teaspoon salt
¼ teaspoon pepper
⅛ teaspoon cayenne pepper

• Sauté mushrooms in butter.
• Whisk in flour and cook 2 minutes.
• Blend in game stock and simmer until thickened.
• Add whipping cream, salt, pepper and cayenne pepper. Blend well.

MARINADE FOR VENISON

Yield: 1 quart

3 cups dry white wine
1¼ cups olive oil
2 onions, sliced
2 carrots, sliced
2 cloves garlic, minced
1 teaspoon salt
1 bay leaf
2 tablespoons chopped fresh
   parsley

¼ teaspoon thyme
8 peppercorns
1 whole clove
6 coriander seeds, optional
6 juniper berries, crushed,
   optional

• Combine all ingredients and pour over meat.
• Cover and marinate in refrigerator overnight, or a few days, turning occasionally.

A great marinade for lamb and beef, too!

MEATS

TENDERLOIN FILETS

Yield: 6 servings

6	tenderloin steaks, 1-inch thick	1	cup dry white wine
	Brandy	1	tablespoon tarragon vinegar
	Salt to taste	1¼	cups beef broth
	Freshly ground pepper		Clarified butter
2	small shallots, finely minced		Vegetable oil
1	teaspoon minced fresh parsley	2	tablespoons whipping cream
1	clove garlic, minced		

• Coat steaks with brandy. Rub well with fingers. Let stand 30 minutes.
• Pat steaks dry and generously coat both sides with salt and pepper.
• Simmer shallots, parsley and garlic in wine and vinegar in heavy saucepan until liquid is reduced by half.
• Add beef broth. Simmer 20 minutes.
• Heat butter and oil in heavy skillet. Add steaks and cook to desired doneness.
• Remove and keep warm while sauce is cooking.
• Pour off excess butter and oil from skillet, if necessary.
• Purée sauce in blender. Add to pan juices, scraping any browned bits from skillet.
• Remove from heat. Blend in cream.
• Serve over warm steaks.

To add to the presentation, sauté 6 slices French bread in butter, place steak on bread and cover with sauce. Sprinkle with sautéed mushrooms, if desired.

MARINATED STEAK TERIYAKI

Yield: 2 servings

¼	cup vegetable oil	2	tablespoons chopped fresh
2	tablespoons soy sauce		ginger root or 1 teaspoon
1	tablespoon cider vinegar		ground ginger
1	tablespoon honey	1	clove garlic, minced
1	tablespoon finely chopped green onion	¾	pound sirloin steak

• Combine oil, soy sauce, vinegar, honey, onion, ginger and garlic. Mix well.
• Pour over meat. Marinate in refrigerator 24 hours, turning occasionally.
• Remove meat. Grill over hot coals 5-7 minutes per side, or broil in oven 6 inches from heat.

NEW YORK STRIP MARINADE

Yield: Marinade for 8 steaks

1½ cups vegetable oil
½ cup soy sauce
¼ cup Worcestershire sauce
2 tablespoons salt
1 teaspoon pepper
½ cup vinegar (wine vinegar may be used)

1½ teaspoons fresh parsley, chopped
2 cloves garlic, crushed
⅓ cup lemon juice
1 cup brown sugar

- Combine all marinade ingredients. Mix well.
- Marinate steaks 6-24 hours in refrigerator, turning occasionally.
- Grill to desired doneness. Baste meat with marinade often while cooking.
  Marinade may be stored in refrigerator and reused.

PEPPER STEAK

Yield: 6 servings

1½ pounds top sirloin steak, about ½-inch thick
Salt and pepper
2 tablespoons margarine
2 cloves garlic, crushed
½ cup sliced green onions with tops
1 large green pepper, cut into strips
1 14½-ounce can tomatoes, drained and chopped, or 2 large fresh tomatoes, diced

1 cup beef broth
¼ cup cold water
3 tablespoons cornstarch
1 tablespoon soy sauce
1 tablespoon Worcestershire sauce
3 cups hot cooked rice

- Cut steak into thin strips. Sprinkle with salt and pepper.
- Heat margarine over medium heat in large skillet or wok.
- Add steak and garlic. Cook until steak is browned, stirring often. Remove steak.
- Stir in onions and green pepper. Cook until just tender.
- Add tomatoes and beef broth. Cover. Simmer 15 minutes.
- Return steak to pan.
- Blend water with cornstarch, soy sauce and Worcestershire sauce.
- Stir into steak mixture. Cook until thickened. (May be frozen at this point.)
- Season with salt and pepper.
- Serve over rice.

STUFFED WINE-BRAISED FLANK STEAK

Yield: 4-6 servings

1½ pounds flank steak	1 teaspoon ground oregano
Salt and pepper	1 medium clove garlic, minced
All-purpose flour	½ teaspoon salt
1 cup finely chopped onion	⅛ teaspoon pepper
½ cup butter, divided	1 egg, beaten
1 cup soft bread crumbs	2 tablespoons all-purpose flour
½ cup finely chopped, cooked ham	1 cup beef broth
	1 cup hearty red wine
½ cup chopped fresh parsley	1 teaspoon cornstarch, optional

• Score beef and pound to tenderize.
• Season beef with salt and pepper, then dust with flour.
• Sauté onion in ¼ cup butter until transparent.
• Combine onion, bread crumbs, ham, parsley, oregano, garlic, salt, pepper and egg.
• Spread bread crumb mixture on flank steak.
• Roll steak from long side, jelly-roll fashion, and tie with kitchen twine.
• Dust steak again with 2 tablespoons flour.
• Brown steak on all sides in remaining ¼ cup butter.
• Add beef broth and wine.
• Cover and simmer 1 hour, or until meat is tender. Baste occasionally.
• To thicken gravy, add cornstarch and blend until smooth.

PEPPERED RIB-EYE ROAST

Yield: 12-14 servings

1 5-6 pound boneless rib-eye roast	1 teaspoon garlic powder
	1 cup soy sauce
⅓ cup coarsely ground pepper	1 cup red wine vinegar
2 tablespoons tomato paste	

• Rub roast with pepper.
• Combine tomato paste, garlic powder, soy sauce and vinegar. Blend well.
• Pour marinade over roast. Cover and refrigerate overnight.
• Remove roast from marinade. Bring to room temperature.
• Place roast fat-side up on rack in roasting pan. Insert meat thermometer. Bake at 325°: 2 hours (140°) for rare, 2½ hours (150°) for medium rare.
• Remove to warm platter.
• Slice and serve.

VITE CARBONNADE de BOEUF

Yield: 6-8 servings

2½ pounds round steak
1 cup all-purpose flour
1 teaspoon salt, divided
½ teaspoon pepper, divided
 Vegetable oil
1 large onion, sliced
½ pound fresh mushrooms, sliced
3 cups beef broth

1¼ cups beer
3 tablespoons red wine vinegar
3 tablespoons tomato paste
2 carrots, thinly sliced
1 tablespoon sugar
½ teaspoon thyme
1 teaspoon chopped fresh parsley
½ teaspoon basil

- Trim steak of all fat. Cut meat into thin strips across the grain.
- Combine flour with ½ teaspoon salt and ¼ teaspoon pepper.
- Dust steak strips with seasoned flour.
- In large skillet, brown meat in small amount of vegetable oil. Continue until all meat is browned, adding oil as needed.
- Drain meat on paper towels.
- Add onion to skillet, browning lightly and stirring often. Add mushrooms and sauté until tender.
- Add broth, beer, vinegar, tomato paste, carrots, sugar, thyme, parsley, basil, ½ teaspoon salt and ¼ teaspoon pepper.
- Bring to a boil.
- Place meat in Dutch oven. Add sauce.
- Cover. Bake at 325° for 1½ hours.

Enjoy this quicker version of beef stew over hot, cooked egg noodles.

FLANK STEAK DIJON

Yield: 4-6 servings

5 tablespoons butter, divided
1 tablespoon vegetable oil
1 1¼-1¾-pound flank steak
 Salt and pepper

6 tablespoons dry vermouth
2 tablespoons Dijon mustard
½ teaspoon Worcestershire sauce
3 tablespoons capers

- In large heavy skillet, melt 1 tablespoon butter and oil over medium-high heat until browned.
- Rub flank steak with salt and pepper.
- Pan-fry steak 3-5 minutes on each side. Remove meat from pan. Keep warm.
- In pan drippings over low heat, melt remaining 4 tablespoons butter.
- Add vermouth, mustard, Worcestershire sauce and capers. Stir until well blended. Remove sauce from heat. Keep warm.
- Thinly slice steak and arrange on serving platter. Pour sauce over steak. Serve immediately.

Try this with CREAMER'S SHRIMP PILAF.

BEEF AND SNOW PEAS

Yield: 2-3 servings

1 pound flank or round steak	8 ounces snow peas
1 clove garlic, minced	1 8-ounce can water chestnuts,
2 tablespoons oil	optional

Marinade:

1 teaspoon cornstarch	1 teaspoon grated fresh
1 tablespoon vegetable oil	ginger root or ¼ teaspoon
1 tablespoon soy sauce	ground ginger
½ teaspoon sugar	

Paste:

1 tablespoon cornstarch	1 teaspoon sugar
2 tablespoons soy sauce	½ cup water

• Cut steak into 3-inch long, very thin strips.
• Combine Marinade ingredients. Pour over steak and marinate 30 minutes.
• Combine Paste ingredients. Set aside.
• Brown garlic in 2 tablespoons oil. Discard garlic.
• Add beef. Brown.
• Add Paste mixture, snow peas and water chestnuts, if desired.
• Cook until gravy has thickened. May thin with water, if needed.

Flank steak is much easier to slice if slightly frozen.

MARINATED BEEF

Yield: 4 servings

⅓ cup wine vinegar	1 teaspoon prepared mustard
2-3 tablespoons ketchup	1 teaspoon salt
2 tablespoons vegetable oil	¼ teaspoon pepper
1 tablespoon soy sauce	¼ teaspoon garlic powder
1 tablespoon Worcestershire	1½ pounds top round steak,
sauce	London Broil or flank steak

• Combine vinegar, ketchup, oil, soy sauce, Worcestershire sauce, mustard, salt, pepper and garlic powder. Blend well.
• Pour marinade over meat and refrigerate several hours or overnight, turning often.
• Allow meat to stand in marinade for 30 minutes at room temperature.
• Grill 8-10 minutes on each side. Cut into thin diagonal slices.

CHINESE BEEF WITH OYSTER SAUCE

Yield: 4 servings

1	pound round steak	½	pound fresh snow peas,
2	tablespoons soy sauce		optional
2	teaspoons cornstarch	2	tablespoons chicken broth
4	tablespoons vegetable oil, divided	1	clove garlic, minced
		4-6	tablespoons oyster sauce
2	large onions, cut into chunks		Rice
2	large green peppers, cut into chunks		

• Slice round steak across the grain into ¼-inch thick strips.
• Blend soy sauce and cornstarch. Marinate meat at least 15 minutes.
• Heat 2 tablespoons oil in large skillet. Stir-fry onions, peppers and snow peas 2 minutes.
• Add chicken broth and continue cooking until liquid evaporates, about 1 minute.
• Remove vegetables and set aside.
• Heat remaining 2 tablespoons of oil. Quickly stir-fry garlic. Discard garlic.
• Add beef to hot oil. Stir-fry about 2 minutes.
• Add reserved vegetables and oyster sauce.
• Heat and serve over fluffy white rice.

BEEF BENGAL

Yield: 6 servings

1½	pounds chuck steak, cut into 1-inch cubes	1½	teaspoons salt
		1	teaspoon instant beef bouillon
2	tablespoons vegetable oil	1½	cups water
2-4	medium onions, sliced	¼	cup vinegar
1	clove garlic, minced	½	cup golden raisins
1	tablespoon curry powder		Rice
1	tablespoon all-purpose flour	1	cup plain yogurt

• In large skillet, brown beef in hot oil.
• Remove beef with slotted spoon.
• Add onions and garlic to hot oil. Cook until tender.
• Stir in curry powder. Cook over low heat 2-3 minutes.
• Stir in flour and salt.
• Add bouillon, water, vinegar, raisins and beef. Stir well.
• Cover. Cook over low heat 1½ hours, stirring occasionally.
• Serve over hot, cooked rice. Top with yogurt.

The yogurt adds an unusual flavor.

SPAGHETTINI BOLOGNESE

Yield: 6 servings

¼ pound fresh mushrooms, sliced
1 carrot, thinly sliced
1 clove garlic, minced
½ cup chopped onion
½ cup chopped celery
½ cup chopped green pepper
2 tablespoons butter
1 pound Italian sausage, hot or mild, casings removed

2 15-ounce cans tomato sauce
½ cup water
¼ cup dry red wine, optional
1 teaspoon sugar
¼ teaspoon Italian seasoning
Vermicelli

• In large Dutch oven, sauté mushrooms, carrot, garlic, onion, celery and green pepper in butter until soft.
• Add sausage. Cook until sausage loses its red color. Drain.
• Add tomato sauce, water, wine, sugar and Italian seasoning. Blend well.
• Simmer, uncovered, 40 minutes. Stir often.
• Serve over hot cooked vermicelli.

A nice change from spaghetti and meatballs.

MEXICAN SPAGHETTI

Yield: 10-12 servings

2 pounds ground round
1 large onion, chopped
1 2-pound jar spaghetti sauce with mushrooms
2 teaspoons salt
¼ teaspoon pepper, or to taste

2 4-ounce cans chopped green chilies
2 teaspoons chili powder, or to taste
12 ounces vermicelli
1 pound Longhorn cheese, grated

• Brown meat. Add onion and cook, stirring frequently, 5 minutes.
• Add spaghetti sauce, salt, pepper, green chilies and chili powder. Simmer 30 minutes.
• Cook vermicelli. Drain.
• Combine sauce and vermicelli.
• Layer half the vermicelli mixture in a 3-quart baking dish.
• Cover with half the cheese. Repeat layers.
• Bake at 300° for 40-50 minutes.

A quick, spicy spaghetti casserole.

MANICOTTI

Yield: 10-12 servings

Pasta:

6   eggs, room temperature
1½ cups all-purpose flour
¼   teaspoon salt

1½ cups water
Melted butter

- Combine eggs, flour, salt and water. Beat until smooth.
- Let stand at least 30 minutes.
- Slowly heat 8-inch skillet. Brush with melted butter as needed.
- Pour in 3 tablespoons batter, rotating quickly to spread evenly.
- Cook over medium heat until top is dry. Do not brown or flip.
- Repeat process with remaining batter.
- Cool on wire rack. Stack, using waxed paper between layers.

Filling:

2   pounds Ricotta cheese
8   ounces Mozzarella cheese,
    cubed
⅓   cup grated Parmesan cheese

2   eggs
1   teaspoon salt
¼   teaspoon pepper
1   tablespoon chopped parsley

- Combine all Filling ingredients. Mix well.

Sauce:

1½ cups chopped onion
1   clove garlic, crushed
⅓   cup vegetable oil
1   28-ounce can Italian tomatoes
1   6-ounce can tomato paste
2   tablespoons chopped parsley
1   teaspoon salt

1   tablespoon sugar
1   teaspoon oregano
1   teaspoon basil
¼   teaspoon pepper
¾   cup red wine
¾   cup water

- In heavy skillet, sauté onion and garlic in heated oil 5 minutes.
- Add all remaining ingredients.
- Bring to a boil. Reduce heat. Simmer, covered, 1 hour, stirring occasionally.

(continued)

Assembly:
½ cup grated Parmesan cheese

• Spoon ¼ cup Filling in center of each Pasta. Roll up.
• Spoon 1½ cups Sauce into each of 2 3-quart shallow baking dishes.
• Place Manicotti, seam side down, in single layer.
• Spoon 1 cup Sauce over each dish.
• Sprinkle each dish with ¼ cup Parmesan cheese.
• Bake at 350° for 30 minutes, or until heated through.

FAJITAS

Yield: 6 servings

2½-3	pounds thin flank steak, skirt steak or rib-eye	1	teaspoon oregano
½	cup olive oil	½	teaspoon salt
¼	cup red wine vinegar	½	teaspoon pepper
⅓	cup fresh lime juice	¼	teaspoon ground cumin
⅓	cup finely chopped onion	3	cloves garlic, minced
1	teaspoon sugar	6	soft flour tortillas

• Pound steak to ¼-inch thickness.
• Combine olive oil, vinegar, lime juice, onion, sugar, oregano, salt, pepper, cumin and garlic. Pour over meat.
• Cover. Marinate overnight in refrigerator, turning often.
• Prepare Toppings.
• Remove steak from marinade and grill to desired doneness. (Meat can be sliced, then stir-fried in a heavy, hot skillet along with chunks of onion, green pepper and tomatoes.)
• Carve into very thin strips. Place strips on large platter and keep warm.
• Warm tortillas according to package directions.
• Place meat and tortillas on table along with any combination of Toppings.
• Allow guests to assemble their own fajitas, putting meat and desired toppings on tortilla, then rolling up.

Toppings:

1 8-ounce jar mild picante sauce	1 cup salsa verde
2 cups guacamole	2 cups shredded lettuce
2 cups chopped tomatoes	1 cup chopped green onions
1 8-ounce carton sour cream	1 cup grated Cheddar cheese

Especially delicious when served with a large pitcher of margaritas and Spanish rice or refried beans.

GOULASH MAYS

Yield: 8-10 servings

10 tablespoons butter, divided	Dash Tabasco
2 onions, chopped	Dash Worcestershire sauce
1 green pepper, chopped	1 12-ounce bottle chili sauce
1 clove garlic, minced	1 8-ounce can sliced mushrooms,
1 pound ground veal	drained
½ pound ground pork	1 10-ounce package extra sharp
3 14½-ounce cans tomatoes	Cheddar cheese, grated, divided
1 teaspoon salt	4 ounces vermicelli, cooked and
½ teaspoon pepper	drained

- Melt 2 tablespoons butter in medium skillet.
- Add onions, green pepper and garlic. Sauté 10 minutes, stirring often.
- In separate skillet, combine veal, pork and water to cover bottom of skillet.
- Brown over low heat 10-15 minutes, stirring often. Drain.
- In large Dutch oven, combine tomatoes, salt, pepper, Tabasco, Worcestershire sauce, chili sauce, remaining butter, mushrooms and half the grated cheese. Mix well.
- Add onion mixture. Simmer 20 minutes.
- Stir in meat and vermicelli. (Sauce may be frozen after adding meat, but do not add vermicelli until ready to serve. An additional can of tomatoes may be needed when reheating frozen sauce to retain juicy consistency.)
- Pour mixture into 3-quart baking dish. Sprinkle with remaining cheese.
- Bake at 350° for 20-30 minutes, or until thoroughly heated.

FETTUCINE MILANO

Yield: 4 servings

1	pound mild Italian sausage,	1	cup chopped green onion
	casings removed	½	cup chopped fresh parsley
¼-½ cup olive oil		1	teaspoon basil, crumbled
½	cup butter	¼	teaspoon rosemary, crumbled
3	cups sliced fresh mushrooms	½	teaspoon oregano, crumbled
2	cloves garlic, minced		Hot cooked fettucine
1	green pepper, chopped		Grated Parmesan cheese

- In large skillet, brown sausage. Remove from skillet and drain well. Pour excess grease from pan.
- Add olive oil and butter to skillet.
- Add mushrooms, garlic, green pepper, onion, parsley, basil, rosemary and oregano. Sauté until soft. Remove from heat. Stir in sausage.
- Toss sausage mixture with fettucine and sprinkle with Parmesan cheese. Serve immediately.

GREEN ENCHILADAS

Yield: 6 servings

Filling:

1 pound ground chuck	1 teaspoon ground cumin
1 large onion, finely chopped	1/8 teaspoon cayenne pepper
3 cloves garlic, minced	2 teaspoons salt
1/2 cup canned tomatoes with juice	1/2 teaspoon pepper
1/2 cup chunky salsa, hot, medium or mild	1 tablespoon Worcestershire sauce
1 tablespoon chili powder	

- In heavy skillet, slowly brown meat with onion and garlic.
- Spoon off excess fat. Add remaining filling ingredients. Simmer until mixture is thickened and no liquid remains.

Sauce:

1/2 pound Velveeta cheese	1 4-ounce can green chilies, chopped (hot or mild)
1 5-ounce can evaporated milk	2 tablespoons chopped pimentos
1 10¾-ounce can cream of chicken soup	

- In double boiler over simmering water, combine cheese and milk. Stir until cheese has melted.
- Add remaining sauce ingredients. Blend well until thoroughly heated.

Assembly:

Vegetable oil	1 pound Longhorn cheese, grated
12 corn or flour tortillas	Chunky salsa, optional

- If using corn tortillas, heat 1/4-inch vegetable oil in skillet.
- Dip tortillas, one at a time, in hot oil, being sure to coat both sides. Blot with paper towels to remove excess oil.
- Immediately fill each tortilla with 2 tablespoons Filling and 2 tablespoons grated cheese. Roll up.
- Place tortillas, seam side down, in 9x13-inch baking dish. Pack tortillas closely to prevent unrolling.
- Pour hot Sauce over tortillas. Sprinkle with remaining grated cheese.
- Bake at 350° for 20-25 minutes, or until thoroughly heated.
- Serve with additional salsa, if desired.

Work quickly with corn tortillas, filling one while another is in hot oil.
If using flour tortillas, use directly from the package or, if dry,
follow hot oil method used for corn tortillas.

MUSTARD GLAZED CORNED BEEF

Yield: 6 servings

1	3-4 pound corned beef brisket	¾	cup honey
10	black peppercorns	½	cup red wine vinegar
2	bay leaves	½	cup firmly packed light
¾	cup Dijon mustard		brown sugar
1¼	teaspoons dry mustard		

- In large pot, place brisket, peppercorns, bay leaves and enough water to cover brisket.
- Cover and simmer 2-2½ hours, or until fork-tender. Cool.
- In saucepan, combine mustards, honey, vinegar and sugar. Simmer 5 minutes.
- Place brisket, fat side up, in shallow baking dish. Spread glaze on top. Bake at 350° for 45 minutes.
- Slice and serve with warm glaze.

VEAL SCALLOPINE

Yield: 4 servings

½	cup all-purpose flour	½	cup beef broth
½	cup grated Parmesan cheese	¼	cup dry sherry
	Salt and pepper to taste	½	pound sliced, fresh
1½	pounds veal scallopine,		mushrooms, sautéed, optional
	pounded thin		Hot, cooked pasta
4	tablespoons butter or		
	margarine		

- Combine flour, cheese, salt and pepper.
- Dust veal, one piece at a time, in seasoned flour until well coated.
- Melt butter in heavy skillet. Brown veal quickly on each side. Transfer to serving platter.
- Add broth, sherry and mushrooms, if desired, to skillet, scraping pan while stirring. Cook 2-3 minutes.
- Pour sauce over veal. Serve immediately over hot, cooked pasta.

VEAL MARENGO

Craig Calvert
Calvert's and C-Grill
Augusta, Georgia
Yield: 12-14 servings

12	slices lean bacon	1	teaspoon fresh minced tarragon
	Vegetable oil		
3	pounds stewing veal, cut into 2-inch cubes and drained on paper towels	1½	bay leaves
		1	ounce chicken base or bouillon to taste
1	pound fresh mushrooms, quartered	2	tablespoons tomato paste
		3	tablespoons all-purpose flour
18-24	small white onions (1-inch in diameter)	3	cups full bodied white wine
	Butter	2	cups veal or chicken stock
2	tablespoons butter	1	pound fresh tomatoes, peeled and seeded
1	tablespoon minced garlic		Tabasco to taste
1	teaspoon fresh minced thyme		

- Brown bacon in large skillet. Remove and break into pieces. Set aside. Reserve drippings.
- In drippings, with a little oil added, brown veal, a small amount at a time, over moderately high heat. Remove veal and set aside.
- Brown mushrooms in remaining drippings.
- Peel onions and cut ¼-inch cross in top of each onion. Brown in small amount of butter. Remove and set aside.
- In Dutch oven, melt 2 tablespoons butter.
- Add garlic, thyme, tarragon and bay leaves. Bring to a slow simmer and cook 3-4 minutes.
- Add chicken base and tomato paste.
- Add flour. Cook 5 minutes.
- Add wine. Cook 5 minutes.
- Add veal stock, bacon pieces, veal, mushrooms and onions. Boil 5 minutes.
- Reduce heat and simmer 2 hours.
- Just prior to serving, add chopped tomatoes and Tabasco to taste.
- Serve with rice, pasta or Duchess potatoes.
- A California Chardonnay or French White Burgundy is excellent with this veal.

Chef's note: in this stew, it is important to properly brown the meat, onions, and mushrooms in the skillet. Always brown small quantities at a time. If too much is added at one time, the process takes much longer.

VEAL CHOPS WITH MUSHROOM WINE SAUCE

Yield: 4 servings

4 veal chops, each ½ to ¾-inch thick
Salt and pepper
2 tablespoons butter, divided
2 tablespoons vegetable oil, divided
½ pound sliced, fresh mushrooms
½ cup hot beef broth

1 cup brown sauce (1.1 ounce package Knorr Hunter Sauce with mushrooms may be substituted for homemade brown sauce. Prepare according to package directions.)
¼ cup red wine
1 teaspoon basil
Salt and pepper to taste

• Dust veal chops with salt and pepper.
• Melt 1 tablespoon butter with 1 tablespoon vegetable oil in large skillet over medium heat.
• Brown chops 3-5 minutes on each side. Transfer chops to 3-quart baking dish.
• Melt remaining 1 tablespoon butter with 1 tablespoon vegetable oil over medium heat.
• Add mushrooms and sauté, stirring often.
• Add hot beef broth. Simmer 10-12 minutes.
• Add brown sauce and red wine. Blend well. Simmer 15-18 minutes or until thickened.
• Stir in basil, salt and pepper.
• Pour sauce over chops. Cover.
• Bake at 325° for 20-30 minutes.

▶ Since the 32nd Masters® concluded, I have had a chance to recover, at least partially, from the excitement and elation generated by my victory and now more fully appreciate how fortunate I was to win such a distinctive sports classic.

Accompanying this realization is a feeling of profound gratitude to you, Mr. Roberts and Mr. Jones, and all the other gentlemen at the Augusta National Golf Club for having had the foresight to initiate such a wonderful tournament, the resourcefulness to conduct it with dignity and the determination to improve it over the years to the point where it now occupies a lofty and special niche among the leading sports events of the world.

From a BOB GOALBY letter
Written May 5, 1968

POT ROAST OF VEAL

Yield: 6 servings

2 teaspoons salt	2 tablespoons vegetable oil
¼ teaspoon pepper	2 carrots, finely chopped
½ teaspoon mace	2 onions, finely chopped
1 4-pound veal roast, boned, rolled, and tied or 1 4-pound veal chuck roast	2 cups chicken broth
	½ cup milk
	1 tablespoon cornstarch

- Combine salt, pepper and mace. Rub mixture over roast.
- In large Dutch oven, heat oil over medium-high heat. Brown roast on all sides. Remove roast.
- Add carrots and onions. Sauté until onions are golden brown, stirring often.
- Return roast to pan. Add chicken broth.
- Cover. Simmer 1½-2 hours, or until tender, turning once.
- Transfer roast to serving platter.
- Purée pan juices and vegetables in blender or food processor.
- Add milk and cornstarch. Blend well.
- Heat gravy thoroughly.
- Slice roast and serve with gravy.

MARINATED LEG OF LAMB

Yield: 8-10 servings

1 leg of lamb	2 tablespoons fresh lemon juice
1 large clove garlic, minced	½ teaspoon ginger
1 large bay leaf, crumbled	½ teaspoon thyme
1 tablespoon salt	½ teaspoon sage
⅔ teaspoon pepper	½ teaspoon marjoram

- Score lamb in diamond shapes through the fat, but not into the meat.
- Combine remaining ingredients to make marinade.
- Rub marinade over lamb and into slits.
- Refrigerate lamb in plastic bag 24 hours, turning occasionally.
- Place lamb, fat side up, in shallow roasting pan. Pour remaining marinade over top.
- Bake at 325° for 25 minutes per pound, or until meat thermometer registers 165°. If necessary, cover with foil to prevent burning.
- Use pan juices to make gravy.

An interesting combination of flavors.

GUVESTI

Roast Leg of Lamb with Orzo
Yield: 8-10 servings

1 large clove garlic, peeled	2 medium onions, thinly sliced
1 6½-7 pound leg of lamb	1 cup boiling water
1 teaspoon oregano	½ cup tomato purée
1 teaspoon salt	Grated Parmesan cheese
Freshly ground pepper	
6 tablespoons fresh lemon juice, divided	

- Sliver garlic into 8 pieces. Insert slivers into ¼-inch deep incisions on fat side of lamb.
- Combine oregano, salt and pepper. Press mixture firmly over entire lamb surface. For best results, insert meat thermometer during roasting. (160°-165° for rare, 165°-175° for medium, 175°-180° for well done.)
- Place lamb, fat side up, in shallow roasting pan. Roast at 450° for 20 minutes, uncovered.
- Reduce heat to 350°.
- Baste lamb with 1 tablespoon lemon juice.
- Place onions in roasting pan.
- Roast 15 minutes. Baste again with 1 tablespoon lemon juice.
- Pour boiling water over onions.
- Continue roasting 1-1½ hours or until lamb is done. Baste occasionally with remaining lemon juice.
- Remove lamb to large heated platter. Let rest at room temperature 10-15 minutes before carving.
- Reserve pan drippings.
- Spoon off all fat except a thin film from reserved pan drippings.
- Stir tomato purée into pan drippings, scraping sides and bottom of pan.
- Stir in cooked orzo. Return pan to 350° oven and bake 10-15 minutes, uncovered. Add additional salt, if needed.
- Spoon orzo around lamb. Serve with Parmesan cheese.

Orzo:

8 cups water	2 cups (about 1 pound) orzo
1 teaspoon salt	(rice shaped pasta)

- Bring water and salt to a boil.
- Add orzo slowly so that water continues to boil. Cook briskly about 10 minutes until orzo is tender. (Be careful not to overcook.)
- Drain orzo.

LAMB CHOPS DIJONNAISE

Yield: 2-4 servings

4 ¾-inch thick loin lamb chops
3 cloves garlic, divided
½ cup olive oil
½ cup brandy
2 tablespoons rosemary, divided
1 teaspoon seasoned pepper
1 tablespoon garlic powder

2 tablespoons Italian bread crumbs
1 tablespoon butter or margarine, melted
½ cup Dijon mustard, divided
Mint jelly

• Rub lamb chops with 1 clove garlic. Place chops in shallow baking dish.
• Mince remaining 2 cloves garlic.
• Combine minced garlic, oil, brandy, 1 tablespoon rosemary, pepper and garlic powder. Blend well.
• Pour mixture over chops. Cover and marinate in refrigerator 2-8 hours, turning chops occasionally.
• Remove chops from marinade. Place on broiler pan.
• Combine bread crumbs, butter and ¼ cup mustard. Blend well.
• Spread mustard mixture on chops. Sprinkle chops with remaining rosemary.
• Broil chops 11 inches from heat for 10 minutes.
• Turn chops over, spread with remaining mustard. Broil an additional 10 minutes.
• Remove from oven. Allow chops to stand 5 minutes. Serve with mint jelly.

BURTON'S LAMB CHOPS

Yield: 8 servings

8 sprigs fresh mint
¼ teaspoon rosemary
1 clove garlic, minced
4 tablespoons white wine
1 tablespoon water

6 tablespoons sugar
6 tablespoons cider vinegar
Salt and pepper
8 1-inch thick lamb chops

• Strip leaves from mint sprigs. Finely chop.
• Combine mint, rosemary, garlic, wine, water, sugar and vinegar. Blend well.
• Allow mint sauce to stand 1 hour.
• Salt and pepper lamb chops.
• Pour mint sauce over chops, turning to coat each side. Marinate 1 hour, turning once.
• Grill chops over medium-hot coals 7 minutes on each side, or until desired doneness. Baste often with remaining sauce.

MARINATED LAMB WITH BÉARNAISE SAUCE

Yield: 8 servings

1 teaspoon rosemary	½ cup fresh lemon juice, optional
1 teaspoon fennel	8 lamb steaks
1 teaspoon salt	Olive oil
½ teaspoon freshly ground pepper	Salt and pepper to taste
⅛ teaspoon thyme	

• Combine rosemary, fennel, salt, pepper, thyme and lemon juice, if desired.
• Pour marinade over lamb steaks. Cover with olive oil. Marinate at least 3 hours.
• Remove steaks from marinade. Salt and pepper steaks.
• Grill over hot coals until desired doneness is reached.
• Serve with Béarnaise Sauce.

Béarnaise Sauce:

1 shallot, finely chopped	2 tablespoons fresh lemon juice
⅛ cup red wine vinegar	1 tablespoon hot water
½ pound butter	⅛ teaspoon fresh tarragon

• In medium saucepan, combine shallot with enough vinegar to cover. Simmer until vinegar is almost evaporated.
• Add butter, lemon juice and water. Whisk until mixture is consistency of mayonnaise.
• Stir in tarragon and serve.

GRILLED PORK TENDERLOIN

Yield: 6-8 servings

¼ cup soy sauce	½ teaspoon cinnamon, optional
3 tablespoons dry sherry	2 pork tenderloins
1 large clove garlic, minced	

• Combine soy sauce, sherry, garlic and cinnamon, if desired.
• Marinate pork in sauce 24 hours, turning often.
• Grill over low heat 45 minutes to 1 hour, turning often.

HARRIET'S PORK TENDERLOIN

Harriet Goldsmith
Augusta, Georgia
Yield: 12 servings

3 pork tenderloins
Salt and pepper
½ cup butter, divided
¾ cup apricot jam

1 cup brown sauce (may use our BROWN SAUCE recipe, or Knorr Swiss Hunter Brown Sauce mix with mushrooms)
Fresh parsley to garnish

- Season tenderloins with salt and pepper.
- Sauté in ¼ cup butter 5-10 minutes, browning all sides. Remove tenderloins.
- Add remaining butter and apricot jam.
- Place meat in shallow roasting pan. Pour apricot sauce over meat.
- Bake at 350° for 40 minutes, basting often.
- Add brown sauce to apricot sauce, mixing well.
- Bake an additional 10 minutes.
- Garnish with fresh parsley. Serve with sauce.

SHERRIED CHOPS WITH RICE

Yield: 6 servings

6 pork loin chops, ¾-inch thick
2 tablespoons oil
1 teaspoon salt
¼ teaspoon pepper
1 clove garlic, minced
2 cups chicken broth
2 tablespoons currant jelly

1 teaspoon bouquet garni, crushed
¼ teaspoon grated orange peel
¾ cup sherry
3 tablespoons cornstarch
¼ cup water
3 cups hot cooked rice

- In heavy skillet, brown pork chops in oil. Transfer to 9x13-inch baking dish.
- Sprinkle chops with salt and pepper.
- Drain skillet. Add garlic and sauté for 1 minute.
- Add broth, jelly, bouquet garni and orange peel. Scrape pan to loosen brown particles. Heat until jelly melts.
- Add sherry.
- Pour sauce over chops.
- Bake, uncovered, at 350° for 1 hour or until tender.
- Remove excess fat from sauce.
- Dissolve cornstarch in water.
- Add to sauce, stirring until clear and thickened, about 2-3 minutes.
- Serve chops and sauce over fluffy white rice.

MARINATED PORK ROAST

Yield: 8-10 servings

1   4-6 pound pork loin, boned,
    rolled and tied
2   tablespoons dry mustard
2   teaspoons thyme

2   cloves garlic, minced
1   teaspoon ginger
½ cup dry sherry
½ cup soy sauce

• Place meat in large plastic bag.
• Combine mustard, thyme, garlic, ginger, sherry and soy sauce. Blend well.
• Pour marinade over roast. Marinate in refrigerator 1-2 days, turning occasionally.
• Place meat in shallow pan. Bake, uncovered at 350°, allowing 30 minutes per pound. Baste often with marinade.
• Serve with Apricot Sauce.

Apricot Sauce:
Yield: 1 ½ cups
1 10-ounce jar apricot preserves
1 tablespoon soy sauce

2 tablespoons dry sherry

• Combine sauce ingredients in small saucepan. Heat slowly until preserves are melted.
• Serve warm.

Easy, yet impressive!

 # TRAIL'S GRILLED PORK CHOPS

Yield: 4 servings

6 ounces soy sauce
1 tablespoon dry mustard
1 tablespoon sugar

2   cloves garlic, minced
4   1-inch loin pork chops

• Combine soy sauce, mustard, sugar and garlic.
• Marinate chops several hours, turning once.
• Grill over medium-hot coals 7-10 minutes per side or until done.

PORK LOIN WITH BOURBON

Yield: 8 servings

1	5-6 pound pork loin, boned and tied	3	cups beef broth Bouquet garni (sage, parsley, thyme, bay leaf)
1	8-ounce jar Dijon mustard		Salt
2	cups firmly packed dark brown sugar		Freshly ground black pepper
3	tablespoons peanut oil	1	6-ounce package dried apricots
1½	cups bourbon, divided		Cornstarch, optional

- Pat meat dry with paper towels.
- Rub meat with mustard, then roll in brown sugar. (Discard any extra mustard and sugar.)
- Heat oil in large Dutch oven. Brown meat on all sides over medium heat, being careful not to burn. Spoon mustard mixture over meat as it browns.
- Add ½ cup bourbon. Allow bourbon to warm, then ignite with match. Allow to burn out.
- Repeat process using ⅓ the bourbon each time, until all bourbon has been used.
- Add beef broth. Cover and bake at 325° for 1 hour, basting often.
- Turn meat over. Add bouquet garni, salt and pepper. Bake an additional 2 hours, basting often.
- Add apricots during last 15 minutes of cooking.
- Place meat on warm platter. Remove bouquet garni and simmer sauce until reduced by half.
- Thicken with cornstarch, if desired.
- Serve sauce over meat.

Always a hit with guests.

> "This is a young man's golf course," said Nicklaus as he accepted congratulations from Tournament Chairman Hord Hardin. "The fast greens, the length, the pins set on knobs—everything about it is suited to the nerves and stamina of younger guys. I'm not as good a player as I was ten or 15 years ago. I just want to be occasionally as good as I was."
>
> Jack Nicklaus April, 1986

BAKED PORK CHOPS WITH CRANBERRY SAUCE

Yield: 6 servings

6 ¾-inch thick pork chops
1 tablespoon shortening
   Salt and pepper
1 8-ounce can sliced pineapple
¾ cup whole berry cranberry sauce
2 chicken bouillon cubes

¾ cup boiling water
3 tablespoons light brown sugar
3 tablespoons vinegar
1 green pepper, cut into rings
3 tablespoons cornstarch
3 tablespoons water

- In large skillet, brown chops in melted shortening.
- Season chops with salt and pepper.
- Drain pineapple, reserving syrup.
- Combine syrup with cranberry sauce. Blend well.
- Dissolve bouillon cubes in boiling water.
- Stir in brown sugar and vinegar.
- Add cranberry mixture and bouillon mixture to pork chops.
- Cover. Simmer 50 minutes, or until tender.
- Top each chop with a pineapple slice, then a green pepper ring.
- Cover. Cook an additonal 10 minutes.
- Carefully remove chops with toppings to serving platter.
- Blend together cornstarch and water. Add to sauce. Stir until thickened.
- Pour sauce over chops. Serve immediately.

Easy, but delicious!

The Augusta National is among the most beautiful and challenging courses in the world. Not only that, but the Masters® has a deserved reputation for being an innovator of improvements in tournament conduct that has done so much for both player and spectator. The Masters® was the first to go to a four day schedule thus making the closing stages more exciting all around; also, you were the first to rope off the fairways and to install multiple scoreboards, later using the red and green numerals which makes it so much easier to relate the standings of the players.

From a BILLY CASPER letter
Written November 5, 1970

STIR-FRIED PORK WITH CASHEWS

Yield: 6 servings

1 tablespoon cornstarch
2 tablespoons dry sherry
2 tablespoons soy sauce
1 pound boneless pork loin, thinly sliced
¼ cup peanut oil
2 tablespoons sliced scallions
1 clove garlic, minced
1 teaspoon finely chopped fresh ginger, optional

½ pound fresh snow peas
4 carrots, sliced and blanched
1 green pepper, cut into 2-inch strips
½ cup chicken broth
1 tablespoon firmly packed dark brown sugar
½ cup unsalted cashews or peanuts
Fried rice

• Combine cornstarch, sherry and soy sauce. Blend well.
• Toss pork slices with sherry mixture. Refrigerate at least 1 hour.
• In large skillet or wok, heat oil over high heat.
• Add scallions, garlic and ginger. Stir-fry 1 minute.
• Add pork and marinade. Stir-fry until meat loses its pink color.
• Stir in peas, carrots and green pepper. Stir-fry 1 minute.
• Blend together chicken broth and brown sugar. Add to skillet, stirring until sauce thickens.
• Stir in nuts.
• Serve over fried rice.

Sliced water chestnuts and bamboo shoots may be added, if desired.

SWEET 'N SOUR RIBS

Yield: 6-8 servings

3 pounds country-style spareribs
Salt and pepper
1 onion, coarsely chopped
2 ribs celery, chopped
½ green pepper, chopped
2 tablespoons vegetable oil

1 tablespoon cornstarch
1 8-ounce can pineapple tidbits, undrained
1 cup water
¼ cup vinegar
1 tablespoon soy sauce

• Place spareribs, meaty side up, in shallow pan. Season with salt and pepper.
• Bake at 400° for 30 minutes. Spoon off grease.
• Combine onion, celery, green pepper and oil in medium saucepan. Cook 5 minutes over medium heat.
• Blend in cornstarch until smooth.
• Stir in pineapple, water, vinegar and soy sauce.
• Bring mixture to a boil, stirring constantly. Pour over spareribs.
• Bake at 350° for 1 hour. Baste occasionally with pan juices.

STROMBOLI

Yield: 6-8 servings

2 loaves frozen bread dough
1 pound ham, thinly sliced
¾ pound hard salami, thinly sliced
1 pound Provolone cheese, sliced
¾ pound Mozzarella cheese, grated

1 onion, thinly sliced, optional
½ pound sliced, fresh mushrooms,
   sautéed, optional
   Oregano
   Basil

• Allow dough to thaw at room temperature, about 2 hours.
• Pulling dough lengthwise, stretch each loaf to form a rectangle about 6x12 inches.
• Down center of rectangle, layer ½ the ham, salami, cheeses, onion and mushrooms, if desired. Be sure to overlap ingredients and mound layers.
• Sprinkle with oregano and basil.
• Fold both sides of dough to meet at the middle. Pinch seams together.
• Repeat with second rectangle and remaining ingredients.
• Place on ungreased baking sheet.
• Bake at 375° for 25-30 minutes.
• Slice and serve immediately.

Light, casual fare with a tossed green salad. Fun to build your own.

BROWN SAUCE

Yield: 2 cups

1 clove garlic, minced
1 onion, chopped
1 carrot, chopped
¼ cup butter
¼ cup all-purpose flour

3 cups beef broth
½ tomato, puréed
   Pinch thyme
   Salt and pepper

• Sauté garlic, onion and carrot in butter until soft.
• Add flour. Stir until golden brown.
• Slowly add beef broth, stirring constantly. (If using canned beef broth, dilute with equal amount of water.)
• Add tomato purée and thyme. Stir constantly until sauce thickens.
• Simmer, stirring occasionally, until sauce is reduced to 2 cups.
• Strain. Season with salt and pepper.

SEAFOOD

SHRIMP FETA

Yield: 8 servings

8	ounces linguini, cooked and drained	1	pound shrimp, peeled and deveined
1	egg, beaten	1	small tomato, peeled and chopped
¾	cup Ricotta cheese		Dash cayenne pepper
¼	cup chopped fresh parsley		
¼	teaspoon salt	1	tablespoon water
¼	teaspoon pepper	2	teaspoons cornstarch
1	tablespoon olive oil	1	8-ounce can tomato sauce
2	tablespoons butter	½	teaspoon basil
3	cloves garlic, minced	¼	teaspoon salt
1½	teaspoons basil		Dash pepper
2	cups sliced fresh mushrooms		Dash cayenne pepper
1	cup chopped onion	½	cup crumbled Feta cheese
½	cup chopped green pepper	1½	cups grated Mozzarella cheese

• Toss pasta with egg, Ricotta, parsley, ¼ teaspoon salt and ¼ teaspoon pepper. Place in buttered 3-quart baking dish.
• In 10-inch skillet, heat oil and butter. Add garlic and basil. Cook 30 seconds.
• Add mushrooms, onion and green pepper. Cook over medium heat 4-5 minutes, or until vegetables are tender.
• Add shrimp, tomato and cayenne pepper. Cook 4-5 minutes or until shrimp are pink.
• Combine water and cornstarch. Add to shrimp mixture. Cook until thickened.
• Spoon shrimp mixture over pasta.
• Combine tomato sauce, basil, ¼ teaspoon salt, dash black and cayenne pepper. Spoon over shrimp mixture.
• Bake at 350° for 20 minutes.
• Remove from oven. Sprinkle with Feta cheese. Cover with Mozzarella cheese.
• Return to oven 5-10 minutes, or until cheese is melted.
• Serve immediately.

SPINACH ROULADE WITH SHRIMP SAUCE

Yield: 8-10 servings

1½ slices day-old bread	1 teaspoon salt
3 10-ounce packages frozen chopped spinach, thawed and drained	½ teaspoon pepper
	1 teaspoon nutmeg
	4 eggs, separated
6 tablespoons butter, cut into pieces	Grated Parmesan cheese

- In food processor with metal blade, process bread until fine crumbs result. Set aside.
- Process spinach, butter, salt, pepper and nutmeg until smooth.
- Add egg yolks one at a time, until well blended.
- Beat egg whites until stiff. Fold into spinach mixture.
- Butter an 11x15x½-inch jelly-roll pan. Line with waxed paper. Butter paper. Sprinkle with bread crumbs.
- Spread spinach mixture in pan with spatula.
- Sprinkle with cheese.
- Bake at 350° for 15-18 minutes.
- Remove from oven. Cover top with buttered waxed paper.
- Invert onto warm platter. Remove paper from roll.
- Spread with Shrimp Filling and roll up carefully. Place seam-side down. (Spinach rolls may be made 1 day ahead. Tightly cover with foil and reheat on low.)
- Serve with Shrimp Sauce.

Shrimp Filling:

2½ pounds shrimp, peeled and deveined	1 cup butter, cut into pieces
	¾ teaspoon onion juice or minced onion
1 clove garlic, minced	
1 bay leaf	½ teaspoon mace
⅓ cup wine vinegar	Salt to taste

- Cook shrimp in boiling salted water with garlic, bay leaf and vinegar until pink. Remove shrimp and cool.
- Reserve ½ pound shrimp and 1½ cups shrimp liquid for sauce.
- With metal blade, process ½ the remaining shrimp, ½ the butter, ½ the onion and ½ the mace until smooth.
- Repeat process.
- Combine and add salt to taste.

(continued)

Shrimp Sauce:

½ cup fresh parsley
1 teaspoon tarragon
½ pound cooked shrimp,
    reserved from Filling
4 tablespoons butter
3½ tablespoons all-purpose flour

1½ cups shrimp water,
    reserved from cooking shrimp
¾ teaspoon salt
½ teaspoon pepper
1 teaspoon paprika
⅛ teaspoon mace

• With metal blade, chop parsley, tarragon and shrimp with on-off pulses until coarsely chopped. Set aside.
• Melt butter. Blend in flour gradually.
• Stir in hot shrimp water and cook on low, stirring until thickened.
• Season with salt, pepper, paprika and mace. Add shrimp mixture.

A true gourmet's dish.

SHRIMP AND RICE CASSEROLE

Yield: 6-8 servings

3 cups cooked rice
2 pounds shrimp, cooked, peeled
    and deveined
¼ cup chopped onion
¼ cup chopped green pepper
3 tablespoons butter or margarine
3 tablespoons all-purpose flour
1 10¾-ounce can chicken broth
1 cup whipping cream

¼ cup dry sherry
½ teaspoon salt
⅛ teaspoon pepper
⅛ teaspoon nutmeg
1 tablespoon fresh lemon juice
2 tablespoons chopped, roasted,
    red bell pepper, or pimento
½ cup slivered almonds

• Combine rice and shrimp. Place in 2-quart baking dish.
• Sauté onion and green pepper in butter 5 minutes, or until soft.
• Add flour and cook, stirring constantly, until bubbly.
• Remove from heat. Gradually add broth.
• Return to heat. Cook, stirring constantly, until thickened.
• Add cream, sherry, salt, pepper, nutmeg, lemon juice and roasted pepper.
• Pour over rice.
• Sprinkle with almonds.
• Bake, uncovered, at 350° for 35 minutes or until heated thoroughly.

SIMPLY ELEGANT SHRIMP

Yield: 6 servings

3 tablespoons unsalted butter	½ cup white wine
3 tablespoons olive oil	½ teaspoon basil
1 large onion, chopped	½ teaspoon oregano
2 cloves garlic, minced	½ teaspoon salt
3 pounds shrimp, peeled and deveined	¼ teaspoon pepper
	⅛ teaspoon cayenne pepper
¾ cup chicken or seafood broth	¼ cup chopped fresh parsley
¾ cup Italian salad dressing	2-3 cups cooked rice or fettucine

• Heat butter and oil in large heavy skillet.
• Add onion and garlic. Sauté until transparent.
• Stir in shrimp, broth, salad dressing, wine, basil, oregano, salt, pepper and cayenne pepper.
• Bring to a boil. Cook until shrimp are pink and opaque. Let stand 5 minutes.
• Stir in parsley.
• Serve over rice or fettucine.

A Louisiana treat. Serve in individual bowls with plenty of crusty French bread to dip into sauce.

DIRTY SHRIMP

Yield: 2 servings

⅓ cup margarine	½ teaspoon thyme
1 teaspoon Worcestershire sauce	1 teaspoon basil
1 clove garlic, minced	½ teaspoon oregano
¼ teaspoon cayenne pepper	1 pound medium shrimp, peeled and deveined
½ teaspoon pepper	
½ teaspoon salt	¼ cup beer

• In heavy skillet, melt margarine. Add Worcestershire sauce, garlic, peppers, salt, thyme, basil and oregano. Cook 1 minute.
• Add shrimp. Cook 2-3 minutes, stirring to coat shrimp evenly.
• Add beer. Cover and cook 1 minute.
• Serve with French bread to dip in sauce, or serve this spicy shrimp over rice.

A shrimp lover's reward.

SHRIMP WITH OUZO AND FETA CHEESE

Yield: 4-6 servings

½ cup fresh parsley, chopped
1 clove garlic, minced
1 medium onion, chopped
3 tablespoons olive oil, divided
1 16-ounce can tomatoes, drained and chopped
⅓ cup dry white wine
1 bay leaf
¼ cup whipping cream
¼ teaspoon pepper
2 pounds shrimp, peeled and deveined
¼ cup ouzo
½ pound Feta cheese
Parsley

- Sauté ½ cup parsley, garlic and onion in 1 tablespoon olive oil until tender.
- Add tomatoes, wine and bay leaf. Cook over medium heat until thickened, about 20 minutes, stirring occasionally.
- Stir in cream and pepper.
- Sauté shrimp in 2 tablespoons oil until pink. Place in 2-quart rectangular baking dish.
- In small saucepan, heat ouzo. Ignite and allow flame to burn out.
- Pour sauce and ouzo over shrimp. Sprinkle with Feta cheese.
- Bake at 425° for 10 minutes or until cheese melts.
- Sprinkle with parsley. Serve hot.

The Greek wine contributes an unusual flavor that will please any palate.

RED BELL PEPPER SHRIMP

Yield: 4 servings

3 tablespoons bacon drippings
5 tablespoons all-purpose flour
1 cup half and half
1 cup fish stock
⅓ cup dry sherry
1 large red bell pepper, roasted
½ teaspoon paprika
⅛ teaspoon cayenne pepper
1 teaspoon salt
Pepper to taste
1 pound shrimp, peeled and deveined

- In 10-inch skillet, melt bacon drippings. Add flour. Cook 3 minutes, stirring constantly.
- Add half and half, stock and sherry. Cook until thickened.
- Mince red pepper in blender or food processor. Add to sauce.
- Add paprika, cayenne pepper, salt, pepper and shrimp.
- Cook 10-12 minutes.
- Serve over hot buttered pasta.

SHRIMP SAUTÉ PROVENÇAL

Michael Jones
Michael's Fine Food
Augusta, Georgia
Yield: 2 servings

24 shrimp, peeled and deveined
    or butterflied
    All-purpose flour
3 tablespoons vegetable oil
2 tablespoons butter, room
    temperature

1 teaspoon chopped shallots
½ teaspoon chopped fresh garlic
1 teaspoon chopped fresh parsley
    Salt and pepper
½ lemon

- Dust shrimp with flour, shaking off excess.
- Heat oil in 10-inch sauté pan over medium-high to high heat until oil is almost smoking hot.
- Slide shrimp into hot oil. Toss, stir or turn shrimp rapidly, about 60 seconds.
- Remove from heat, drain and discard excess oil.
- Return pan to heat, immediately adding butter, shallots, garlic, parsley, salt and pepper, to make garlic butter sauce. Toss or stir 60 seconds or until done.
- Squeeze lemon over shrimp.
- Remove to serving plate. Pour garlic butter sauce over shrimp.
- Serve immediately.

Michael often serves this dish with rice pilaf, broiled tomatoes, and a California Chardonnay or French Montrachet. Mushrooms may be added initially with the shrimp.

⛳ NEW ORLEANS BARBEQUE-STYLE SHRIMP

Yield: 10 servings

5 pounds shrimp
2 cups margarine, melted
½ cup pepper

1 16-ounce bottle Italian dressing
    Juice of 4 lemons

- Place shrimp in large, deep roasting pan.
- Combine margarine, pepper, dressing and lemon juice. Pour over shrimp. Cover.
- Roast at 350° for 45 minutes, stirring occasionally.

Serve with lots of hot French bread and plenty of napkins. Peel the shrimp and dip the bread into the sauce. A spicy reminder of old New Orleans.

SHRIMP BARSAC

Yield: 3-4 servings

12 jumbo or 1 pound medium
   shrimp, peeled and deveined
½ cup butter, divided
1 teaspoon minced garlic
2 tablespoons chopped
   fresh parsley

4   ounces Barsac wine
½ cup bread crumbs
½ teaspoon salt
   Egg noodles

• Sauté shrimp in 4 tablespoons butter 3-5 minutes or until cooked.
• Add garlic, parsley and wine. Cook 1 minute.
• Remove shrimp to 2-quart baking dish.
• Reduce pan juices by ½. Pour over shrimp.
• Sprinkle with bread crumbs and salt. Drizzle with remaining 4 tablespoons melted butter.
• Broil 6 inches from heat until slightly brown.
• Serve over egg noodles.

Barsac is a sweet dessert wine from the Sauterne region. Any French Sauterne or slightly sweet white wine may be used.

SHRIMP AND SAUSAGE VERANDAH

The Verandah, Wild Dunes
Isle of Palms, South Carolina
Yield: 4 servings

1   cup chopped onion
5   tablespoons butter, divided
½ pound smoked sausage, cut
   into ½-inch slices
1   pound shrimp, peeled
   and deveined
1   red pepper, roasted, peeled,
   seeded and cut into strips

   Kernels from 2 ears fresh corn
⅛ teaspoon cayenne pepper
⅛ teaspoon black pepper
⅛ teaspoon white pepper
   Pinch each of thyme, oregano
   and garlic powder
½ teaspoon salt
   Pasta

• Sauté onion in 1 tablespoon butter until transparent.
• Add sausage. Cook on high until done.
• Add shrimp, red pepper, corn, cayenne pepper, black and white pepper, thyme, oregano, garlic powder and salt.
• When shrimp are cooked, remove all ingredients from pan juices to warm platter.
• Reduce pan juices by half. Whisk in remaining butter to make sauce.
• Pour sauce over all ingredients. Serve hot with cooked pasta.

ASPARAGUS WITH SHRIMP AND MUSHROOMS

Yield: 4-6 servings

½	pound fresh mushrooms, sliced	¼-½	teaspoon dill weed
2	tablespoons sliced green onion	¼	teaspoon Worcestershire sauce
4	tablespoons butter, divided	½	teaspoon salt
2	tablespoons all-purpose flour	¼	teaspoon white pepper
¾	cup half and half	1	pound shrimp, cooked, peeled and deveined
2	tablespoons white wine or dry vermouth	1½	pounds fresh asparagus, steamed tender crisp
	Juice of ½ lemon		Parsley, chopped

• In large skillet, sauté mushrooms and onion in two tablespoons butter.
• Make a roux with remaining 2 tablespoons butter and flour. Add half and half, and stir until thickened.
• Add wine, lemon juice, dill weed, Worcestershire sauce, salt and pepper.
• In skillet, combine cream sauce with mushrooms and onions. Add shrimp and stir until hot and well mixed.
• Arrange asparagus in serving dish. Top with shrimp mixture. Sprinkle with chopped parsley. Serve immediately.

This delicate combination of flavors serves well as a beef or veal accompaniment. It is also good served as a light supper.

SHRIMP DE JONGHE

Yield: 4 servings

2	pounds large shrimp	½	teaspoon tarragon
1	cup butter	½	teaspoon thyme
1	cup fine bread crumbs	¼	teaspoon nutmeg
1	clove garlic, minced	¼	teaspoon pepper
2	scallions, minced	¼	teaspoon salt
1½	tablespoons chopped fresh parsley		Pinch of cayenne pepper
		¾	cup dry sherry

• Steam shrimp 5 minutes. Peel and devein, leaving tails intact.
• Arrange shrimp in single layer in 9x13-inch baking dish. Set aside.
• Melt butter. Add remaining ingredients. Mix well.
• Sprinkle shrimp with crumb mixture.
• Bake at 400° for 15 minutes, or until thoroughly heated.

Also delicious as an appetizer or first course!

SHRIMP AND ASPARAGUS CASSEROLE

Yield: 10-12 servings

¾ cup butter, divided
½ cup all-purpose flour
3 cups half and half
1½ cups milk
½ cup sherry
¾ cup grated sharp Cheddar cheese
½ cup grated Parmesan cheese
Juice of 1 lemon
1½ tablespoons grated onion
1 tablespoon chopped parsley

1 tablespoon prepared mustard
2½ teaspoons salt
Pepper to taste
1 cup mayonnaise
¾ pound vermicelli
1 pound fresh mushrooms, sliced
2 pounds shrimp, cooked, peeled and deveined
2 15-ounce cans asparagus, drained

- In heavy saucepan, melt ½ cup butter. Blend in flour. Cook 2 minutes.
- Add half and half, milk and sherry. Cook until thickened, stirring constantly.
- Add cheeses, lemon juice, onion, parsley, mustard, salt and pepper. Heat until cheeses are melted.
- Remove from heat. Add mayonnaise.
- Cook vermicelli according to package directions. Drain.
- Sauté mushrooms in remaining butter until tender. Set aside.
- Combine sauce, vermicelli and shrimp. Mix well.
- In two 2-quart baking dishes, arrange layers in the following order: ⅓ the shrimp mixture, ½ the sautéed mushrooms and ½ the asparagus.
- Repeat layers ending with shrimp.
- Bake, uncovered, at 350° for 30 minutes, or until thoroughly heated.

An elegant casserole for a large dinner party.

▶ As you know, I made a special trip from Johannesburg five years ago to respond to my first invitation to play in the Masters®. Each year since I've returned to Augusta and the experience gained there has been a most important factor in shaping up my golfing career. I cannot tell you what it means to someone from my part of the world to play in a championship as fabulous as the Masters®, let alone to be victorious in it.
From a GARY PLAYER letter
Written April 18, 1961

EAT-CETERA'S CREOLE GUMBO

Terry Wick
Eat-Cetera Delicatessen
Augusta, Georgia
Yield: 10-12 servings

2 pounds medium shrimp	¼ teaspoon cayenne pepper
4-5 pounds chicken thighs	1 tablespoon Worcestershire
1 pound country ham	sauce
¼ pound diced smoked bacon	2 bay leaves
2½ pounds onions, chopped	1 tablespoon thyme
3 large green peppers, chopped	1 tablespoon chili powder
1 bunch celery, chopped	1 teaspoon celery salt
2 pounds okra, sliced	1 teaspoon onion powder
2 bunches fresh parsley, chopped	1 teaspoon garlic powder
2 bunches green onions,	½ tablespoon lemon-pepper
thinly sliced	marinade
4 pounds tomatoes, peeled	
and diced	

- Cook shrimp in boiling water until pink. Remove, peel and devein. Reserve broth.
- Cook chicken in simmering water until tender. Cool. Remove meat from bone. Reserve broth.
- In large soup pot, sauté ham and bacon. Remove. Reserve 2-3 tablespoons drippings.
- Sauté onion, green peppers and celery in reserved drippings until transparent.
- Add okra, parsley, green onions, tomatoes and reserved broth from shrimp and chicken to reach desired consistency. Simmer 10 minutes.
- Add cayenne pepper, Worcestershire sauce, bay leaves, thyme, chili powder, celery salt, onion powder, garlic powder and lemon-pepper marinade. Simmer 30 minutes.
- Add shrimp and chicken. Simmer 10 minutes.
- Serve over hot cooked rice.

If gumbo is too thick, thin with more chicken broth.

To roast red peppers:
Core, seed and cut into thirds. Lay on pan, skin side up and broil 5 inches from heat until skin is blackened. Remove from oven. Cover with paper towel. When cool, strip off skin.

JAMES RIVER SHRIMP CREOLE

Yield: 12-15 servings

½ cup corn oil
½ cup olive oil
2 cups chopped celery
1 cup chopped celery leaves
2 cups chopped green pepper
3 cups chopped onion
1 cup golden raisins
½ cup chopped fresh parsley
2 14½-ounce cans tomatoes, chopped
1 cup chili sauce
1 teaspoon sugar

1 teaspoon thyme
1 teaspoon curry powder
Salt and pepper to taste
3 large bay leaves
1 cup white wine
5 pounds medium shrimp, cooked, peeled and deveined
Cooked white rice
1 cup toasted slivered almonds
3 pounds kielbasa, grilled and cut into 3-inch pieces

• Heat oils in Dutch oven. Sauté celery, celery leaves, green pepper and onion until tender.
• Add raisins, parsley, tomatoes, chili sauce, sugar, thyme, curry powder, salt, pepper, bay leaves and wine.
• Simmer, covered, 30 minutes.
• Just before serving, add shrimp and heat well.
• To serve, spoon sauce over rice. Sprinkle with almonds. Surround with grilled sausage.

The best Creole ever.

SHRIMP AND CRAB CASSEROLE

Yield: 6-8 servings

1 cup chopped celery
1 cup chopped onion
1 cup chopped green pepper
2 tablespoons butter or margarine
1 10-ounce package frozen peas, thawed
2 pounds shrimp, cooked, peeled and deveined

1 pound claw crabmeat
1-1½ cups mayonnaise
Juice of 2 lemons
2 cups cooked rice
Salt and pepper to taste
⅓ cup fresh chopped parsley, optional
1 cup cracker crumbs

• Sauté celery, onion and green pepper in butter until tender.
• Combine with peas, shrimp, crab, mayonnaise, lemon juice, rice, salt, pepper and parsley, if desired. Toss gently.
• Pour into 2-quart baking dish. Sprinkle with cracker crumbs. Best if made early in the day, covered and refrigerated until cooking.
• Bake at 350° for 30 minutes or until heated thoroughly.

187

JAMBALAYA

Yield: 6-8 servings

4	celery ribs, sliced	½	teaspoon poultry seasoning
1	large green pepper, chopped		Salt and pepper to taste
2	large onions, chopped	1	pound medium shrimp
2	cloves garlic, minced	3	lemon slices
2-4	tablespoons butter	2	bay leaves
2	28-ounce cans tomatoes	2	pounds smoked sausage
	Tabasco to taste		Rice

• In Dutch oven, sauté celery, green pepper, onions and garlic in butter 10 minutes.
• Add tomatoes, Tabasco, poultry seasoning, salt and pepper. Simmer 30 minutes, stirring frequently.
• Boil shrimp in water with lemon slices and bay leaves 5-7 minutes. Cool, peel and devein.
• Slice sausage into ½-inch pieces. Brown lightly in skillet. Drain.
• Add shrimp and sausage to tomato mixture. Simmer 30 minutes.
• Serve over hot rice.

LOW COUNTRY SHRIMP PIE

Yield: 6 servings

2½-3	pounds shrimp	1	teaspoon pepper
2	14½-ounce cans tomatoes	2	large onions, chopped
2	tablespoons Worcestershire sauce	½	cup butter, divided
1	teaspoon salt	2	pie crusts, unbaked
			Milk

• Peel and devein shrimp. Steam until pink.
• In saucepan, cook tomatoes until thickened.
• Add Worcestershire sauce, salt and pepper. Cook 15 minutes.
• Sauté onions in 2 tablespoons butter until transparent. Add to tomato mixture.
• Place 1 pie crust in a 10-inch square baking dish. Prick 3-4 times with fork.
• Bake at 375° for 8-10 minutes.
• Place shrimp in cooked crust.
• Pour tomato mixture over shrimp. Dot with remaining butter.
• Cover with remaining crust. Brush lightly with milk. Prick with fork.
• Bake at 375° for 45-50 minutes, or until crust is golden brown.
• Let stand 10-15 minutes before serving.

CURRIED SHRIMP WITH CONDIMENTS

Amelia Cartledge
Augusta, Georgia
Yield: 8-10 servings

6 tablespoons butter	1 cup whipping cream
2 large onions, finely chopped	2½ teaspoons salt
2 large apples, cored, peeled and chopped	½ teaspoon pepper
1½ cups water	⅛ teaspoon cayenne pepper
2-3 tablespoons curry powder	1 tablespoon fresh lemon juice
½ cup all-purpose flour	3 pounds shrimp, peeled and deveined
4 cups fresh chicken broth or 2 10¾-ounce cans chicken broth, heated	

- Melt butter in large heavy saucepan.
- Add onion, apples and water. Cook over medium heat until all water has evaporated and onions and apples are soft.
- Stir in curry powder. Cook 2 minutes.
- Stir in flour. Blend until smooth. Cook 3 minutes longer.
- Stir in hot broth. Bring to a boil. Reduce heat and simmer 10-15 minutes, stirring occasionally. (Sauce may be prepared to this point, sealed with plastic wrap and refrigerated.)
- Stir in cream, salt, pepper, cayenne pepper and lemon juice.
- Add shrimp. Bring to a boil. Reduce heat and simmer 2-5 minutes or until shrimp are cooked. (Do not double this recipe. Make sauce twice if preparing for more than ten people.)
- Serve any combination of the following Condiments presented in individual bowls.

Condiments:

Chutney	Sliced green onions
Shredded coconut	Cooked crumbled bacon
Raisins, plumped in cognac	Sliced bananas sprinkled with
Chopped peanuts	lemon juice
Toasted slivered almonds	

Chutney is the classic accompaniment to curried dishes, but any combination of condiments enhances the flavor.

CRAB SOUFFLÉ

Yield: 4-6 servings

1 tablespoon butter
1 tablespoon all-purpose flour
1 cup milk
½ teaspoon salt
White or cayenne pepper to taste

Nutmeg to taste
2 eggs, separated
2 tablespoons sherry
1 pound fresh crabmeat
Butter cracker crumbs

- In double boiler, melt butter. Add flour to make a paste.
- Add milk, stirring constantly.
- Add salt, pepper and nutmeg. Cook until thickened. Cool.
- Beat egg whites until stiff. Set aside.
- Stir slightly beaten egg yolks into sauce.
- Add sherry.
- Fold in egg whites and crabmeat.
- Place in greased 1½-quart baking dish.
- Top with cracker crumbs.
- Place baking dish in pan of hot water.
- Bake at 325° for 45 minutes.
- Serve immediately.

Nutmeg gives this soufflé a special taste. Rich and delicious.

STUFFED CRAB

Yield: 4 servings

1 medium onion, finely chopped
½ cup finely chopped green pepper
6 tablespoons unsalted butter
4 slices white bread, broken and
   dampened with water
2 bay leaves

½ teaspoon salt
¼ teaspoon black pepper
⅛ teaspoon cayenne pepper
¾ pound crabmeat
1 tablespoon chopped fresh
   parsley

- In 9-inch skillet, sauté onion and green pepper in butter until tender.
- Add bread pieces and continue cooking 3-5 minutes.
- Add bay leaves, salt, pepper, cayenne pepper, crabmeat and parsley. Mix thoroughly and heat well.
- Remove from heat. Remove bay leaves. Pack stuffing into 4 shell ramekins.
- Arrange shells in shallow baking pan.
- Bake at 350° for 15-20 minutes.

CRAB STUFFING

Yield: stuffing for 6-7 pounds of flounder

Crab Stuffing:

½ cup chopped onion
⅓ cup chopped celery
⅓ cup chopped green pepper
2 cloves garlic, minced
⅓ cup margarine, melted
1 pound crabmeat

2 cups soft bread crumbs
2-3 eggs, beaten
1 tablespoon chopped fresh parsley
1 teaspoon salt
½ teaspoon pepper

• Sauté onion, celery, green pepper and garlic in margarine until tender.
• Combine all ingredients. Mix well.
• Stuff flounder filets or prepare Crab Cakes.

Crab Cakes:

1 teaspoon horseradish
1 teaspoon Worcestershire sauce
¼ teaspoon dry mustard

2 tablespoons mayonnaise
Bread crumbs

• Add all ingredients except bread crumbs to Crab Stuffing.
• Form cakes. Roll in bread crumbs.
• Fry in vegetable oil over moderate heat until browned.

CRABMEAT IMPERIAL

Chef Emil Waldis
La Maison on Telfair
Augusta, Georgia
Yield: 4 servings

4 eggs
1 cup mayonnaise
1 cup grated Swiss cheese
1 cup white lump crabmeat
1 tablespoon chopped chives or chopped parsley

1 teaspoon Worcestershire sauce
1 tablespoon finely chopped shallots
Salt and pepper to taste
4 English muffin halves, toasted

• Beat eggs.
• Add mayonnaise. Mix until smooth.
• Gently fold in cheese, crabmeat, chives, Worcestershire sauce, shallots, salt and pepper.
• Spread filling on muffin halves.
• Bake at 425° for 8-10 minutes or until lightly browned.

CRABMEAT SYCAMORE

Yield: 6-8 servings

2	pounds white lump crabmeat	2½	cups milk
¾	pound Swiss cheese, diced	4	tablespoons sherry
2	8½-ounce (drained weight) cans artichoke hearts, drained	4	dashes Tabasco
2	tablespoons chopped shallots	2	teaspoons Worcestershire sauce
2	teaspoons chopped fresh parsley		Salt and pepper to taste
6	tablespoons butter	1	cup bread crumbs
4	tablespoons all-purpose flour		Parsley sprigs and lemon slices to garnish

- In buttered 3-quart baking dish, layer crabmeat, cheese and artichoke hearts. Set aside.
- In heavy saucepan, sauté shallots and parsley in butter until shallots are tender.
- Stir in flour. Cook 2 minutes.
- Remove from heat. Gradually stir in milk. Return to heat and cook until thickened.
- Add sherry, Tabasco, Worcestershire sauce, salt and pepper.
- Spoon sauce evenly over artichoke hearts.
- Sprinkle with bread crumbs.
- Bake at 350° for 35-40 minutes.
- Garnish with parsley sprigs and lemon slices.

Elegant!

SCALLOPED OYSTERS

Yield: 4 servings

½	cup white bread crumbs	Salt and pepper to taste
1	cup fine cracker crumbs	3-6 tablespoons whipping cream
½	cup butter, melted	Tabasco to taste, optional
1	pint oysters	

- Combine bread crumbs and cracker crumbs with butter.
- Layer ½ the crumb mixture on bottom of buttered 1-quart baking dish.
- Cover with half the oysters.
- Sprinkle with salt and pepper.
- Top with half the cream.
- Repeat oyster and cream layers.
- Sprinkle with remaining bread crumbs.
- Bake at 400° for 30 minutes.

GRAM'S OYSTER PIE

Yield: 10 servings

1 cup finely chopped celery	¼ teaspoon garlic salt
½ cup butter or margarine, divided	1½ quarts oysters
2 cups crushed oyster crackers	2 eggs, beaten
1 teaspoon salt	1 cup milk
1 teaspoon pepper	2 slices bread, cubed
	Paprika

• Sauté celery in 4 tablespoons butter until tender. Set aside.
• Combine cracker crumbs, salt, pepper and garlic salt. Set aside.
• In 2-quart baking dish, layer ⅓ the oysters with their juice, ⅓ the cracker crumbs and all the celery.
• Repeat layers of oysters and cracker crumbs.
• Beat together eggs and milk. Pour over layers.
• Melt remaining 4 tablespoons butter and toss with bread cubes. Spread over pie.
• Bake at 325° for 45 minutes. Serve immediately.

A wonderful accompaniment to the traditional holiday turkey.

NEW OYSTERS ROCKEFELLER

Yield: 6-8 servings

1 small onion, chopped	¼ cup chopped fresh parsley
½ cup chopped celery	1½ pints fresh oysters, well drained
¼ cup butter	1½ cups sour cream
1 10-ounce package frozen whole green beans, cooked, or 1 pound cooked fresh green beans, puréed	½ cup grated Parmesan cheese
	⅛ teaspoon Tabasco
	2 slices white bread, crumbled
	Paprika to taste

• Sauté onion and celery in butter until onion is transparent.
• Add puréed green beans and parsley.
• Transfer mixture to buttered 1½-quart baking dish.
• Place oysters on top of green bean mixture.
• Combine sour cream, Parmesan cheese, Tabasco and bread crumbs. Spread over oysters.
• Sprinkle with paprika.
• Bake at 350° for 30 minutes.
• Serve immediately.

COQUILLES ST. JACQUES

Yield: 6 servings

1½ pounds scallops, preferably
    bay scallops
1   cup dry white wine
1   small onion, sliced
1   tablespoon chopped fresh
    parsley
2   teaspoons fresh lemon juice
½   teaspoon salt

7   tablespoons butter, divided
6   tablespoons all-purpose flour
1   cup half and half
2   ounces Gruyère cheese,
    cut into cubes
    Dash of pepper
½   pound mushrooms, sliced
1½ cups soft bread crumbs

- In large saucepan, combine scallops, wine, onion, parsley, lemon juice and salt. Bring to a boil.
- Reduce heat and simmer 5 minutes. Drain, reserving 1 cup liquid.
- In another saucepan, melt 4 tablespoons butter. Stir in flour. Cook 2 minutes.
- Add half and half and 1 cup reserved liquid from scallops. Cook over medium heat until thickened, stirring constantly.
- Remove from heat. Add cheese and pepper. Stir until cheese is melted.
- Sauté mushrooms in 2 tablespoons butter. Add to sauce.
- Melt 1 tablespoon butter. Toss with bread crumbs.
- Spoon scallops into 6 ramekins.
- Cover scallops with sauce. Sprinkle with bread crumbs.
- Bake at 350° for 25 minutes, or until thoroughly heated.

♪LINGUINI WITH WHITE CLAM SAUCE

Chuck Ballas
Luigi's Restaurant
Augusta, Georgia
Yield: 4 servings

3   green onions, chopped
4   cloves garlic, minced
2   tablespoons chopped
    fresh parsley

½ cup butter
2   tablespoons all-purpose flour
4   6½-ounce cans minced clams
    Linguini

- Sauté onions, garlic and parsley in butter 1-2 minutes.
- Remove from heat. Add flour. Return to heat, stirring constantly 2 minutes or until roux has thickened.
- Add clams and their liquid. Heat well.
- Serve over hot, buttered linguini.

SEAFOOD VERMOUTH WITH PASTA

Yield: 6-8 servings

1	16-ounce package fettucine	2	teaspoons rosemary, crushed
½	cup butter	1½	tablespoons fresh lemon juice
2	tablespoons olive oil	¼	cup vermouth
½	cup chopped green onion	½	cup whipping cream
1	clove garlic, minced	2	teaspoons chopped, fresh
½	pound sliced, fresh		parsley
	mushrooms	1	egg, optional
3	pounds raw seafood, any 1 or a		Salt and pepper to taste
	combination of shrimp, lobster,		Grated Parmesan cheese
	scallops, clams or oysters		

• Cook fettucine according to package directions. Drain.
• Melt butter and oil in heavy skillet. Add green onion, garlic and mushrooms. Sauté until tender.
• Add seafood, rosemary, lemon juice and vermouth. Cook 5 minutes.
• Add cream and parsley. Continue cooking on medium-high heat until sauce thickens, about 10-15 minutes. If sauce becomes too thin, add one beaten egg. If sauce is too thick, thin with additional cream.
• Add salt and pepper.
• Toss pasta with seafood mixture. Serve immediately with grated Parmesan cheese.

It is extremely difficult, if not impossible, for me to put into words what I feel about the Masters® Tournament and the Augusta National Golf Course. I can recall that as a young boy, prior to attending Wake Forest College, the Masters® was something I read about in the papers, and it was my burning ambition to some day be able to play this great course, particularly as a participant in the tournament. One incident in particular stands out in my memory. The Wake Forest golf team was scheduled to play a spring match in Georgia. In an effort to get to see the Masters®, we offered our services to the officials in charge. Unfortunately for us, arrangements had already been made, and our offer was turned down. To say that we were disappointed would be a mild understatement, but it made us all, and myself in particular, even more desirous of finding a way to be invited to your great classic.

From an ARNOLD PALMER letter
Written January 10, 1961

PASTA WITH RED SEAFOOD SAUCE

Chef Jim Watts
St. Louis, Missouri
Yield: 4-6 servings

2	28-ounce cans whole tomatoes, crushed	1	large green pepper, diced
1	15-ounce can tomato sauce	1	large onion, diced
1	bay leaf	½	pound mushrooms, sliced
½-1	teaspoon basil	1	cup dry white wine
1¼	teaspoons salt	1	pound shrimp, peeled and deveined
¼	teaspoon pepper	½	pound scallops
	Crushed red pepper to taste	2	6½-ounce cans clams with juice
5	cloves garlic, minced		Freshly grated Romano cheese
½	cup shrimp stock		Linguini
3-4	tablespoons olive oil		

- Combine tomatoes and tomato sauce. Simmer 30 minutes.
- Add bay leaf, basil, salt, pepper, red pepper, garlic and stock. Simmer 45 minutes.
- In olive oil, sauté green pepper, onion and mushrooms. Add to sauce. Simmer 15 minutes.
- Add wine. Heat thoroughly.
- Just prior to serving, remove bay leaf and add shrimp, scallops, clams and juice. Cook until seafood is done, about 2-5 minutes. (If desired, add half and half to lighten sauce.)
- Serve over hot, cooked linguini.
- Sprinkle each serving with Romano cheese.

A delightful seafood entrée.

To make a shrimp stock, cover shrimp shells with water. Add onion, celery, a pinch of salt and a pinch of pepper. Simmer, covered, for 30 minutes.

FILET OF SOLE FLORENTINE

Yield: 4 servings

2 pounds fresh spinach, cooked and drained, or 2 10-ounce packages frozen chopped spinach, thawed and drained	1½ tablespoons chopped, fresh parsley
½ teaspoon onion powder	2 tablespoons butter
1 teaspoon salt, divided	2½ tablespoons all-purpose flour
White pepper to taste	⅔ cup half and half
Dash mace	½ cup white wine
4 filets of sole	¼ cup grated Gruyère cheese, divided
1½ teaspoons seasoned salt	Paprika

- Combine spinach, onion powder, ½ teaspoon salt, pepper and mace.
- Spread in buttered 1½-quart baking dish.
- Sprinkle filets with seasoned salt and parsley. Roll and place on spinach.
- In heavy saucepan, melt butter. Add flour. Blend well.
- Gradually add half and half. Cook, stirring constantly, until thickened.
- Add wine and remaining ½ teaspoon salt. Cook until sauce boils. Remove from heat.
- Stir in 3 tablespoons cheese. Stir until melted.
- Spoon sauce over filets and spinach.
- Sprinkle with remaining cheese and paprika.
- Bake at 350° for 25 minutes or until filets are done.
- Serve immediately.

Any fresh fish filets may be substituted.

FISH FILETS IN CONSOMMÉ

Yield: 4 servings

1 pound fish filets	1 10½-ounce can beef consommé
½ teaspoon salt	1 lemon, sliced, to garnish
3 green onions, thinly sliced	3-4 sprigs fresh parsley to garnish
Pinch thyme	
Pinch basil	

- Place fish, skin-side down, in flat, greased baking dish.
- Sprinkle with salt, onions, thyme and basil.
- Pour consommé over fish until it just covers filets.
- Bake at 350° for 20-30 minutes depending on thickness of fish.
- Garnish with lemon slices and parsley.

A low-calorie delight.

FISH STEAKS IN ORANGE JUICE

Yield: 4 servings

2 pounds fresh fish steaks
½ cup finely chopped onion
2 cloves garlic, minced
2 tablespoons vegetable oil
2 tablespoons chopped fresh
   cilantro or parsley

1 teaspoon salt
⅛ teaspoon pepper
½ cup fresh orange juice
1 tablespoon fresh lemon juice
   Paprika
   Orange slices

• Arrange fish in a 12x7½x2-inch baking dish.
• In small skillet, sauté onion and garlic in oil until tender.
• Add cilantro, salt and pepper. Spread over fish.
• Combine orange juice and lemon juice. Pour over fish.
• Bake at 400°, covered, for 20-25 minutes or until fish flakes easily.
• Sprinkle with paprika. Garnish with orange slices.

*Tickle your tastebuds while watching your waist-line
with this low-calorie dish.*

GROUPER BRETAGNE

Yield: 1 serving

1-2 ounces vegetable oil
1 6-8 ounce grouper filet
   All-purpose flour
1 ounce dry white wine
1 tablespoon butter
2 ounces small shrimp, peeled
   and deveined

1 ounce fresh mushrooms, sliced
½ ounce green onions, finely
   chopped
   Chopped fresh parsley
   Salt and pepper to taste

• Heat oil in oven-proof skillet.
• Dredge filet lightly in flour.
• Brown on meaty side first, then turn and brown skin side.
• Deglaze pan with white wine. Add a small amount of water.
• Place pan in oven and cook at 450° for 5 minutes, or until done.
• Remove fish to warm platter. Discard remaining liquid in pan.
• Add butter to pan. Sauté shrimp, mushrooms, green onions, parsley, salt
  and pepper until done.
• Spoon shrimp mixture over filet.
• Serve immediately.

SOLE TALLEYRAND

Harriet Goldsmith
Augusta, Georgia
Yield: 8 servings

8 sole or flounder filets	Dash of salt and pepper
1 teaspoon fennel	2 tablespoons butter
1 teaspoon rosemary	3 tablespoons white vermouth

• Cut filets in half.
• Sprinkle a buttered 3-quart baking dish with fennel and rosemary.
• Place filets in prepared dish. Sprinkle with salt and pepper. Dot with butter.
• Sprinkle with vermouth. Cover with buttered waxed paper.
• Bake at 400° for 10 minutes.

TROUT MEUNIÈRE

Yield: 4 servings

4 trout filets	All-purpose flour
Milk	½ teaspoon white pepper
2 drops Tabasco	½ cup unsalted butter, clarified
1 teaspoon salt, divided	2 tablespoons vegetable oil

• In flat pan, cover filets with milk. Add Tabasco and ½ teaspoon salt.
• Soak 30 minutes.
• Season flour with ½ teaspoon salt and pepper.
• Remove filets from milk. Coat with flour mixture.
• In small saucepan, heat butter and oil. Keep warm.
• In large, heavy skillet, pour butter mixture to ⅛-inch depth.
• When hot, fry filets, a few at a time, until they flake with a fork. Add more butter mixture as needed to maintain proper depth.
• Remove filets to heated platter. Keep hot while preparing Sauce.
• Pour Sauce over fish. Serve immediately.

Sauce:

½ cup unsalted butter	1 teaspoon salt
1-2 tablespoons fresh lemon juice	2 tablespoons chopped fresh
2 tablespoons Worcestershire sauce	parsley

• Wipe any burned flour from skillet.
• Melt butter and add remaining ingredients.
• Blend well. Heat thoroughly.

GRILLED STUFFED SALMON WITH MUSTARD DILL SAUCE

Mary Ann Baggs
Augusta, Georgia
Yield: 8 servings

1 5-pound whole fresh salmon, cleaned (do not remove head and tail)	2 tablespoons fresh lemon juice 2 tablespoons dry white wine Salt and pepper

• Wash fish and pat dry inside and outside.
• Make 2 slashing incisions on each side of fish.
• Rub inside of fish with lemon juice and wine.
• Sprinkle with salt and pepper.
• Spoon Mushroom Filling into fish opening. Close with metal skewers.
• Brush fish with Parsley Butter.
• Place in fish grill. Grill over medium heat 10 minutes per inch of thickness, turning once while grilling.
• Baste frequently with Parsley Butter.
• Serve salmon with Mustard Dill Sauce.

Mushroom Filling:

¼ cup butter	1½ pounds fresh mushrooms, thinly sliced
1 large onion, finely chopped	
2 celery ribs with leaves, finely chopped	2 teaspoons minced fresh dill Salt and pepper
½ cup chopped fresh parsley	

• In large skillet, melt butter and sauté onion and celery until golden.
• Add parsley and mushrooms. Sauté 3-5 minutes. Add dill, salt and pepper.

Parsley Butter:
Yield: 1 cup

1 cup butter	2 tablespoons fresh lemon juice
¼ cup chopped fresh parsley	Pepper

• Cream butter and remaining ingredients.

Mustard Dill Sauce:
Yield: 2½ cups

½ cup sugar	⅓ cup wine vinegar
1 cup fresh dill	½ cup mayonnaise
1 cup Dijon mustard	2 tablespoons vegetable oil

(continued)

- Combine sugar, dill, mustard, vinegar and mayonnaise in blender or food processor. Blend until smooth.
- While blending, add oil, one drop at a time, until totally absorbed.
- Cover. Store in refrigerator until ready to use.

A most impressive entrée.

GRILLED KING MACKEREL

Yield: ¾ cup marinade

½ cup olive oil
¼ cup soy sauce
1 tablespoon Worcestershire sauce

King Mackerel steaks or filets
Salt and pepper

- Combine olive oil, soy sauce and Worcestershire sauce. Pour into flat pan.
- Lay fish in marinade. Sprinkle with salt and pepper. Turn and repeat on other side.
- Marinate in refrigerator at least 2-4 hours, turning at least twice.
- Grill over hot coals, about 8 minutes per side. Be careful not to overcook.

A wonderful new flavor for fresh fish.

FLOUNDER FLORENTINE

Yield: 2-3 servings

1 10-ounce package frozen chopped spinach, thawed and drained
1 pound flounder filets
2 tablespoons butter, melted
⅓ cup sour cream

⅓ cup mayonnaise
¼ cup vermouth
½ teaspoon lemon-pepper marinade
Grated Parmesan cheese
Paprika

- Spread spinach in buttered 9-inch square baking dish.
- Cover with filets. Brush with melted butter.
- Combine sour cream, mayonnaise, vermouth and lemon-pepper marinade.
- Spread over filets.
- Sprinkle generously with Parmesan cheese and paprika.
- Bake at 350° for 25 minutes or until bubbly.

MUSTARD-MARINATED SWORDFISH

Yield: 2 servings

8 tablespoons Grey Poupon
   mustard
   Juice of 1 lemon
6 tablespoons vegetable oil
1 tablespoon chopped fresh
   parsley

⅛ teaspoon pepper
20 green peppercorns, crushed
2 swordfish steaks

• Combine mustard and lemon juice.
• Add oil, 1 tablespoon at a time, stirring vigorously after each addition.
• Add parsley, pepper and peppercorns. Mix well.
• Pour marinade over steaks. Marinate 4 hours.
• Grill over hot coals or mesquite wood.
• Serve immediately.

NICK'S SPECIAL FISH

Yield: 6 servings

6 boneless fresh fish filets
   Salt and pepper
   Juice of one lemon
1 clove garlic, minced
½ cup chopped onion
½ pound fresh mushrooms,
   sliced

3 tablespoons butter
1½ cups grated sharp Cheddar
   cheese
1 10¾-ounce can cream of
   mushroom soup
1 8-ounce carton sour cream
⅛ teaspoon cayenne pepper

• Place fish filets in buttered 9x13-inch baking dish.
• Sprinkle with salt, pepper and lemon juice. Set aside.
• In skillet, sauté garlic, onion and mushrooms in butter until tender.
• Sprinkle over fish filets.
• Sprinkle with cheese.
• Combine soup (one cup mayonnaise may be substituted), sour cream and
  cayenne pepper.
• Pour over fish.
• Bake at 325° for 45 minutes.

VEGETABLES AND ACCOMPANIMENTS

ASPARAGUS DIVINE

Yield: 6-8 servings

1½ pounds fresh asparagus,
    trimmed
½ cup mayonnaise

Grated Parmesan cheese
Paprika

- Blanch asparagus in boiling water 3 minutes. Plunge into cold water. Remove.
- Layer asparagus in buttered 9x13x2-inch baking dish. Spread mayonnaise over all.
- Sprinkle with Parmesan cheese and paprika.
- Bake, uncovered, at 350° for 20 minutes.

Easy, but elegant!

ITALIAN STYLE ASPARAGUS

Yield: 4 servings

¼ cup butter, melted
1 pound fresh asparagus, trimmed
¼ cup minced onion
¼ cup chopped celery
4 tablespoons grated Parmesan
    cheese
2 tablespoons bread crumbs

1 14½-ounce can Italian-style
    tomatoes, drained and diced
¼ teaspoon thyme
¼ teaspoon oregano
¼ teaspoon basil
    Salt and pepper to taste

- Pour butter into bottom of 9x13x2-inch baking dish.
- Line bottom of dish with asparagus, alternating tips to each side.
- Sprinkle asparagus with onion, celery, cheese, bread crumbs and tomatoes.
- Season with thyme, oregano, basil, salt and pepper.
- Cover and bake at 375° for 45 minutes, or until tender.

A wonderful combination.

ARTICHOKE PARMESAN

Yield: 8-10 servings

¼ cup olive oil, divided
4 8½-ounce (drained weight) cans artichoke hearts, drained and quartered
½ cup dry white wine
1 teaspoon onion powder

Salt to taste
Cayenne pepper to taste
1 cup grated Parmesan or Romano cheese
1 cup seasoned bread crumbs
½ cup butter

• Grease 2-quart baking dish with olive oil.
• Combine artichokes, wine, remaining olive oil, onion powder, salt, cayenne pepper and cheese.
• Place in baking dish, sprinkle with bread crumbs and dot with butter.
• Cover and bake at 350° for 30 minutes.
• Uncover and broil 5 minutes.

Rich and delicious with roast pork!

BEST-IN-THE-WEST BAKED BEANS

Yield: 12-14 servings

1 pound bacon, chopped
1 medium onion, chopped
1 pound ground beef
½ cup ketchup
½ cup barbeque sauce
4 tablespoons molasses
4 tablespoons prepared mustard
1 teaspoon chili powder

½ teaspoon salt
½ teaspoon pepper
1 16-ounce can pork and beans, undrained
1 16-ounce can lima beans, undrained
1 16-ounce can kidney beans, undrained

• In large heavy skillet, brown bacon, onion and ground beef. Drain.
• Add ketchup, barbeque sauce, molasses, mustard, chili powder, salt and pepper. Mix well.
• Add all beans. Mix well.
• Pour mixture into greased 9x13-inch baking dish.
• Bake at 350° for 1 hour.

MASTERS® ITALIAN BAKED BEANS

Chef Jim Watts
St. Louis, Missouri
Yield: 20 servings

1 15-ounce jar Ragu spaghetti
   sauce
2 14½-ounce cans stewed
   tomatoes
1 16-ounce jar Hot Thick and
   Chunky Salsa
1 cup barbeque sauce
¼ cup brown sugar
¼ cup molasses
2 cloves garlic, minced

1 teaspoon Italian spice
   Pepper to taste (if needed)
¼ pound bacon
1 green pepper, diced
1 red pepper, diced
1 large onion, diced
1 pound fresh mushrooms, sliced
1 pound Italian sausage
4 28-ounce cans Bush's Best
   Deluxe pork and beans

• In an 8-quart pot, combine spaghetti sauce, tomatoes, salsa, barbeque
  sauce, sugar, molasses, garlic, Italian spice and pepper, if needed. Simmer
  30 minutes.
• Cook bacon until crisp. Crumble and set aside. Reserve drippings.
• In drippings, sauté peppers, onion and mushrooms until tender. Set aside.
• Remove casings from sausage. Break into pieces and cook until done.
• Add sautéed vegetables to sauce. Simmer an additional 15 minutes.
• Add pork and beans and sausage. Simmer 30 minutes.
• Stir in bacon.

APPLE SOUFFLÉ

Yield: 8 servings

1 16-ounce can unsweetened
   applesauce
½ cup sugar
1 cup graham cracker crumbs

1 cup milk
2 eggs, slightly beaten
¼ cup butter, melted

• Combine applesauce, sugar, cracker crumbs, milk and eggs. Pour into
  greased 2-quart baking dish.
• Drizzle with butter.
• Bake, uncovered, at 350° for 1 hour and 15 minutes.

A refreshing change from sweet potatoes.

SWISS GREEN BEANS

Yield: 6-8 servings

4 tablespoons butter, divided
2 tablespoons all-purpose flour
1 cup milk
½ teaspoon minced onion

1 teaspoon salt
2 cups fresh green beans, cooked
8 ounces Swiss cheese, grated
2 cups bread crumbs

- In heavy saucepan, melt 2 tablespoons butter. Add flour. Cook 2 minutes, stirring constantly.
- Slowly add milk, stirring with whisk until thickened.
- Add onion and salt. Mix well.
- In a 1½-quart baking dish, layer 1 cup green beans and half the grated cheese. Repeat layers.
- Pour sauce on top. Set aside.
- Sauté bread crumbs in remaining 2 tablespoons butter. Sprinkle on top of sauce.
- Bake at 350° for 20-30 minutes, or until bubbly.

SNAPPY GREEN BEANS

Yield: 6 servings

8 slices bacon
1 small onion, chopped
½ pound fresh mushrooms, sliced

1½ pounds fresh green beans, snapped and cooked
2 cups grated sharp Cheddar cheese

- Fry bacon until crisp. Drain and crumble, reserving 3 tablespoons of drippings.
- Sauté onion and mushrooms in reserved drippings.
- Add beans and cheese. Heat to melt cheese, stirring often. Add bacon.
- Bake in greased 1½-quart baking dish at 350° for 20 minutes.

BROCCOLI SUPREME

Barbara Nicklaus
wife of Jack Nicklaus,
6 time Masters® Champion
Yield: 6 servings

2 cups coarsely chopped fresh broccoli
3 carrots, sliced
1 8½-ounce (drained weight) can artichoke hearts, drained and quartered
1 10¾-ounce can cream of mushroom soup
½ cup Hellmann's mayonnaise

2 eggs, slightly beaten
1 tablespoon fresh lemon juice
1 tablespoon Worcestershire sauce
1 cup grated sharp Cheddar cheese
1 cup herb-seasoned stuffing mix
¼ cup butter, melted

- Cook broccoli and carrots in boiling water until tender crisp. Drain. Set aside.
- Place quartered artichokes in bottom of greased 8-inch square baking dish.
- Combine soup, mayonnaise, eggs, lemon juice and Worcestershire sauce. Mix well.
- Combine soup mixture, broccoli and carrots.
- Pour broccoli mixture over artichoke hearts.
- Sprinkle cheese and stuffing over top of casserole.
- Pour butter over topping.
- Bake at 350° for 25 minutes or until heated through.

▶ From start to finish, the 1980 Masters® Tournament belonged to Severiano Ballesteros. The performance by this gifted Spaniard was notable not only by the fact that he became the youngest champion in the history of the Tournament, but that he won with such relative ease.

BROCCOLI MOLD WITH LEMON VELOUTÉ SAUCE

Martha Fleming
Augusta, Georgia
Yield: 6-8 servings

Vegetable oil
1 cup bread crumbs, divided
2 10-ounce packages frozen chopped broccoli
2 tablespoons chicken broth
6 tablespoons butter, divided
½ cup chopped onion
1 cup grated Swiss cheese
Salt and pepper to taste
Nutmeg to taste
1 cup milk
5 eggs, beaten
Fresh broccoli florets and lemon slices to garnish

- Generously grease a 6-cup ring mold with vegetable oil.
- Sprinkle ½ cup bread crumbs in ring mold.
- Cook broccoli in chicken broth until just tender.
- Melt 2 tablespoons butter in large skillet. Add onion and cook until transparent.
- Add broccoli to onion. Remove from heat.
- Add cheese, remaining bread crumbs, salt, pepper and nutmeg. Set aside.
- In saucepan, combine remaining 4 tablespoons butter and milk. Bring to a boil.
- Slowly add milk mixture to beaten eggs, stirring constantly with a whisk.
- Add egg mixture to broccoli mixture. Blend well.
- Place mixture in prepared ring mold.
- Place mold in baking pan. Add enough boiling water to pan to cover bottom half of mold.
- Bake at 325° for 1 hour or until set.
- Allow mold to stand 5 minutes before unmolding.
- Steam broccoli florets.
- Fill center of mold with broccoli and lemon slices.
- Serve with Lemon Velouté Sauce.

(continued)

Lemon Velouté Sauce:

4 tablespoons butter
4 tablespoons all-purpose flour
2 cups hot chicken broth

1 tablespoon fresh lemon juice
Salt and pepper to taste

• In saucepan, melt butter over medium heat.
• Slowly add flour, stirring constantly with whisk until mixture is smooth and thickened.
• Remove from heat. Add hot chicken broth.
• Return to heat. Whisk mixture until it boils. Continue to stir until mixture is smooth, about 2 minutes.
• Add lemon juice, salt and pepper. (Sauce can be made ahead. Reheat slowly before serving with Broccoli Mold.)

SPICY BROCCOLI

Yield: 6 servings

5 tablespoons butter, divided
1½ tablespoons all-purpose flour
½ cup milk
2 cups grated sharp Cheddar cheese, divided
¼ cup grated Parmesan cheese

1 16-ounce package frozen broccoli cuts, thawed and drained
1 10-ounce can Ro-Tel tomatoes, partially drained
½ cup Ritz cracker crumbs

• In heavy saucepan, melt 2 tablespoons butter. Add flour. Cook 2 minutes.
• Gradually add milk. Stir until smooth and thickened.
• Add 1½ cups Cheddar cheese and Parmesan cheese. Stir until melted.
• Combine sauce, broccoli and tomatoes.
• Pour into greased 1½-quart baking dish.
• Combine reserved cheese and cracker crumbs.
• Sprinkle over casserole.
• Dot with remaining 3 tablespoons butter.
• Bake at 450° for 15 minutes or until bubbly.

BROCCOLI SOUFFLÉ

Yield: 4 servings

3 eggs
1 cup cottage cheese
3 tablespoons all-purpose flour
1 10-ounce package frozen chopped broccoli, cooked and drained

1 tablespoon chopped green onion
¼ cup butter, cubed
4 ounces American cheese, grated and divided
Salt and pepper to taste

• Stir eggs well with a fork.
• Add cottage cheese. Sprinkle with flour. Mix well.
• Add broccoli, onion, butter and half the grated cheese.
• Season with salt and pepper. Stir well.
• Pour into buttered 1-quart baking dish. Sprinkle with remaining grated cheese.
• Bake at 325° for 1 hour.
• Serve immediately.

RED CABBAGE WITH APPLES

Yield: 6 servings

2-2½ pounds red cabbage, shredded
⅔ cup red wine vinegar
2 tablespoons sugar
2 teaspoons salt
2 tablespoons bacon drippings
2 medium apples, peeled and cut into ⅛-inch wedges

½ cup finely chopped onion
1 whole onion, peeled and pierced with 2 whole cloves
1 small bay leaf
2 cups boiling water
3 tablespoons dry red wine
3 tablespoons red currant jelly

• Combine cabbage, vinegar, sugar and salt. Toss until evenly coated.
• In Dutch oven, melt drippings. Add apples and chopped onion. Sauté until lightly browned, approximately 5 minutes.
• Add cabbage, whole onion and bay leaf. Stir thoroughly.
• Pour in boiling water. Return to a boil, reduce heat, cover and simmer for 45 minutes to 1 hour, stirring occasionally.
• Keep moist while simmering, but when done there should be almost no water left in pan.
• Remove onion and bay leaf.
• Stir in wine and currant jelly.

CURRIED CABBAGE

Yield: 3-4 servings

8   slices bacon
1   pound white cabbage, shredded
½ cup whipping cream

Salt and pepper to taste
Curry powder to taste
1   tablespoon fresh lemon juice

• Cook bacon until crisp. Crumble. Reserve ⅓ cup drippings.
• In drippings, sauté shredded cabbage 5 minutes.
• Stir in cream, salt, pepper and curry powder. Cook 2 minutes, stirring constantly.
• Add lemon juice. Stir well.
• Sprinkle with crumbled bacon.
• Serve immediately.

CARROTS MADEIRA

Yield: 8-10 servings

¼ cup butter
2   pounds carrots, cut into
    thin strips
1   teaspoon sugar

1   teaspoon salt
⅓ cup Madeira wine
8   sprigs parsley, finely chopped
¼ teaspoon dried tarragon leaves

• Melt butter in heavy saucepan.
• Add carrots, sugar, salt and wine.
• Bring to a boil. Cover and simmer 15-20 minutes or until carrots are tender.
• Drain. Sprinkle with parsley and tarragon.

*A special way to enhance a
year 'round vegetable.*

APRICOT CARROTS

Yield: 4 servings

2½ cups thinly sliced carrots
1½ tablespoons butter
¼ cup apricot preserves
¼ teaspoon grated orange rind

1 teaspoon fresh lemon juice
¹⁄₁₆ teaspoon nutmeg
Salt to taste

• Steam carrots until tender. Drain. (Carrots may be cooked in microwave for 6 minutes or until just tender.)
• Combine butter, preserves, orange rind, lemon juice, nutmeg and salt in small saucepan. Heat until preserves are melted.
• Pour mixture over carrots.
• Toss and serve immediately.

CARROTS FETTUCINE

Yield: 8 servings

2 pounds carrots
½ cup butter
1 teaspoon sugar
½ teaspoon salt
½ teaspoon nutmeg

2 tablespoons chopped fresh parsley
2 teaspoons fresh lemon juice
¼ cup slivered almonds, toasted

• With vegetable peeler, peel cleaned whole carrots in long fettucine-like strands (or with food processor, cut into thin strips).
• Rinse in cold water.
• Plunge in boiling salted water for 1 minute.
• Rinse under cold water. Drain. (May be prepared ahead to this point and stored in refrigerator in colander.)
• Combine butter, sugar, salt, nutmeg, parsley and lemon juice in small saucepan. Heat until butter is melted.
• Toss sauce with carrots and heat well.
• Sprinkle with almonds.

A beautiful and unique way to serve carrots.

ISRAELI CARROTS

Yield: 6 servings

1½ pounds young carrots, peeled and cut into ¼-inch slices
4 tablespoons butter
⅓ cup dry white wine

½ teaspoon nutmeg
⅔ cup golden raisins
3 tablespoons light brown sugar

• Cook carrots, covered, in medium saucepan with butter, wine and nutmeg over low heat until tender.
• Stir in raisins and sugar. Cook a few minutes longer until raisins are plump and carrots are glazed.

Not too sweet!

BEST CAULIFLOWER

Yield: 4 servings

1 medium head cauliflower, cut into florets
½ cup mayonnaise
½ cup grated extra sharp Cheddar cheese

½ teaspoon dry mustard
½ teaspoon salt
¼ teaspoon cayenne pepper

• Cook cauliflower in boiling salted water 10-15 minutes, or until tender crisp. Drain.
• Place cauliflower in 1-quart baking dish.
• Combine remaining ingredients. Stir well.
• Spoon over cauliflower.
• Bake, uncovered, at 400° for 10 minutes or until bubbly.

CURRIED CAULIFLOWER

Yield: 6 servings

1 head cauliflower, cut into florets
1 cup grated sharp Cheddar cheese
⅓ cup mayonnaise

1 10¾-ounce can cream of chicken soup
1 teaspoon curry powder
¾ cup dry bread crumbs
3 tablespoons butter, melted

- Cook cauliflower in 3 cups boiling salted water. Drain well.
- Combine cheese, mayonnaise, soup and curry powder. Add cauliflower. Mix well.
- Place in greased 2-quart baking dish.
- Combine crumbs and butter. Sprinkle on top.
- Bake at 350° for 30 minutes or until bubbly.

CAPTAIN'S CELERY

Yield: 6-8 servings

1 whole bunch celery
¾ cup chopped onion
3 tablespoons vegetable oil
¾ cup chopped green pepper
1 clove garlic, minced
1 14½-ounce can tomatoes, chopped

1½ teaspoons salt
⅛ teaspoon pepper
½ teaspoon dried basil
Rice, optional

- Cut celery into ¼-inch diagonal slices. (This will be approximately 1½ quarts.)
- Sauté onion in oil and cook until transparent.
- Add celery, green pepper, garlic, tomatoes, salt and pepper.
- Bring to a boil. Cover and simmer 20 minutes or until celery is tender crisp.
- Stir in basil and cook for another minute.
- May be served over rice.

A unique way to prepare celery!

CRISP BAKED EGGPLANT

Yield: 4-6 servings

1 large eggplant, approximately
  1 pound
½ cup mayonnaise
¼ teaspoon salt
⅛ teaspoon cayenne pepper

¼ cup finely chopped onion
⅓ cup seasoned bread crumbs
⅓ cup grated Parmesan cheese
½ teaspoon Italian seasoning

- Slice eggplant crosswise into ½-inch slices.
- Combine mayonnaise, salt, pepper and onion. Set aside.
- Combine bread crumbs, Parmesan cheese and Italian seasoning.
- Spread both sides of eggplant slices with mayonnaise mixture, then coat with bread crumb mixture.
- Place on baking sheet.
- Bake at 425° for 15-17 minutes, or until golden brown.

EXCITING EGGPLANT

Yield: 8 servings

1 large eggplant, peeled and
  chopped
1 egg
3 slices of bread, torn into pieces
  Milk
1 cup butter or margarine, divided
1 large onion, chopped

3 cups grated sharp Cheddar
  cheese, divided
1 teaspoon salt
¼ teaspoon pepper
  Pinch cayenne pepper
12 saltine crackers, crushed

- Cook eggplant in salted water until tender. Drain.
- Beat egg until foamy. Add bread pieces and enough milk to saturate bread. Allow to stand while preparing onion.
- Melt ½ cup butter in heavy skillet. Sauté onion in butter until transparent.
- Combine onion, eggplant, bread mixture, 2 cups cheese, salt and peppers. Blend well.
- Place mixture in greased 1½-quart baking dish.
- Combine crushed crackers with remaining cheese. Sprinkle on top of eggplant mixture. Dot with remaining butter or margarine.
- Bake at 400° for 20-30 minutes, or until top is golden brown.

This recipe is equally as delicious when made with squash!

HOLIDAY BAKED FRUIT

Vera Stewart
Vera Stewart Occasions
Augusta, Georgia
Yield: 8 servings

16 dried coconut macaroon cookies, crumbled	¾ cup pecans, toasted
4 cups canned fruit, drained (peaches, pears and pineapple chunks)	¼ cup light brown sugar
	½ cup golden sherry
	¼ cup butter, melted

• In a greased 2½-quart baking dish, layer ¼ the crumbled cookies, ⅓ the fruit, ¼ cup nuts, and ⅓ of the brown sugar. Repeat all layers twice more.
• Top with remaining cookie crumbs.
• Combine sherry and butter. Pour over all. May be prepared to this point the day before.
• Bake, uncovered, at 350° for 30 minutes.

The aroma of this dish will arouse the appetites of all your guests...plan to heat it last for this reason.

BEST-EVER GRITS

Yield: 8 servings

½ pound bacon	1½ cups regular white grits
1 medium onion, chopped	½ cup butter
1 medium green pepper, chopped	½ cup sour cream
8 medium tomatoes, peeled and cut into wedges	1 cup grated extra sharp Cheddar cheese
	2 cups finely chopped ham

• Fry bacon until crisp. Crumble and set aside. Reserve 3 tablespoons drippings.
• In drippings, sauté onion and green pepper.
• Add tomatoes and simmer 20 minutes.
• Cook grits as directed.
• To grits add butter, sour cream, cheese and ham. Fold in tomato mixture.
• Sprinkle crumbled bacon on top.

This hearty dish is creamier when stone-ground grits are used.
A great accompaniment to fish.

OKRA-RICE PILAF

Yield: 6 servings

2 cups cooked rice
2 tablespoons butter, melted
6 slices bacon, cooked and
  crumbled
2 tablespoons bacon drippings

2 cups sliced okra
1 medium onion, chopped
1 green pepper, chopped
  Salt and pepper to taste

• Combine rice and butter. Set aside.
• In reserved bacon drippings, sauté okra, onion and green pepper
  until tender.
• Combine rice, bacon, salt, pepper and okra mixture. Pour into
  1 ½-quart baking dish. Cover.
• Bake at 350° for 30 minutes.

POPPY'S ONION CASSEROLE

Yield: 6-8 servings

3 cups sliced onions,
  preferably Vidalia
¼ cup butter or margarine
1 cup grated sharp Cheddar
  cheese
3 eggs
1 cup milk

¼ teaspoon thyme
½ teaspoon salt
¼ teaspoon pepper
½ cup crushed cheese crackers
8 slices bacon, cooked and
  crumbled
  Poppy seeds

• Sauté onions in butter or margarine. Place in greased 2-quart baking dish.
• Sprinkle cheese over onions.
• Beat eggs and milk together. Add thyme, salt and pepper.
• Pour egg mixture over onions.
• Sprinkle with cheese crackers, bacon and poppy seeds.
• Bake, uncovered, at 350° for 30 minutes.

Vidalia onions from Georgia are delightfully sweet and delicious.

BAKED ORANGE CUPS

Yield: 24 servings

12 juice oranges
12 apples, peeled, cored and diced
1 14-ounce can crushed pineapple,
   drained

2 cups sugar
24 pecan halves
   Butter

- Slice oranges in half and clean out pulp. Remove as much membrane as possible.
- Combine orange pulp, apples, pineapple and sugar in heavy saucepan and cook on low 1-2 hours.
- Spoon mixture into orange cups.
- Top each cup with a pecan half and dot with butter.
- Bake at 350° for 20 minutes.

Delicious with holiday meals.

SHERYL'S PINEAPPLE CASSEROLE

Yield: 4-6 servings

1 20-ounce can pineapple chunks
½ cup sugar
3 tablespoons all-purpose flour

1 cup shredded sharp Cheddar
   cheese

- Drain pineapple, reserving 3 tablespoons juice.
- Combine sugar and flour. Stir in pineapple juice.
- Add cheese and pineapple chunks. Mix well.
- Spoon into 1-quart baking dish.
- Bake at 350° for 20-30 minutes.

An interesting mixture of tastes. This is a delicious accompaniment to any meat dish. Good with crisp vegetables.

MEXICAN MACARONI

Yield: 8 servings

2 10-ounce cans Ro-Tel
   tomatoes, undrained
1 medium onion, chopped
½ teaspoon salt
¼ teaspoon pepper
1 tablespoon Worcestershire
   sauce

1 8-ounce box small macaroni
   shells
1 pound Cheddar cheese, grated
½ cup cracker crumbs
   Butter

• Combine tomatoes, onion, salt, pepper and Worcestershire sauce in heavy
  saucepan.
• Cook over medium heat 20-30 minutes to reduce liquid.
• Cook macaroni according to package directions.
• In greased 2-quart baking dish, layer macaroni, tomato sauce and cheese.
  Repeat.
• Top with cracker crumbs. Dot with butter.
• Bake at 375° for 20-30 minutes.

A new twist to an old favorite.

FETTUCINE ALFREDO

Yield: 4-6 servings

1 8-ounce package fettucine
1 clove garlic, minced
2 tablespoons butter

½ cup half and half
¼ cup grated Parmesan cheese
   Salt and pepper to taste

• Cook fettucine as directed. Drain.
• Sauté garlic in butter.
• On medium-low heat, add fettucine. Slowly stir in half and half and
  Parmesan cheese. Blend until thickened.
• Season with salt and pepper.
• For a main course dish, one or more of the following may be added:
  ½ cup cooked shrimp; ½ pound blanched fresh asparagus; ½ cup
  blanched fresh broccoli, squash, carrots, or pea pods; or ½ cup
  sliced, sautéed mushrooms.

PASTA WITH ARTICHOKES AND MUSHROOMS

Yield: 6 servings

1 8½-ounce (drained weight) can artichoke hearts, drained and sliced
2 cups sliced, fresh mushrooms
6 tablespoons olive oil
4 tablespoons dry white wine
½ cup sliced green onions

½ teaspoon crushed basil
¼ teaspoon salt
1 8-ounce package fettucine, cooked and drained
¼ cup grated Parmesan cheese
⅛ teaspoon cracked pepper

• Sauté artichoke hearts and mushrooms in olive oil about 2 minutes.
• Add wine, onions, basil and salt. Cover. Simmer 2-3 minutes.
• Serve over cooked pasta. Top with Parmesan cheese and pepper.

GRATIN DAUPHINOIS

Yield: 8 servings

2 pounds white potatoes, peeled
2 cups milk
1½ cups whipping cream
1 large or 2 small cloves garlic, minced

¾ teaspoon salt
½ teaspoon freshly ground white pepper
4 tablespoons butter, divided
2-4 ounces grated Swiss cheese

• Wash the potatotes well and dry thoroughly.
• Slice potatoes ⅛-inch thick and place in a large saucepan.
• Add milk, cream, garlic, salt and pepper. Bring to a boil over moderate heat, stirring to prevent scorching.
• Remove pan from heat.
• Pour potato mixture into 2-quart baking dish that has been buttered with 1 tablespoon butter. Sprinkle grated cheese on top.
• Place baking dish on baking sheet.
• Dot with remaining 3 tablespoons butter.
• Bake at 400° for 30 minutes. Reduce heat to 350° and continue baking 30 minutes. (Potatoes are done when they are nicely browned and the tip of a knife pierces a potato easily.)
• Allow dish to stand 15-20 minutes before serving.

SOUR CREAM POTATOES

Yield: 8 servings

3   pounds medium potatoes, peeled and sliced
2½ cups grated sharp Cheddar cheese
¼   cup butter, melted
1⅛ teaspoons salt
¼   teaspoon pepper

⅓   cup chopped green onion, including tops
1   16-ounce carton sour cream
⅛   teaspoon cayenne pepper
½   cup fresh bread crumbs
2   tablespoons butter

• In heavy saucepan, boil potatoes until just tender. Drain.
• While potatoes are hot, stir in cheese, melted butter, salt and pepper. Be careful not to break potato slices.
• Combine onion, sour cream and pepper. Add to potatoes. Stir carefully.
• Place mixture in buttered 9x13-inch baking dish. Sprinkle with bread crumbs. Dot with butter.
• Bake at 325°, uncovered, for 25 minutes, or until hot and bubbly.

SWISS POTATOES

Yield: 6-8 servings

4-5 medium potatoes, peeled and thinly sliced
¼   teaspoon salt
¼   teaspoon pepper
1   clove garlic
¼   cup butter, divided

1½ cups grated Swiss cheese, divided
1   small bunch parsley, chopped
1   small onion, chopped
2   cups whipping cream

• Season potatoes with salt and pepper.
• Rub 2-quart glass baking dish with garlic and 2-3 tablespoons butter.
• Alternately layer potatoes, 1 cup cheese, parsley and onion, ending with potatoes.
• Cover with cream.
• Sprinkle with remaining ½ cup cheese.
• Dot with remaining butter.
• Bake at 375° for 45 minutes to 1 hour, or until potatoes are done.

Rich and so good!

221

SWEET POTATOES SAUTERNE

Yield: 12-14 servings

6-8 large sweet potatoes
½ cup butter, melted
1 cup brown sugar

2 teaspoons vanilla
½ cup sauterne
½ pint whipping cream

- Peel potatoes and boil until done.
- Mash through potato ricer or with a fork.
- Add butter, sugar and vanilla. Mix well.
- Add sauterne.
- Beat cream until stiff and fold into potato mixture.
- Place in 2-quart baking dish and refrigerate several hours. Serve cold.

A sophisticated approach to sweet potatoes.

BOURBON SWEET POTATOES

Yield: 10-12 servings

4 pounds sweet potatoes
½ cup butter, softened
½ cup bourbon
⅓ cup orange juice
¼ cup firmly packed light
  brown sugar

1 teaspoon salt
½ teaspoon cinnamon
⅓ cup chopped pecans

- Cook potatoes, covered, in boiling salted water until tender, approximately 35 minutes. Drain and cool slightly.
- Peel and mash potatoes.
- Combine potatoes, butter, bourbon, orange juice, sugar, salt and cinnamon. Beat until fluffy and smooth.
- Spoon into buttered 1½-quart baking dish. Sprinkle nuts around the edges.
- Bake at 350° for 45 minutes or until slightly browned.

BOURBON YAMS

Yield: 6 servings

6 sweet potatoes
2 cups light brown sugar, divided

½ cup butter, divided
½ cup bourbon

- Cook potatoes in boiling water until barely tender. Drain. Cool slightly.
- Peel and cut into large pieces.
- In buttered 1½-quart baking dish, layer one half the potatoes, one cup brown sugar, and 4 tablespoons of butter, sliced. Repeat.
- Pour bourbon over all.
- Bake, uncovered, at 350° for 30-45 minutes or until bubbly and browned.

Old-fashioned Southern yams.

WILD RICE AND CHEESE

Yield: 10-12 servings

½ cup butter
2 tablespoons all-purpose flour
1 cup milk
1 3-ounce package cream cheese, cubed

½ teaspoon salt
1 6-ounce box Uncle Ben's Long Grain and Wild Rice, cooked
½ pound mushroom caps, sautéed

- Melt butter in double boiler. Add flour, stirring constantly.
- Slowly add milk, stirring until thickened.
- Add cream cheese and salt. Blend until smooth.
- Alternate layers of rice, mushrooms and cream sauce. Repeat until 1½-quart dish is filled, ending with a generous amount of sauce.
- Bake, uncovered, at 325° for 20-30 minutes.

Very rich and flavorful!

BETTER THAN HOPPIN' JOHN

Yield: 8 servings

1 18-ounce package frozen
  black-eyed peas
1 cup raw rice
1 pound hot sausage
1 pound mild sausage
1 large onion, chopped

2 medium green peppers, chopped
1 cup fresh chopped mushrooms
1 tablespoon garlic powder
1 teaspoon salt
1 tablespoon pepper
2 bay leaves

- Cook black-eyed peas as directed. (Do not overcook.) Drain.
- Cook rice as directed.
- Crumble and cook sausage. Drain, reserving 3 tablespoons drippings.
- Sauté onion, peppers and mushrooms in drippings.
- Add garlic powder, salt, pepper, and bay leaves to vegetables.
- Combine rice, peas, sausage and vegetables in large baking dish.
  (May refrigerate or freeze at this point.)
- Heat, covered, at 300° for 1-1½ hours.

*According to Southern tradition, eating black-eyed peas on New Year's Day
brings good luck throughout the year.*

RICE-A-ROSIE

Yield: 4-6 servings

1   cup long grain rice
2   cups chicken broth
2   tablespoons butter
1   tablespoon vegetable oil
1   6-ounce can sliced
    mushrooms
½   cup chopped green pepper

4-5 spring onions, chopped with
     some tops
1   rib celery, chopped
2   tablespoons chopped
     pimento
¼-½ teaspoon thyme
     Dash Tabasco
     Salt and pepper to taste

- Cook rice in chicken broth until liquid is absorbed, about 20-25 minutes.
- Melt butter and oil in heavy skillet.
- Sauté mushrooms, green pepper, onions and celery until tender crisp.
  (Do not overcook.)
- Add sautéed vegetables, pimento, thyme, Tabasco, salt and pepper to rice.
- Toss gently.
- Place in greased 2-quart glass baking dish. Bake, covered, at 350° for
  20 minutes.

A colorful accompaniment to chicken or pork.

SARA ANN'S WILD RICE CASSEROLE

Yield: 12 servings

½	pound fresh mushrooms, sliced	1	14½-ounce can tomatoes, drained and chopped
½	cup chopped onion	1	teaspoon salt
½	cup butter	1	cup hot water
6½-7	cups cooked wild rice		
1	cup grated sharp Cheddar cheese		

• Sauté mushrooms and onion in butter for 5 minutes.
• Toss rice with mushrooms, onion, cheese, tomatoes, salt and water.
• Place in greased 2-quart baking dish.
• Cover and bake at 350° for 1 hour.

Uncle Ben's Long Grain and Wild Rice may be substituted for wild rice. Omit hot water and bake at 350° for 30 minutes or until thoroughly heated.

DELIGHTFUL RICE

Yield: 8 servings

½ pound sausage	1	10¾-ounce can cream of chicken soup
1 cup sliced fresh mushrooms		
½ cup chopped onion	1	teaspoon salt
1 5-ounce package Uncle Ben's Brown and Wild Rice, cooked	1	teaspoon pepper
		Dash Tabasco

• Brown sausage. Drain, reserving 3 tablespoons drippings.
• Sauté mushrooms and onion in reserved drippings.
• Combine rice and remaining ingredients.
• Add sausage, mushrooms and onion.
• Bake, uncovered, in 2-quart baking dish at 350° for 25-30 minutes.

Add one cup chopped, cooked chicken to create a main dish.

FRUITED RICE CURRY

Yield: 4 servings

1 cup raw rice
1 tablespoon instant onion
2 teaspoons curry powder
2 beef bouillon cubes, crushed to a fine powder
½ teaspoon salt

¼ cup mixed dried fruits, finely chopped
¼ cup blanched slivered almonds
2½ cups water
2 tablespoons butter

- Combine rice, onion, curry powder, bouillon, salt, fruit and almonds.
- Add water and butter.
- Cover and bring to a boil.
- Reduce heat and simmer, covered, 20 minutes.

The dry ingredients can be packaged in individual packets.
A great gift for holiday giving.
A perfect dish with roast pork.

CREAMER'S SHRIMP PILAF

Yield: 4-6 servings

4 slices bacon
1 cup raw rice
½ cup finely chopped celery
2 tablespoons chopped green pepper
½ cup butter

2 cups shrimp, peeled and deveined
1 tablespoon Worcestershire sauce
1 tablespoon all-purpose flour
Salt and pepper to taste

- Fry bacon until crisp, reserving drippings. Add drippings to the water in which rice is to be cooked.
- Cook rice as directed.
- Sauté celery and green pepper in butter until tender.
- Sprinkle shrimp with Worcestershire sauce and flour. Add shrimp to skillet.
- Stir gently. Simmer until flour is cooked and shrimp are pink.
- Add rice, salt and pepper to shrimp mixture. Blend together.
- Stir in crumbled bacon. Spoon into greased 2-quart baking dish.
- Bake, covered, at 350° for 15-25 minutes. Remove cover and bake 5 minutes.

This is a great accompaniment to FLANK STEAK DIJON.

BRAZIL NUT DRESSING

Yield: 6-8 servings

1 medium onion, chopped
3/4 cup chopped celery with leaves
1/3 cup butter
8 cups soft bread crumbs
1/2 pound Brazil nuts, coarsely chopped
1/3 cup minced fresh parsley

1 teaspoon thyme
1 teaspoon marjoram
1 teaspoon salt
1/2 teaspoon pepper
2 eggs, beaten
2/3 cup chicken broth

• Sauté onion and celery in butter until golden.
• Add bread crumbs, nuts, parsley, thyme, marjoram, salt, pepper and eggs.
• Add broth and mix well. If a moister dressing is desired, add more broth.
• Place in buttered 9x9-inch baking dish.
• Bake at 375° for 45 minutes.

This is a dry dressing with a nice crunch! Delicious served with giblet gravy.

SPECIAL SAUSAGE DRESSING

Yield: 20 squares

1 pound mild or hot bulk pork sausage
2 cups diced onion
1 cup diced celery
1/2 cup butter, melted
2 1/2 quarts bread crumbs made from good French loaves
3/4 teaspoon salt

1/2 teaspoon black pepper
1/4 teaspoon cayenne pepper
1/4 teaspoon thyme
1/4 teaspoon sage
1 14 1/2-ounce can clear chicken broth
4 eggs, beaten

• Brown sausage. Drain, reserving 2 tablespoons drippings.
• Sauté onion and celery in drippings.
• Drizzle butter over bread crumbs.
• Toast bread crumbs.
• Combine all ingredients and press into a 17 1/4x11 3/4x2 1/4-inch aluminum pan.
• Bake, covered, at 350° for 30 minutes.
• Can be made and frozen.

A new tradition for the holiday meal.

227

SQUASH FRITTERS

Yield: 6-8 servings

2 cups cubed yellow squash
1 cup chopped onion
1 cup chopped green pepper
1 cup chopped fresh mushrooms
1 teaspoon salt, or to taste

¼ teaspoon pepper, or to taste
1 egg, beaten
1 cup sour cream
1 cup all-purpose flour
½ cup vegetable oil

• Combine squash, onion, green pepper, mushrooms, salt and pepper.
• Add egg, sour cream and flour. Blend well.
• Shape into patties.
• Fry in hot oil until browned.

Divine!!!

SPINACH AND BROWN RICE, GREEK STYLE

Yield: 6 servings

2 tablespoons olive oil
2 medium onions, chopped
1 clove garlic, minced
1 10-ounce package frozen
   chopped spinach, thawed and
   drained well
½ teaspoon salt

1 cup brown rice, cooked
1 medium tomato, peeled and
   chopped
1 tablespoon fresh lemon juice
½ teaspoon grated lemon rind
1 cup grated Swiss cheese,
   divided

• Heat oil in a 10-inch skillet.
• Add onions and garlic. Cook until onion is transparent.
• Add spinach and salt. Stir and cook until spinach is tender, about
  5 minutes.
• Add hot rice, tomato, lemon juice and rind to spinach mixture.
• Stir in ½ cup of cheese.
• Place in serving dish and sprinkle with remaining cheese.
• Serve immediately.

SPINACH-ARTICHOKE CASSEROLE

Yield: 8-10 servings

1 6-ounce can whole mushroom crowns
6 tablespoons butter or margarine, divided
1 tablespoon all-purpose flour
½ cup milk
½ teaspoon salt
¼ teaspoon dry mustard
⅛ teaspoon cayenne pepper

1 6-ounce can mushroom pieces
2 10-ounce packages frozen spinach, thawed and well drained
1 8½-ounce (drained weight) can artichoke hearts, drained
½ cup sour cream
½ cup mayonnaise
2 tablespoons fresh lemon juice

• Sauté 8 mushroom crowns in 3 tablespoons butter. Remove mushrooms and set aside.
• Coarsely chop remaining mushrooms. Add to pan and sauté until tender. Remove and set aside.
• Add remaining butter. Add flour and cook until bubbly, stirring constantly.
• Blend in milk, salt, mustard, pepper, chopped mushrooms, mushroom pieces and spinach. Mix well.
• Place artichoke hearts in buttered 1½-quart baking dish.
• Spread spinach mixture over artichoke hearts. Set aside.
• Combine sour cream, mayonnaise and lemon juice.
• Spread over spinach layer.
• Arrange mushroom crowns on top.
• Bake at 350° for 30 minutes or until heated thoroughly.

SQUASH-TOMATO-ASPARAGUS SAUTÉ

Yield: 6 servings

4 yellow squash, sliced
¼-½ pound fresh asparagus, sliced on diagonal with tough ends removed
2-3 tomatoes, cut into wedges

2-3 tablespoons butter
Herbs to taste (any combination of dill, basil, tarragon or oregano)
Morton Nature's Seasons

• Blanch squash and asparagus.
• Sauté squash, asparagus and tomatoes in butter with herbs and Nature's Seasons.
• Serve when vegetables are bright and fork tender.

Very colorful! Broccoli florets can be substituted for fresh asparagus.

CLASSIC STUFFED SQUASH

Yield: 8 servings

4 large yellow squash	½ pound fresh mushrooms, sliced
2 medium onions, chopped	6 slices bacon, diced
1 green pepper, chopped	Parsley sprigs to garnish

- Steam squash until barely tender, about 10 minutes.
- Sauté onions, green pepper, mushrooms and bacon together until bacon is browned. Drain off excess grease.
- Cut squash in half lengthwise. Remove seeds.
- Carefully remove pulp leaving a thin shell.
- Mash pulp and add to onion mixture.
- Spoon pulp mixture into shells. Place in baking dish.
- Bake at 350° for 30 minutes.

RITZY ZUCCHINI BOATS

Yield: 8 servings

4 small zucchini	1 egg, beaten
1 small onion, chopped	¼ cup chopped fresh parsley
3 tablespoons vegetable oil	½ cup grated Parmesan cheese,
1 clove garlic, minced	divided
½ cup chopped fresh mushrooms	½ teaspoon salt
3 ounces cream cheese, cut into pieces	¼ teaspoon pepper

- Parboil zucchini, covered, 5-7 minutes or until just tender. Drain. Cool slightly.
- Cut zucchini lengthwise. Carefully scoop out pulp.
- Sauté onion in oil. Add zucchini pulp, garlic and mushrooms. Cook 5 minutes, stirring until liquid is absorbed.
- Add cream cheese, egg and parsley. Stir in Parmesan cheese, reserving 1 tablespoon for topping.
- Cook slowly, stirring constantly, about 5 minutes.
- Add salt and pepper.
- Spoon mixture into zucchini shells. Sprinkle with reserved 1 tablespoon Parmesan cheese.
- Place zucchini in baking dish. Bake at 350° for 15-20 minutes. Place under broiler to brown.

Rich and delicious!

NOONIE'S ZUCCHINI

Yield: 4 servings

4 small zucchini	¼ cup grated Parmesan cheese
⅔ cup mayonnaise	Dash of cayenne pepper
2 tablespoons crumbled	Salt
Blue cheese	Oregano
¼ teaspoon garlic salt	

• Parboil whole zucchini in salted water until just tender. Drain.
• Cut zucchini in half, lengthwise. Cool slightly.
• Combine mayonnaise, Blue cheese, garlic salt, Parmesan cheese and cayenne pepper. Blend well.
• Sprinkle zucchini halves with salt. Spread mayonnaise mixture on cut halves.
• Sprinkle with oregano.
• Bake at 350° for 20 minutes.

An intriguing combination of flavors.

BUTTERNUT SQUASH CASSEROLE

Yield: 6 servings

2 large butternut squash	1 teaspoon vanilla
1 cup sugar	½ cup milk
2 eggs, beaten	½ cup butter, melted

• Cut squash in half, lengthwise. Remove seeds.
• Fill shallow baking pan half full of water.
• Place squash in water, cut side up. Cover with foil.
• Bake at 375° until tender, approximately 1-1½ hours. Cool slightly. Drain well.
• Scoop out pulp and mash. (There should be about 3 cups.)
• Combine squash pulp, sugar, eggs, vanilla, milk and butter.
• Pour into buttered 1½-quart baking dish.
• Bake at 350° for 45 minutes, or until mixture is firm and lightly browned.

SAUCY ZUCCHINI

Yield: 6 servings

1 pound zucchini, thinly sliced	1 cup half and half
2 medium onions, thinly sliced	⅛ teaspoon cayenne pepper
2 tablespoons butter or margarine	1 tablespoon basil
2 tablespoons all-purpose flour	1 cup grated sharp Cheddar
1 teaspoon salt	cheese, divided
¼ teaspoon pepper	½ cup buttered bread crumbs

- Cook zucchini and onions in boiling salted water until just tender. Drain well.
- In heavy saucepan, melt butter. Blend in flour, salt and pepper. Cook until bubbly.
- Add half and half. Cook, stirring constantly, until mixture thickens and bubbles.
- Add cayenne pepper, basil and ½ cup cheese.
- Add cooked vegetables to sauce. Mix gently.
- Pour into greased 1½-quart baking dish.
- Top with remaining ½ cup cheese and bread crumbs.
- Bake at 350° for 25 minutes.

TOMATO PUDDING

Mrs. Hord Hardin
wife of the Chairman of Augusta National Golf Club
Yield: 12 servings

3 10-ounce cans Hunt's tomato purée	1 6-ounce can spicy hot V-8 juice
1½ cups brown sugar	12 slices white bread
¼ teaspoon salt	¾ cup butter, melted

- Combine purée, brown sugar, salt and V-8 juice in saucepan. Bring to a boil. Reduce heat and simmer 5 minutes.
- Cut bread into 1-inch cubes. Line a buttered 9x12-inch baking dish with cubes.
- Pour melted butter over bread.
- Pour tomato mixture over butter.
- Bake at 375°, covered, 30 minutes. Remove cover and bake an additional 15 minutes.

Tomato pudding is great with beef and lamb. Men love this spicy delight!

TANTALIZING STUFFED TOMATOES

Yield: 6 servings

¼ cup chopped onion
4 tablespoons butter
6 medium tomatoes
½ teaspoon salt
¼ teaspoon pepper
¼ teaspoon basil

1 teaspoon chopped fresh parsley
2 cups crushed cheese crackers
1 8½-ounce (drained weight) can artichoke hearts, drained and cut in half

- Sauté onion in butter.
- Core tomatoes, remove pulp and mash.
- Combine mashed tomato pulp, onion, salt, pepper, basil, parsley and crackers. Mix well.
- Divide tomato mixture among each of the six tomatoes.
- Top each with ½ artichoke heart.
- Use any remaining tomato pulp mixture to firmly fill tomatoes.
- Place tomatoes in baking dish. Cover with foil.
- Bake at 350° for 5 minutes. Remove foil and bake 10 minutes longer.

Enjoy this recipe when local tomatoes are at their best.

RICE FILLED TOMATOES

Yield: 8 servings

8 medium tomatoes
1 6-ounce package Jane's Krazy Mixed Up Rice, cooked
1 medium onion, chopped

1 cup grated sharp Cheddar or Swiss cheese
4-5 slices bacon, cooked and crumbled

- Core tomatoes, remove pulp and reserve.
- Invert tomatoes to drain.
- Chop half of pulp, discarding remaining pulp.
- Combine pulp with rice and onion.
- Spoon rice mixture into tomatoes.
- Top with cheese and bacon.
- Bake, uncovered, at 350° for 15-20 minutes. May be served cold or warm.

Any other herbed rice may be substituted.

BAKED TOMATOES WITH ASPARAGUS SPEARS

Yield: 8 servings

4 large tomatoes
24 spears fresh asparagus, steamed
1 cup mayonnaise
2 cups grated sharp Cheddar cheese

2 dashes Tabasco
1 tablespoon Dijon mustard
3 tablespoons grated onion

- Cut tomatoes in half and remove large core at stem end.
- Place in buttered baking dish, cut side up.
- Top each tomato with 3 asparagus spears, cut into 6-inch lengths.
- Combine mayonnaise, cheese, Tabasco, mustard and onion.
- Spoon sauce on top of each tomato.
- Bake at 350° for 10-15 minutes or until cheese is melted and tomato is heated through.

Absolutely wonderful!
Canned asparagus may be used if fresh is not available.

 # CHERRY TOMATO SAUTÉ

Yield: 6-8 servings

3 tablespoons butter
3 tablespoons extra virgin olive oil
1 clove garlic, minced
1½ teaspoons dried basil (or 3 teaspoons fresh)
½ teaspoon dried thyme

½ teaspoon salt
¼ teaspoon pepper
⅛ teaspoon Tabasco
4 tablespoons dry sherry
2 pints cherry tomatoes
¼ cup grated Parmesan cheese

- Melt butter in heavy skillet over medium heat.
- Add oil, garlic, basil, thyme, salt, pepper, Tabasco and sherry.
- Roll tomatoes in mixture over heat for 5 minutes, no longer!
- Sprinkle with Parmesan cheese.
- Serve immediately.

This dish makes a colorful and attractive accompaniment for any meal.

TEMPTING TOMATO PIE

Yield: 6-8 servings

1 9-inch pie crust, baked and cooled	½ teaspoon basil
2-3 large tomatoes, peeled and sliced	1 teaspoon chives
½ teaspoon salt	3 green onions, chopped
¼ teaspoon pepper	1 cup mayonnaise
	1 cup grated sharp Cheddar cheese

• Place tomatoes in pie crust and sprinkle with salt, pepper, herbs and onions.
• Combine mayonnaise and cheese. Spread over tomatoes.
• Bake at 350° for 30 minutes.

This is an excellent brunch dish!

RAW CRANBERRY RELISH

Yield: 2 quarts

1 quart fresh cranberries	Peel and rind from ½ orange
2 red or yellow Delicious apples, cored and unpeeled	2 large oranges
	2 cups sugar

• Coarsely chop berries, apples, orange rind and peel in food grinder or processor. Remove to bowl.
• Section oranges and cut into small pieces. Add to berry mixture.
• Add sugar. Mix well.

This tart relish is a wonderful accompaniment to any holiday meal.
It will keep in the refrigerator for six weeks.

HORSERADISH SAUCE

Yield: 2 cups

4	tablespoons butter	1	medium onion, grated
2	teaspoons horseradish	1½	cups mayonnaise
1	teaspoon Dijon mustard	1	tablespoon wine vinegar
1	teaspoon salt	2	drops Tabasco

• Combine all ingredients in double boiler.
• Heat only enough to blend.
• Serve over fresh asparagus or other fresh green vegetables.

An excellent alternative to Hollandaise.

PEACH CHUTNEY

Yield: 4-5 pints

3	pounds peaches, peeled and sliced	1	tablespoon cayenne pepper
1	pound seedless raisins	1	clove garlic, minced
¼	pound candied ginger, finely chopped	2	teaspoons salt
4	large, tart apples, cored and chopped	1	teaspoon ginger
		4	cups sugar

• Combine all ingredients in large canning pot. Slowly bring to a boil.
• Simmer one hour, stirring often.
• Pour into sterilized jars and seal.

Simply wonderful served with baked ham.

DESSERTS

DESSERTS

MIAMI BEACH BIRTHDAY CAKE

Yield: 1 9-inch cake

Cake:

1 6-ounce package semi-sweet chocolate chips, divided	1 teaspoon salt
½ cup graham cracker crumbs	½ cup butter, softened
⅓ cup butter, melted	1⅔ cups sugar
½ cup chopped pecans	2 eggs
2 cups all-purpose flour	1 teaspoon vanilla
1 teaspoon baking soda	1¼ cups buttermilk

• Melt ⅓ cup chocolate chips. Set aside.
• Combine cracker crumbs, butter, pecans and ⅔ cup chocolate chips. Set aside.
• Sift together flour, baking soda and salt.
• Cream butter and sugar.
• Add eggs one at a time, beating well after each addition.
• Blend in melted chocolate and vanilla.
• At low speed, add dry ingredients alternately with buttermilk.
• Pour batter into 2 greased and floured 9-inch cake pans.
• Sprinkle each with crumb mixture.
• Bake at 375° for 30-40 minutes. Cool completely.
• Spread Icing between layers and on sides, leaving top unfrosted.
• Keep refrigerated.

Icing:

1 cup whipping cream	2 tablespoons sugar

• Beat cream with sugar until stiff.

Take a second slice when no one is looking.

> ◤ The theatrical nature of his victory stands in contrast to the demeanor of this unpretentious young man with the smooth, classical swing. However, Larry Mize is an entirely fitting Masters® champion. After all, it was another soft spoken Georgian with a rhythmic swing who founded the Augusta National Golf Club.
>
> Hord Hardin, April, 1987

HENRY STREET HEAVEN

Yield: 1 9-inch cake

Cake:

¾ cup butter, softened
2 cups sugar
3 cups sifted cake flour
3 teaspoons baking powder
½ teaspoon salt

½ cup milk
½ cup water
1 teaspoon vanilla
6 egg whites

• Cream butter and sugar until fluffy.
• Sift together flour, baking powder and salt three times.
• Mix together milk, water and vanilla.
• Add flour to creamed mixture alternately with milk mixture, beating well after each addition.
• Beat egg whites until stiff, but not dry, and fold into cake mixture.
• Pour into 3 9-inch cake pans which have been lined with waxed paper.
• Bake at 350° for 25 minutes or until tester inserted in center comes out clean.
• Remove cake from oven and cool.
• Spread Cream Filling between layers.
• Spread Frosting on top and sides.

Cream Filling:

½ cup butter, softened
1 cup powdered sugar

1 egg white

• Cream butter until very soft. Add sugar gradually.
• Beat egg white until very stiff and add one teaspoon at a time to butter mixture, mixing well after each addition.

Frosting:

1 cup sugar
¼ cup water
Pinch cream of tartar

2 egg whites
½ cup slivered almonds, browned in 1 tablespoon butter

• In medium saucepan, combine sugar, water and cream of tartar.
• Cook, stirring constantly, over medium heat until sugar is dissolved and syrup is clear. Continue cooking, without stirring, to 240° (or until a small amount of mixture spins thread 6-8 inches long when dropped from tip of spoon).
• Beat egg whites until soft peaks form.
• Add hot syrup in thin stream to egg whites, beating at high speed.
• Continue beating until stiff peaks form and frosting is thick enough to spread.
• Fold in almonds.

Worth every calorie!

CHOCOLATE CHIP MOCHA CUPCAKES

Yield: 12 cupcakes

½	cup butter or margarine	⅔	cup milk
½	cup light brown sugar	1¾	cups all-purpose flour
½	cup sugar	1	tablespoon baking powder
3	tablespoons instant coffee powder or granules	½	teaspoon salt
		1	cup mini-chocolate chips
2	teaspoons vanilla	1	cup chopped pecans
2	eggs		

• Combine butter and sugars. Beat until creamy. Add coffee and vanilla. Beat well. Set aside.
• In a separate bowl, beat together eggs and milk.
• Combine flour, baking powder and salt.
• Add dry ingredients alternately with egg mixture to butter mixture. Stir just until blended.
• Stir in chocolate chips and pecans.
• Spoon into greased and floured muffin cups until ⅔ full.
• Bake at 350° for 20-25 minutes.

Sinful before noon, but oh-h-h so-o-o good! A perfect birthday party treat.

CHIP 'n CHERRY CAKE

Yield: 1 loaf

½	cup butter	1-1½	cups chopped pecans
1	cup sugar	1	cup chopped dates
3	eggs	1	cup candied cherries
1½	cups all-purpose flour		All-purpose flour
1½	teaspoons baking powder		Rum or bourbon
1	cup chocolate chips		

• Cream butter and sugar.
• Add eggs. Beat until blended.
• Slowly add flour and baking powder. Mix well.
• Combine chocolate chips, pecans, dates and cherries in separate bowl. Coat lightly with flour. Fold into batter.
• Grease a 9x5-inch loaf pan and line bottom with brown paper. Pour in batter.
• Bake at 325° for 1½-2 hours, or until crusty and browned. A pan of water on lower shelf of oven during baking will help keep cake moist.
• Remove from pan. Wrap in rum or bourbon soaked cloth.
• Store 1-2 weeks before serving.

CHERRY CUPCAKES

Yield: 36 miniature muffins

4 tablespoons butter, softened
½ cup sugar
½ cup light brown sugar
2 eggs, separated
1 cup all-purpose flour
¼ teaspoon baking powder

2 tablespoons cherry juice
Pecans, finely ground
1 12-ounce bottle maraschino cherries
Powdered sugar

• Cream butter and sugars.
• Beat egg yolks. Add to creamed mixture.
• Sift together flour and baking powder. Add to creamed mixture.
• Stir in cherry juice.
• Beat egg whites until stiff. Fold into batter.
• Sprinkle nuts in bottom of greased miniature muffin pans.
• Add 1 teaspoon batter, then 1 cherry. Top with another teaspoon batter.
• Sprinkle with more pecans.
• Bake at 400° for 10 minutes.
• Roll in powdered sugar while still warm.
• Store in airtight container 1-2 weeks before serving.

A change from the usual muffins – a surprise inside.

"There is one point you can gamble on, as far as anyone can look ahead. The Augusta National's annual Masters® Tournament is on its way to becoming one of the big fixtures of golf, presenting Bobby Jones again next spring in his second start since 1930.

"The opening act was an amazing success. There were automobiles parked around the club from 38 states and Canada. Eighteen thousand more words were telegraphed from the Augusta battlefield than the last United States Open at Chicago sent spinning over the wires. Thousands of people came from all over the country to see what the Mop-up star of 1930 could do against a fast moving field of young stars and veterans, after four years rest from the wars."

Comment by Grandland Rice 1934

GRAND DIPLÔME CHOCOLATE ROULADE

Craig Calvert
Calvert's
Augusta, Georgia
Yield: 10 servings

6 ounces semi-sweet chocolate, broken into small pieces	1 pint whipping cream
3-4 tablespoons water	½ cup powdered sugar
5 eggs, separated	Powdered sugar
1 cup sugar	1 cup nuts, finely chopped, optional
1-2 egg whites, beaten, optional	Chocolate sauce
½ teaspoon cream of tartar	Whipped cream

- Grease 15x10-inch jelly-roll pan. Cover with waxed paper. Grease paper. Set aside.
- Melt chocolate in water in double boiler, stirring until creamy. Remove from water. Cool.
- Beat egg yolks with sugar 5 minutes or until thick and light colored. Stir in chocolate.
- Beat egg whites with cream of tartar until stiff peaks form. Fold into chocolate mixture. (If a lighter cake is desired add additional egg whites.)
- Spread mixture into prepared pan.
- Bake at 350° for 15 minutes or until cake springs back when lightly pressed.
- When cake is done, remove from oven. Cool slightly. Cover with dish towel which has been dipped in cold water and wrung out well.
- Refrigerate 12 hours or overnight.
- Just prior to serving, whip cream with powdered sugar. Set aside.
- Sprinkle a sheet of waxed paper with powdered sugar. Turn roulade onto paper.
- Trim edges of roulade.
- Spread whipped cream over entire surface. If desired, 1 cup toasted, finely chopped nuts may be added.
- Roll jelly-roll fashion.
- Spoon chocolate sauce onto platter. Place roulade in center. Sprinkle heavily with powdered sugar.
- Drizzle with chocolate sauce and garnish with whipped cream. May decorate with fresh fruit, if desired.

This Augusta favorite deserves applause.

MILKY WAY CAKE

Yield: 1 9-inch cake

Cake:

6   1¹¹/₁₆-ounce Milky Way candy bars
½   cup butter or margarine
2   cups sugar
1   cup shortening
4   eggs

2½   cups all-purpose flour
1   teaspoon salt
1½   cups buttermilk
½   teaspoon baking soda
1   teaspoon vanilla

• Melt candy bars and butter over low heat, stirring constantly. Set aside.
• Cream together sugar and shortening.
• Add eggs and continue beating until light and fluffy.
• Combine flour and salt.
• Combine buttermilk and baking soda.
• Add dry ingredients to creamed mixture, alternately with buttermilk. Beat well after each addition.
• Stir in vanilla and candy mixture.
• Pour batter into 3 greased and floured 9-inch cake pans.
• Bake at 350° for 30 minutes.
• Cool and frost with Chocolate Marshmallow Frosting.

Chocolate Marshmallow Frosting:

2   cups sugar
1   5-ounce can evaporated milk
½   cup butter or margarine

1   6-ounce package chocolate chips
1   cup marshmallow cream

• Combine sugar, milk and butter in saucepan.
• Cook over medium heat until mixture reaches soft ball stage (236°).
• Remove from heat. Add chocolate chips and marshmallow cream.
• Stir until melted.

▶   Dignity is the keynote of the Masters® Tournament where the game of golf is elevated to the high position it deserves. I am happy and very proud to play a small part in it.

From a BEN HOGAN letter
Written January 12, 1954

CHOCOLATE RUM CAKE

Yield: 1 10-inch cake

1 18½-ounce package Betty
   Crocker Devil's Food cake mix
1 3½-ounce package instant
   chocolate pudding mix
½ cup sour cream
4 eggs

1 cup vegetable oil
½ cup dark rum
½ cup strong coffee
1 12-ounce package semi-sweet
   chocolate chips

• Sift together cake mix and pudding mix into large mixing bowl.
• Combine sour cream, eggs, oil, rum and coffee in small bowl. (If using
  instant coffee, dissolve 2 tablespoons coffee in ½ cup hot water.) Beat on
  low speed 1 minute.
• Pour liquid ingredients into dry ingredients. Beat at high speed 1 minute.
  Scrape sides of bowl and beat 1 more minute.
• Fold in chocolate chips.
• Pour batter into greased and floured 10-inch tube or Bundt pan.
• Bake at 325° for 55 minutes or until cake springs back when touched.
• Remove from oven. Cool in pan 30 minutes.
• Remove cake from pan. Cool completely.
• Wrap tightly in foil and allow to age 48 hours.

GRANNY'S POUND CAKE

Yield: 1 10-inch cake

1 cup butter, softened
3 cups sugar, sifted
6 eggs
3 cups cake flour, sifted
1 8-ounce carton sour cream

¼ teaspoon salt
¼ teaspoon baking soda
1 teaspoon fresh lemon juice
1 teaspoon vanilla

• Cream butter. Add sugar, 2 tablespoons at a time.
• Add, in this order: 1 egg, 2 heaping tablespoons of flour and 1 heaping
  teaspoon of sour cream. Mix well.
• Repeat in order until all ingredients are used.
• Add salt and baking soda with last teaspoon of sour cream.
• Stir in lemon juice and vanilla.
• Pour batter into greased and floured 10-inch tube pan.
• Bake at 325° for 1 hour and 20 minutes, or until cake tests done.

A light and delicate pound cake.

CHOCOLATE POUND CAKE

Yield: 1 10-inch cake

Cake:

1 cup butter, softened
½ cup shortening
3 cups sugar
5 eggs
3 cups sifted cake flour
½ teaspoon baking powder
½ teaspoon salt
½ cup cocoa
1 cup milk
2 teaspoons vanilla
    Powdered sugar, optional

- Cream butter, shortening and sugar.
- Add eggs one at a time, beating until smooth.
- Combine flour, baking powder, salt and cocoa. Sift together 3 times.
- Add sifted ingredients to creamed mixture alternately with milk. Blend well. Add vanilla.
- Pour batter into greased and floured 10-inch tube or Bundt pan.
- Bake at 300° for 1 hour and 20 minutes.
- When cake is cool, sprinkle with powdered sugar or drizzle with Chocolate Icing.

Chocolate Icing:

Yield: ⅔ cup

1 tablespoon butter
4 ounces semi-sweet chocolate
6 tablespoons whipping cream
1½ cups sifted powdered sugar, or more if needed
1 teaspoon vanilla

- In double boiler, combine butter and chocolate. Melt over simmering water.
- Add cream and beat well.
- Add powdered sugar and vanilla.
- Beat until icing reaches desired consistency.

This is a chocolate-lover's treat, without too much fuss.

COCONUT POUND CAKE

Yield: 1 10-inch cake

Cake:

2	cups cake flour	5	eggs
½	teaspoon salt	¼	cup milk
1½	teaspoons baking powder	1	teaspoon vanilla
1	cup vegetable oil	1	teaspoon coconut flavoring
2	cups sugar	1	cup shredded coconut

• Sift together flour, salt and baking powder.
• Cream oil and sugar.
• Add eggs one at a time, beating until smooth.
• Add sifted ingredients to creamed mixture, a small amount at a time.
• Add milk, vanilla, coconut flavoring and coconut.
• Bake in greased and floured tube or Bundt pan at 325° for 1 hour.
• Remove cake from oven and immediately pour Glaze over cake.
• Allow cake to cool in pan before removing.

Glaze:

1	cup sugar	4	tablespoons margarine
½	cup milk	1	teaspoon coconut flavoring

• Combine glaze ingredients over medium heat. Boil 3 minutes.

CREAM CHEESE POUND CAKE

Yield: 1 10-inch cake

1½	cups butter or margarine, softened	1½	teaspoons vanilla
		½	teaspoon almond extract
3	cups sugar	6	eggs
1	8-ounce package cream cheese, softened	3	cups sifted cake flour

• In large bowl, cream butter, sugar and cream cheese.
• Add vanilla and almond extract.
• Add eggs, one at a time, beating until smooth.
• Add flour. Mix well.
• Spoon batter into greased and floured 10-inch tube or Bundt pan.
• Bake at 325° for 1½ hours.
• Cool in pan 10 minutes. Remove to wire rack and cool completely.

SHERRY CAKE

Yield: 1 10-inch cake

1	angel food cake	1	pint whipping cream, divided
1	envelope unflavored gelatin		Sugar to taste
½	cup sherry		Vanilla to taste
1	3⅛-ounce package vanilla pudding mix (regular)		Nuts or seasonal fruits to garnish
1½	cups milk		

- Break cake into bite-size pieces.
- Dissolve gelatin in sherry.
- Prepare pudding according to package directions, using only 1½ cups milk.
- Add gelatin mixture to pudding. Mix well. Cool.
- Whip ½ pint cream. Fold into pudding mixture.
- Combine cake pieces and pudding mixture.
- Pour into lightly-oiled 10-inch tube pan.
- Refrigerate at least 12 hours before unmolding.
- Whip remaining ½ pint cream.
- Add sugar and vanilla to taste.
- Ice cake with whipped cream.
- Refrigerate until ready to serve.
- Garnish with nuts or seasonal fruits.

ANGEL FOOD CAKE

Yield: 1 10-inch cake

1¼	cups sifted cake flour	1¼	teaspoons cream of tartar
2	cups sifted sugar, divided	1	teaspoon vanilla
1½	cups egg whites (10-12)	1	teaspoon almond extract
1	teaspoon salt		

- Sift together flour and ½ cup sugar 4 times. Set aside.
- In large bowl, beat egg whites until foamy.
- Add salt, cream of tartar, vanilla and almond extract. Beat until soft peaks form, but remain moist and glossy.
- Add remaining 1½ cups sugar, sprinkling 5 tablespoons at a time over whites and beating well after each addition.
- Sift flour mixture over egg whites in 4 small additions, folding each in well.
- Gently pour batter into ungreased 10-inch tube pan.
- Bake at 375° approximately 30 minutes.
- Remove cake from oven. Invert pan onto neck of bottle. Cool 1½ hours.

The flavor and texture of a perfect angel food cake.

FRESH COCONUT CAKE

Yield: 1 9-inch cake

Cake:

¾ cup shortening	½ teaspoon salt
1½ cups sugar	¾ cup milk
3 eggs	1¼ teaspoons vanilla
2¼ cups sifted cake flour	1 cup grated fresh coconut
2½ teaspoons baking powder	

- In large mixing bowl, cream shortening and sugar. Beat until light and fluffy.
- Add eggs one at a time, beating well after each addition.
- Combine flour, baking powder and salt.
- Add flour mixture to creamed mixture alternately with milk, beginning and ending with flour mixture.
- Stir in vanilla.
- Pour batter into 2 greased and floured 9-inch cake pans.
- Bake at 375° for 20-25 minutes or until a straw inserted in center comes out clean.
- Cool cake in pans 10 minutes. Remove from pans to wire rack and cool completely.
- Cut each layer in half horizontally, making 4 layers.
- Spread Custard Filling between layers. Frost with Snow Peak Frosting.
- Sprinkle with coconut. Keep refrigerated.

Custard Filling:

2 cups milk	3 tablespoons orange-flavored liqueur or 1 teaspoon orange flavoring
4 egg yolks	
½ cup sugar	
⅓ cup cornstarch	1 cup grated fresh coconut

- Combine milk, egg yolks, sugar and cornstarch in heavy saucepan. Stir with a wire whisk until well blended.
- Cook over medium heat until smooth and thickened, stirring constantly.
- Stir in liqueur or orange flavoring.
- Chill mixture thoroughly.
- When chilled, add coconut. Blend well.

Snow Peak Frosting:

1¼ cups light corn syrup	⅛ teaspoon salt
2 egg whites	1 teaspoon vanilla

(continued)

- Bring syrup to a boil.
- Combine egg whites and salt in large mixing bowl. Beat until soft peaks form.
- Continue beating and slowly add syrup.
- Add vanilla. Continue beating until stiff peaks form and frosting is thick enough to spread.

This cake is well worth the time and effort spent.
The cook will get rave reviews.

PRUNE CAKE

Yield: 1 10-inch cake

Cake:

3	eggs	1	teaspoon ground allspice
1	cup vegetable oil	1	teaspoon salt
1½	cups sugar	1	cup buttermilk
2	cups all-purpose flour	1	cup chopped prunes, cooked
1	teaspoon baking soda	1	teaspoon vanilla
1	teaspoon cinnamon	1	cup chopped nuts
1	teaspoon nutmeg		

- Beat eggs until thick.
- Add oil and sugar. Beat well.
- Sift together flour, baking soda, cinnamon, nutmeg, allspice and salt.
- Add flour mixture to egg mixture alternately with buttermilk.
- Fold in prunes, vanilla and nuts.
- Pour into greased 10-inch tube or Bundt pan.
- Bake at 350° for 1 hour or until cake pulls away from side of pan.
- Pour hot Buttermilk Icing over hot cake. Allow icing to soak into cake before removing from pan.

Buttermilk Icing:

1 cup firmly packed light brown sugar	½ teaspoon baking soda
	½ teaspoon vanilla
½ cup buttermilk	1 tablespoon light corn syrup
¼ cup butter	

- Combine all ingredients in saucepan. Bring to a boil.

This old-fashioned cake is even better if made 2 days before serving.

BANANA NUT CAKE

Yield: 1 9-inch cake

Cake:

½ cup shortening	½ teaspoon salt
1⅓ cups sugar	½ cup buttermilk
2 eggs	½ cup finely chopped pecans
2 cups all-purpose flour	1 teaspoon vanilla
1 teaspoon baking soda	1 cup mashed ripe bananas
1 teaspoon baking powder	

- Cream shortening and sugar.
- Add eggs to creamed mixture. Beat well.
- Sift together flour, baking soda, baking powder and salt.
- Add flour mixture to creamed mixture alternately with buttermilk. Beat well.
- Add pecans and vanilla. Blend well.
- Add bananas, mixing well.
- Pour into 2 greased and floured 9-inch cake pans. Bake at 350° for 20 minutes.
- When cool, split each layer in half.
- Fill and frost layers with Cream Cheese Icing.

Cream Cheese Icing:

1 8-ounce package cream cheese, softened	Milk as needed
½ cup butter, softened	1 teaspoon vanilla
1 16-ounce box powdered sugar	1 cup chopped pecans

- Cream together cream cheese and butter.
- Add powdered sugar, a small amount at a time. Beat well.
- Add milk as needed to make spreading consistency.
- Add vanilla.
- Fold in pecans.

▶ Today he had earned it. Long after the presentation, Larry Mize was still on the grounds of Augusta National, just as he had been the night before. This time, though, he was wearing the green jacket that Jack Nicklaus had put on him. His wife and son were with him, and winning the Masters® was no longer a childish dream but an indelible memory.

April, 1987

BARBARA NICKLAUS'S OATMEAL CAKE

Barbara Nicklaus
wife of Jack Nicklaus
6 time Masters® Champion
Yield: 1 9x13-inch cake

Cake:

1½ cups boiling water
1 cup quick oats
1 cup firmly packed light brown sugar
1 cup sugar
½ cup vegetable oil

2 eggs
1½ cups all-purpose flour
1 teaspoon cinnamon
1 teaspoon baking soda
½ teaspoon salt

• Pour boiling water over oats. Let stand.
• Cream sugars and oil.
• Add eggs one at a time, beating well after each addition.
• Combine flour, cinnamon, baking soda and salt. Add to creamed mixture.
• Add oat mixture. Mix well.
• Pour batter into greased 9x13-inch cake pan.
• Bake at 350° for 35 minutes.
• Prick top of cake with a fork. Pour Glaze over warm cake.

Glaze:

½ cup butter or margarine
1 cup firmly packed light brown sugar
½ cup milk

1 teaspoon vanilla
1 3½-ounce can shredded coconut

• Melt butter in saucepan over medium heat.
• Add sugar and milk.
• Cook until mixture reaches soft ball stage, stirring constantly.
• Remove from heat. Stir in vanilla and coconut.

This cake gets better as it ages.

GOOEY BUTTER CAKE

Mrs. Sarah Goalby
wife of Bob Goalby,
1968 Masters® Champion
Belleville, Illinois
Yield: 1 9x13-inch cake

1 box yellow cake mix	1 16-ounce box powdered sugar
1 cup butter, melted and divided	½ cup chopped pecans
3 eggs, divided	
1 8-ounce package cream cheese, softened	

- Combine cake mix, ½ cup butter and 1 egg. Beat well.
- Press into a 9x13-inch baking pan.
- Combine cream cheese, remaining 2 eggs, remaining ½ cup butter and powdered sugar. Blend until smooth.
- Spread cream cheese mixture over cake.
- Sprinkle with pecans.
- Bake at 350° for 35-45 minutes.
- Cool. Cut into squares.

"Belleville is known for its white asparagus, horseradish, Stag Beer in buckets and Gooey Butter Cake. I wanted to send you a Gooey Butter Cake from my favorite Belleville bakery, but I couldn't fit one into an envelope. Hope you enjoy baking your own!"
Sarah Goalby

▶ Seve Ballesteros has admitted to being troubled by homesickness when he plays the U.S. tour but he feels differently about Augusta.

"I feel very much at home there," he said after winning the 1980 Masters. "You can breathe the spring there. It is a good feeling. I like the flowers and the trees and the green color. It is a very special thing. Everything is green. It is very much like my home in the spring in the north of Spain."

When he was eleven years old, Seve heard about the Masters® for the first time. He heard about its tradition, its colorful environment and its golf course.

He has found the atmosphere and the gallery at the Masters® to be exceptional. "It makes you feel good when they clap for your shots. Winning the Masters® means the people will always remember you. Golf history will always include you for winning the Masters®. I like the people, I like the tournament and I feel very comfortable at Augusta.

Severiano Ballesteros 1980, 1983 Masters® Champion

LEMON CHIFFON CAKE

Yield: 1 10-inch cake

Cake:

2	cups sifted all-purpose flour	¾	cup cold water
1½	cups sugar	2	teaspoons vanilla
3	teaspoons baking powder	2	teaspoons grated lemon rind
1	teaspoon salt		or 1 teaspoon lemon extract
½	cup vegetable oil	1	cup egg whites (7-8)
7	egg yolks, unbeaten	½	teaspoon cream of tartar

- Sift together flour, sugar, baking powder and salt into mixing bowl.
- Make well in center. Add oil, egg yolks, water, vanilla and lemon rind, in that order.
- Beat with a spoon until smooth.
- Beat egg whites and cream of tartar until stiff, but not dry.
- Slowly pour egg yolk mixture over whites. Gently fold together with a spatula until just blended.
- Pour into ungreased 10-inch tube pan.
- Bake at 325° for 55 minutes. Increase temperature to 350°. Bake 10-15 minutes longer.
- When cake tests done with a straw, remove and invert over neck of bottle until completely cooled.
- Ice with Lemon Butter Icing.

Lemon Butter Icing:

4	cups sifted powdered sugar	1	teaspoon grated lemon rind,
½	cup butter, softened		optional
4	tablespoons fresh lemon juice		Dash salt
1	teaspoon vanilla		Yellow food coloring, optional
1	teaspoon lemon extract		

- Beat together powdered sugar and butter.
- Stir in lemon juice, vanilla, lemon extract, lemon rind if desired, and salt.
- If needed, add more powdered sugar to reach desired spreading consistency.
- Add food coloring if desired.

This is a light lemon cake for any special occasion.
The icing is smooth, creamy and unforgettable.

PIÑA COLADA CAKE

Yield: 1 9x13-inch cake

Cake:

1 18½-ounce package Duncan Hines Golden Butter cake mix
¼ cup vegetable oil
3 eggs
1 8-ounce carton sour cream
1 8½-ounce can cream of coconut

- Combine cake mix, oil, eggs, and sour cream. Mix well.
- Pour into greased and floured 9x13-inch cake pan.
- Bake at 350° for 35 minutes. Cool 10 minutes.
- Poke holes in top of cake with fork. Pour cream of coconut over cake.

Icing:

1 8-ounce package cream cheese, softened
2 tablespoons milk
1 16-ounce box powdered sugar
1 teaspoon vanilla
Coconut, shredded

- Beat together cream cheese and milk.
- Add powdered sugar, a small amount at a time. Beat well.
- Stir in vanilla.
- Ice cake.
- Sprinkle with Coconut.

This cake is best if made the day before serving

For many tournaments it is the weekends that bring out the crowds, but at the Masters® there are those who traditionally schedule their visits to the Augusta National to begin on Monday.

They walk with a favorite. They stake out a hole and sit. They are true golf fans. More than that, they're Masters® fans, and they are special.

They not only identify with the players, they appreciate the freshness of a springtime among tall pines and azaleas that form a perfect setting for a golf championship.

It is not only the thrill of golf shots that they remember. They relish the experience, the splendor and the atmosphere that can be found only at the Masters®.

FAT TUESDAY CAKE

Yield: 1 9-inch layer cake

Cake:

¾	cup butterscotch morsels	½	teaspoon baking powder
¼	cup water	¼	cup shortening
2¼	cups sifted all-purpose flour	1¼	cups sugar
1	teaspoon salt	3	eggs
1	teaspoon baking soda	1	cup buttermilk

- Combine butterscotch morsels and water in saucepan. Cook over low heat until melted. Cool.
- Sift together flour, salt, baking soda and baking powder. Set aside.
- In large mixing bowl, cream shortening. Slowly add sugar.
- Add eggs, one at a time, beating well after each addition.
- Add cooled butterscotch mixture.
- Using low speed of mixer, add dry ingredients alternately with buttermilk, beginning and ending with dry ingredients. Blend well after each addition.
- Pour batter into 2 greased and floured 9-inch cake pans.
- Bake at 375° for 25-30 minutes. Cool on wire rack.
- Spread Butterscotch Filling between layers and on top layer to within ½-inch of edge.
- Frost sides and top outer edge of cake with Sea Foam Frosting.

Butterscotch Filling:

½ cup sugar	1 egg yolk, beaten
1 tablespoon cornstarch	2 tablespoons butter
½ cup evaporated milk	1 cup shredded coconut
⅓ cup water	1 cup chopped pecans
¼ cup butterscotch morsels	

- Combine sugar and cornstarch in saucepan.
- Stir in milk, water, butterscotch morsels and egg yolk.
- Cook over medium heat, stirring constantly, until thickened.
- Remove from heat. Add butter, coconut and pecans. Cool.

Sea Foam Frosting:

⅓ cup sugar	1 tablespoon corn syrup
⅓ cup light brown sugar	1 egg white
⅓ cup water	¼ teaspoon cream of tartar

(continued)

- In saucepan, combine sugar, brown sugar, water and corn syrup.
- Cook until mixture reaches soft ball stage (236°).
- Meanwhile, beat egg white with cream of tartar until soft peaks form.
- Add hot syrup mixture to egg white in slow, steady stream, beating constantly until thick enough to spread.

Cake may be frosted with whipped cream instead of Sea Foam Frosting. This variation must be refrigerated.

CARROT CAKE

Craig Calvert
Calvert's and C-Grill
Augusta, Georgia
Yield: 1 9-inch cake

Cake:

2	cups plus 1 tablespoon all-purpose flour	1	teaspoon salt
2	cups sugar	1¼	cups vegetable oil
2	teaspoons baking powder	4	eggs
2	teaspoons cinnamon	2	teaspoons vanilla
1	teaspoon baking soda	2	cups grated carrots
		½	cup chopped pecans

- Sift together flour, sugar, baking powder, cinnamon, baking soda and salt into large bowl.
- Add oil. Beat 2 minutes, beginning at medium speed and increasing to high. Scrape bowl several times.
- Add eggs and vanilla. Beat 2 minutes.
- Fold in carrots and pecans.
- Pour into 2 9-inch round, greased and floured cake pans.
- Bake at 325° for 40-50 minutes, or until tester comes out clean.
- Ice cake and serve.

Icing:

2	3-ounce packages cream cheese, room temperature	½	teaspoon salt
3	tablespoons whipping cream	1	16-ounce box powdered sugar
1½	teaspoons vanilla	¾	cup chopped pecans
		½	cup coconut

- In small bowl, combine cream cheese, cream, vanilla and salt. Beat 5-7 minutes.
- Gradually add sugar, 1 cup at a time, blending well after each addition.
- Fold in pecans and coconut.

LUCILLE'S FRUITCAKE

Yield: 2 cakes or 5 loaves

½ pound crystallized pineapple, chopped
½ pound crystallized cherries, chopped
½ cup candied orange peel, chopped
½ cup candied lemon peel, chopped
2 pounds golden raisins

½ pound citron, chopped
1 cup whiskey
2 pounds pecans, chopped
6 cups all-purpose flour, divided
1 tablespoon baking powder
1 teaspoon salt
1 pound butter
3 cups sugar
6 eggs

- Place pineapple, cherries, orange peel, lemon peel, raisins and citron in large bowl.
- Pour enough boiling water over fruit to cover. Stir 20-30 seconds. Drain and return fruit to bowl. Pour whiskey over all. Let stand overnight.
- Add pecans and 3 cups flour.
- Combine remaining flour, baking powder and salt. Stir into fruit mixture.
- Cream butter and sugar until light and fluffy.
- Add eggs one at a time. Beat 30 seconds after each addition.
- Fold butter mixture into fruit mixture. (It takes a large bowl and strong hands!)
- Grease two 10-inch tube pans or five 9x5-inch loaf pans. Line bottom with waxed paper. Grease and flour paper.
- If using tube pans, fill with batter to within ¼-inch of rim. For loaf pans, fill ⅔ full.
- Bake at 275°. In tube pans bake for 2-2½ hours. In loaf pans bake for 1-1½ hours.
- Remove from oven. Cool 20-25 minutes.
- Remove from pan and peel off paper.
- When completely cool, wrap in plastic wrap and aluminum foil. Age in refrigerator at least 2 weeks.
- Cake may be wrapped in brandy-moistened cheesecloth. Add more brandy each week.

This truly is an old-fashioned fruit cake. Just like grandmother used to make.

WHISKEY CAKE

Yield: 2 loaves

1 cup butter	2 cups all-purpose flour
2 cups sugar	½ teaspoon baking soda
6 eggs, beaten	½ cup molasses
1 tablespoon baking powder	2 cups seedless raisins
½ teaspoon salt	4 cups chopped pecans
2 teaspoons nutmeg	⅔ cup bourbon
½ cup milk	

- Cream butter and sugar.
- Add eggs.
- Combine baking powder, salt and nutmeg. Reserve enough to dust raisins and pecans. Add remaining nutmeg mixture to creamed mixture.
- Add milk, then flour. Blend well.
- Stir baking soda into molasses. Add to batter.
- Dust raisins and nuts with reserved nutmeg mixture, then stir into batter.
- Add bourbon. Mix well.
- Pour into 2 greased and floured 9x5-inch loaf pans.
- Bake at 300° for 1½-2 hours.
- Cool in pans, then turn onto racks. When completely cool, wrap in plastic wrap and store in cool place indefinitely.

DECORATOR ICING

Yield: Icing for a 2-layer cake,
25-30 cupcakes, or
5-6 dozen cookies

1 egg white	1 teaspoon vanilla
¾ cup shortening	¼-½ cup water
2 16-ounce boxes 10-X powdered sugar	Food coloring, optional

- Beat egg white until frothy.
- Add shortening. Beat until mixture resembles cottage cheese.
- Slowly add powdered sugar and continue beating.
- Add vanilla. Slowly add water until icing reaches desired spreading consistency.
- Add food coloring, if desired
- Freezes beautifully.

LEMON SAUCE

Yield: 1½ cups

½ cup sugar
2 tablespoons cornstarch
⅛ teaspoon salt
1 cup water

2 teaspoons grated lemon rind
½ cup fresh lemon juice
1 tablespoon margarine

• Combine sugar, cornstarch, salt and water in small saucepan.
  Blend until smooth.
• Cook over medium heat, stirring constantly until smooth and thickened.
• Add lemon rind, lemon juice and margarine.
• Cook until thoroughly heated.
• Serve warm over pound cake, gingerbread or spice cake.

THE VERY BEST CARAMEL ICING

Yield: Icing for a 9x13-inch cake or a 2-layer cake

½ cup butter (no substitute)
1 16-ounce box light brown sugar
1 cup sugar

1 cup evaporated milk
1 teaspoon vanilla

• Melt butter over low heat.
• Add sugars and milk. Stir constantly until completely melted.
• Cook over medium heat until mixture reaches soft ball stage (234°-240°).
• Remove from heat.
• Add vanilla.
• Beat until icing reaches spreading consistency.

PUMPKIN CHIFFON PIE

Yield: 1 9-inch pie

⅔ cup sugar
1 envelope unflavored gelatin
½ teaspoon salt
1 teaspoon cinnamon
½ teaspoon nutmeg
3 eggs, separated
¾ cup milk

1 cup canned pumpkin
⅓ cup sugar
1 9-inch graham cracker
  pie crust, chilled
½ cup whipping cream, whipped
  and sweetened

- Combine sugar, gelatin, salt, cinnamon and nutmeg in saucepan.
- Beat egg yolks. Add to gelatin mixture. Blend well. Add milk. Stir.
- Cook over low heat, stirring constantly, until mixture thickens slightly.
- Stir in pumpkin.
- Chill until mixture mounds slightly when spooned.
- Beat egg whites until soft peaks form.
- Gradually add ⅓ cup sugar, beating to form stiff peaks.
- Fold in pumpkin mixture.
- Spoon mixture into crust.
- Refrigerate until firm.
- When serving, top each piece with whipped cream.

*Many people who do not care for traditional pumpkin pie are
surprised to find that they enjoy this lighter version.*

PINEAPPLE PIE

Yield: 2 9-inch pies

1 8-ounce can crushed pineapple
½ cup shredded coconut
½ cup butter or margarine, melted
2 teaspoons cornmeal
2 teaspoons all-purpose flour

2 teaspoons vanilla
2 cups sugar
4 eggs, beaten
2 9-inch pie crusts, unbaked

- Combine pineapple, coconut, butter, cornmeal, flour, vanilla, sugar and
  egg in mixing bowl. Blend well.
- Pour into pie crusts.
- Bake at 350° for 30-35 minutes, or until pies are set.

*These easy pies are delicious served hot or cold.
Keep one for your family and share one with a friend.*

SOUR CREAM APPLE PIE

Yield: 1 9-inch pie

2 tablespoons all-purpose flour	1 teaspoon vanilla
⅛ teaspoon salt	¼ teaspoon nutmeg
¾ cup sugar	2 cups tart apples, peeled
1 egg	and diced
1 cup sour cream	1 9-inch pie crust, unbaked

- Sift together flour, salt and sugar.
- Add egg, sour cream, vanilla and nutmeg.
- Beat until batter is smooth and thin.
- Fold in apples. Pour mixture into pie crust.
- Bake at 400° for 15 minutes.
- Reduce oven temperature to 350°. Continue baking 30 minutes.
- Remove from oven. Adjust oven temperature to 400°.
- Sprinkle with Topping. Bake 10 minutes or until browned.

Topping:

⅓ cup sugar	1 teaspoon cinnamon
⅓ cup all-purpose flour	¼ cup cold butter

- Combine sugar, flour and cinnamon.
- Cut in butter with pastry blender.

A scrumptious change from traditional apple pie.

In 1936, during a practice round for the third Masters® Tournament, Bob Jones did what no other man has ever done. Five full years had passed since his abrupt and unequivocal retirement from competitive golf, and Jones was comfortably ensconced in the role of Southern gentleman and genial Masters® host. But Jones was also Jones, the finest golfer of his time. And so it was on this day of April of 1936, that Bob Jones completed 18 holes at the Augusta National in 64 strokes, the lowest score the course had ever yielded...

BLUEBERRY CREAM PIE

Yield: 1 9-inch pie

Filling:

1 cup sour cream	1 egg, beaten
2 tablespoons all-purpose flour	1 pint fresh blueberries
¾ cup sugar	(approximately 2½ cups),
1 teaspoon vanilla	rinsed and stemmed
¼ teaspoon salt	1 9-inch pie crust, unbaked

• Combine sour cream, flour, sugar, vanilla, salt and egg in mixing bowl. Beat until smooth, about 3-4 minutes.
• Fold in blueberries. Pour mixture into pie crust.
• Bake at 400° for 25 minutes.
• Sprinkle Topping over pie.
• Bake an additional 10 minutes.
• Chill and serve.

Topping:

3 tablespoons all-purpose flour	3 tablespoons chopped pecans
3 tablespoons butter, softened	

• Combine flour and butter in mixing bowl with pastry blender.
• Add pecans. Mix well.

FRESH BLUEBERRY PIE

Yield: 1 9-inch pie

1 cup sugar	4 cups fresh blueberries, rinsed
3 tablespoons fresh lemon juice	and stemmed
2 teaspoons quick-cooking	1 9-inch double pie crust, unbaked
tapioca	2 tablespoons margarine

• Sprinkle sugar, lemon juice and tapioca over fresh blueberries. Let stand 15 minutes.
• Turn mixture into unbaked pie crust.
• Dot with margarine.
• Cover with remaining pie crust. Prick well with a fork.
• Bake at 450° for 10 minutes.
• Reduce heat to 350°. Continue baking 35-40 minutes or until top is golden brown.
• Let pie stand 15 minutes before serving.

The perfect ending to a summer supper.

DUTCH APPLE CRISP PIE

Yield: 1 9-inch deep-dish pie

1 9-inch deep-dish pie crust, unbaked

Filling:

½ cup sugar	2½ pounds tart apples, peeled,
2 tablespoons all-purpose flour	cored and thinly sliced
½ teaspoon nutmeg	(about 7 cups, sliced)
½ teaspoon cinnamon	2 tablespoons fresh lemon juice
	½ cup chopped pecans

• Combine sugar, flour, nutmeg and cinnamon.
• Toss sugar mixture with apples.
• Pour into pie crust. Sprinkle with lemon juice.
• Sprinkle Topping over apples.
• To prevent overflow in oven, place pie pan on cookie sheet.
• Bake at 350° for 35 minutes.
• Remove pie and sprinkle with pecans. Bake an additional 20 minutes.

Topping:

½ cup sugar	½ cup butter, softened
½ cup all-purpose flour	

• Combine sugar and flour. Cut in butter until mixture is crumbly.

Welcome fall with this fruit pie.

MANGE'S PEACH PIE

Yield: 6 servings

5-6 fresh ripe peaches,	1 cup sugar
peeled and sliced	¼ teaspoon salt
1 9-inch pie crust, unbaked	1 teaspoon cinnamon
3 tablespoons all-purpose flour	½ pint whipping cream

• Place peach slices in pie crust, covering bottom completely.
• Combine flour, sugar, salt and cinnamon. Sprinkle over peaches.
• Pour whipping cream over all.
• Bake at 400° for 10 minutes. Lower heat to 350° and bake 35 minutes or until peaches are tender.

An unforgettable flavor when Georgia peaches are used.

BRANDY ALEXANDER PIE

Yield: 1 9-inch pie

Chocolate Wafer Crust:
1 ¼ cups chocolate wafer crumbs   ⅓ cup butter, melted

• Combine wafer crumbs and melted butter. Blend well.
• Line 9-inch pie pan with mixture. Chill.

Filling:

½ cup cold water
1   envelope unflavored gelatin
⅔ cup sugar, divided
    Pinch salt
3   eggs, separated
¼ cup Cognac or other brandy

¼ cup Creme de Cacao
1   cup whipping cream, whipped
    and divided
1-2 tablespoons sugar, optional
    Chocolate curls to garnish

• In saucepan, pour cold water over gelatin.
• Add ⅓ cup sugar, salt and 3 egg yolks.
• Stir over low heat until gelatin dissolves and mixture begins to thicken.
  Do not boil.
• Remove from heat. Stir in Cognac and Creme de Cacao.
• Refrigerate until mixture begins to mound slightly.
• Beat 3 egg whites until soft peaks form.
• Gradually add remaining ⅓ cup sugar, beating until stiff.
• Fold egg white mixture into gelatin mixture.
• Fold in half of the whipped cream.
• Spoon mixture into chilled pie crust.
• Chill several hours.
• Sweeten remaining whipped cream with sugar, if desired.
• Top pie with whipped cream. Garnish with chocolate curls.

Fit for a king.

▶ It was a victory for dreamers, for dreamers who realize that anything is possible, as long as the dream is pursued with passion, with purpose, and most of all with hard work.
On Larry Mize's 1978 Masters® victory

MOCHA MERINGUE PIE

Yield: 1 9-inch pie

Meringue Crust:

3 egg whites, room temperature
½ teaspoon baking powder
¾ cup sugar
   Pinch salt

1 cup chocolate wafer crumbs
¾ cup chopped pecans
1 teaspoon vanilla

- Beat egg whites until frothy.
- Add baking powder, beating slightly.
- Gradually add sugar and salt. Continue beating until thick and glossy.
- Fold in cookie crumbs, pecans and vanilla.
- Spoon meringue into buttered 9-inch pie pan.
- Using back of a spoon, shape meringue up sides of pan.
- Bake at 350° for 30 minutes. Cool completely.

Filling:

1 quart coffee ice cream, softened
1 cup whipping cream
½ cup powdered sugar

Chocolate curls to garnish
Kahlúa, optional

- Spread ice cream evenly over crust.
- Cover with aluminum foil. Freeze overnight.
- Combine whipping cream and powdered sugar. Beat until light and fluffy.
- Spread over ice cream.
- Garnish with chocolate curls. Freeze.
- Let stand at room temperature 10 minutes before slicing.
- Pour 1 tablespoon Kahlúa over each serving, if desired.

Rich and sinful.

FROZEN MOCHA PIE

Yield: 1 9-inch pie

1¼ cups chocolate wafer crumbs
¼ cup sugar
¼ cup margarine, melted
1 8-ounce package cream cheese, softened
1 14-ounce can sweetened condensed milk

⅔ cup chocolate syrup
2 tablespoons instant coffee
1 teaspoon hot water
1 cup whipping cream, whipped
  Whipped cream to garnish

• Combine cookie crumbs, sugar and margarine. Press on bottom of a 9-inch springform pan or pie pan.
• Beat cream cheese until fluffy.
• Add milk and chocolate syrup. Blend well.
• Dissolve coffee in hot water. Add coffee to chocolate mixture.
• Fold in whipped cream.
• Pour into prepared crust. Freeze.
• When ready to serve, garnish with whipped cream.

FUDGE NUT PIE

Yield: 1 9-inch pie

Crust:
¼ cup margarine, softened
¼ cup sugar

1 tablespoon all-purpose flour
1 cup chopped pecans

• Blend together all ingredients.
• Line bottom and sides of 9-inch pie pan.
• Chill.

Filling:
½ cup margarine, melted
1 cup sugar
3 eggs
1 teaspoon vanilla
2 ounces unsweetened chocolate, melted

⅓ cup sifted all-purpose flour
½ teaspoon baking powder
⅛ teaspoon salt

• Combine all ingredients in medium bowl. Mix with spoon until smooth.
• Pour into prepared crust.
• Bake at 325° for 35-40 minutes. (Filling should look moist.)
• Serve warm or cool.

COCONUT PIE

Yield: 1 9-inch pie

6 tablespoons butter, melted
3 eggs, well beaten
1 cup sugar
1 teaspoon vanilla

¼ cup buttermilk
1 cup shredded coconut
1 9-inch pie crust, unbaked

• Combine butter, eggs, sugar, vanilla, buttermilk and coconut. Blend well.
• Pour mixture into pie crust.
• Bake at 350° for 35-40 minutes.

Easy and delicious!

PECAN-CHEESE PIE

Yield: 1 9-inch pie

1 9-inch pie crust, unbaked

Cheese layer:
1 8-ounce package cream
  cheese, softened
⅓ cup sugar
¼ teaspoon salt

1 teaspoon vanilla
1 egg
1½ cups chopped pecans

• Combine cream cheese, sugar, salt, vanilla and egg. Beat until smooth.
• Pour into crust.
• Sprinkle with pecans.

Custard:
¼ cup sugar
1 cup light corn syrup

1 teaspoon vanilla
3 eggs

• Combine sugar, corn syrup, vanilla and eggs.
• Pour over pecans.
• Bake at 375° for 35-40 minutes or until top is firm.
• Cool and refrigerate before serving.

The best of two old favorites – cheesecake and pecan pie.

PECAN PIE

Yield: 1 9-inch pie

Crust:

1½ cups all-purpose flour
½ teaspoon salt

½ cup shortening
3-6 tablespoons cold water

• Combine flour and salt.
• Cut in shortening until mixture resembles coarse corn meal.
• Add water, one tablespoon at a time until dough sticks together.
  Refrigerate 30 minutes.
• Roll dough on floured board to make a 9-inch pie crust.
• Place in pie pan.

Filling:

¾ cup plus 2 tablespoons light
  brown sugar
2 tablespoons all -purpose flour
1 tablespoon butter, softened
1 cup light corn syrup

3 eggs, beaten
¼ teaspoon salt
1 teaspoon vanilla
1 cup coarsely chopped pecans

• Combine sugar and flour. Add butter. Beat until creamy.
• Add syrup and eggs. Beat until frothy.
• Add salt and vanilla. Stir in pecans.
• Pour into pie crust.
• Bake at 325° for 45 minutes.

A Southern favorite.

▶ Art Wall birdied five of the last six holes in the 1959 final round. We are unable to find anything in the Record Books pertaining to major tournaments that equals this driving finish. It might be added that Art scored a total of eight birdies in that history-making final day of the Masters®.

At the end of fifty four holes, Wall was six shots back of Stan Leonard and Arnold Palmer who were tied for the lead. Art then won his first Masters® with a one-stroke margin by scoring a 66 which equals the closing round record established by Doug Ford in 1957.

1959 Masters®

WHIPPED CREAM PIE

Yield: 1 9-inch pie

1 8-ounce package cream cheese, softened
1 cup sugar
1 tablespoon fresh lemon juice
½ pint whipping cream, whipped
1 9-inch graham cracker pie crust
Fresh strawberries to garnish

• Combine cream cheese, sugar and lemon juice. Beat until smooth and creamy.
• Fold cheese mixture into whipped cream. Pour into pie crust.
• Refrigerate.
• Garnish with fresh strawberries.

A delicious pie served with any fresh fruit.

PEANUT BUTTER PIE

Chuck Baldwin
The French Market Grille
Augusta, Georgia
Yield: 12 servings

1 8-ounce package cream cheese, softened
2 cups powdered sugar
1 8-ounce container non-dairy whipped topping, thawed
12 ounces creamy peanut butter
2 tablespoons vanilla
2 9-inch graham cracker pie crusts
Whipped cream and lightly salted peanuts to garnish
Hot caramel sauce or hot chocolate sauce for topping

• Whip cream cheese 10 minutes.
• Add powdered sugar. Whip 10 minutes more.
• Blend in whipped topping, peanut butter and vanilla. Beat 5 minutes.
• Pour into pie crusts. Freeze at least 2 hours.
• Before serving, garnish with whipped cream and peanuts.
• For a special touch, top pie with hot caramel or chocolate sauce.

Enjoy this award-winning pie from the French Market Grille.

ORANGE ALASKA PIE

Yield: 1 9-inch pie

1 cup crushed rice cereal
7 tablespoons butter or
  margarine, melted
⅓ cup plus 6 tablespoons sugar,
  divided
⅓ cup shredded coconut

1 pint vanilla ice cream, softened
1 pint orange sherbet, softened
3 egg whites
¼ teaspoon cream of tartar
½ teaspoon vanilla

• Toast cereal at 350° for 10 minutes or until lightly browned.
• Combine butter and ⅓ cup sugar.
• Add cereal and coconut. Blend thoroughly.
• Press firmly on bottom and up sides of buttered 9-inch pie pan.
• Chill 45 minutes.
• Combine ice cream and sherbet.
• Pour into pie crust.
• Freeze until firm, 4-6 hours or overnight.
• Beat egg whites with cream of tartar and vanilla until soft peaks form.
• Gradually add remaining sugar.
• Continue beating until meringue is stiff and glossy and all sugar is
  dissolved.
• Spread meringue on top of frozen filling, sealing all edges.
• Bake pie at 475° for 1½-2 minutes, or until meringue is lightly browned.
• Serve at once or return to freezer.

*Freeze this pie until ready to serve, or prepare meringue quickly and serve
hot. Be versatile with the cold filling and use any favorite ice cream or
sherbet.*

When Jack Nicklaus turned professional, everyone knew he would be one of the greats. The only question was how great. Over the quarter-century between 1961 and 1986 he has answered that question beyond any doubt. Jack Nicklaus is the greatest champion golfer ever to play the game... Indeed, it's unlikely that any athlete has dominated any sport as long or as certainly as Jack Nicklaus has dominated the game of golf.

LEMON-CHEESE PIE

Yield: 1 9-inch pie

Ladyfinger Crust:

18 unfilled ladyfingers   ½ cup butter, melted

- Split ladyfingers and spread on cookie sheet.
- Bake at 225° for 15-20 minutes, or until dry.
- Remove from oven. Crumble.
- Blend crumbs with butter.
- Line a 9-inch pie pan with crumb mixture. Press down firmly.
- Chill until ready to fill.

Filling:

1 8-ounce package cream cheese, softened	½ cup sour cream
	1 teaspoon grated lemon rind
½ cup sugar	2 tablespoons fresh lemon juice
1 egg	½ teaspoon vanilla

- Beat cream cheese until smooth. Add sugar and beat until fluffy.
- Beat in egg, sour cream, lemon rind, lemon juice and vanilla.

Glaze:

½ cup sugar	1 teaspoon grated lemon rind
1½ tablespoons cornstarch	3 tablespoons fresh lemon juice
Pinch salt	1 tablespoon butter
½ cup water	½ teaspoon vanilla
2 egg yolks, beaten	

- Combine sugar, cornstarch and salt in saucepan.
- Whisk in water and egg yolks.
- Cook slowly until thickened.
- Boil 2 minutes. Remove from heat.
- Add lemon rind, lemon juice, butter and vanilla. Blend well.
- Allow mixture to cool.

Assembly:
- Pour Filling into Ladyfinger Crust.
- Bake at 375° for 20 minutes, or until set. Cool completely.
- Cover with Glaze.
- Chill until ready to serve.

A lemon lover's delight.

SURPRISE DELICIOUS

Yield: 1 9-inch pie

3 egg whites
½ teaspoon baking powder
¼ teaspoon salt
1 cup sugar
1 teaspoon vanilla

16 Ritz crackers, crushed
½ cup chopped pecans
½ pint whipping cream, whipped
½ a 1.65-ounce Hershey bar, grated

- Beat egg whites with baking powder and salt until soft peaks form.
- Add sugar, one tablespoon at a time, beating until stiff.
- Fold in vanilla, crackers and nuts.
- Spoon mixture into greased 9-inch pie pan.
- Bake at 325° for 30 minutes. Cool completely.
- Ice pie with whipped cream.
- Sprinkle with grated chocolate.
- Refrigerate overnight.

The name says it all!

SPICED CHERRIES

Mary Ann Baggs
Augusta, Georgia
Yield: 4 cups

1 16-ounce can pitted black cherries
1½ cups red wine
1 10-ounce jar red currant jelly
1 3-inch cinnamon stick

4 whole cloves
1 tablespoon cornstarch, optional
2 tablespoons brandy
1½ quarts vanilla ice cream

- Drain cherries, reserving juice.
- Combine cherry juice, wine, jelly, cinnamon stick and cloves in double boiler over simmering water.
- Cook until thickened and reduced to 2 cups. If too thin, add cornstarch.
- Remove cinnamon stick and cloves.
- Add cherries. Simmer 15 minutes longer. Cool.
- Add brandy.
- Cherries may be served hot over vanilla ice cream. If preferred, cherries may be served cold in individual bowls with whipped sour cream, topped with cinnamon sugar.

POACHED PEARS IN ORANGE SAUCE

Yield: 6 servings

6 large pears, ripe but firm	2 teaspoons cornstarch
2 tablespoons fresh lemon juice	¾ cup orange juice, divided
1½ cups sugar	1 cup red currant jelly
1 3-inch cinnamon stick	1-2 teaspoons sugar
1 3-inch vanilla bean	½ cup Cointreau
Zest of 2 oranges, cut into	2 tablespoons brandy
julienne strips	¼ teaspoon ground cinnamon

- Peel pears and core from bottom leaving stems intact. To prevent discoloring put pears in water to which lemon juice has been added.
- Combine 6 cups water, sugar, cinnamon stick and vanilla bean. Heat to boiling.
- Remove pears from lemon water and add to boiling mixture. Reduce heat.
- Cover and simmer until tender, about 25 minutes.
- Transfer pears to bowl. Pour liquid over pears and let cool.
- Blanch zest in boiling water 5 minutes.
- Drain and reserve zest.
- Combine cornstarch with 2 tablespoons orange juice. Set aside.
- Melt jelly. Add remaining orange juice and 1-2 teaspoons sugar. Heat to boiling. Continue cooking slowly until reduced to 1 cup, being careful not to caramelize mixture.
- Whisk in cornstarch mixture and stir until thickened, about 3 minutes.
- Reduce to low, stir in Cointreau and brandy. Simmer 2 minutes.
- Stir in ground cinnamon and orange zest.
- Cover and refrigerate. (May be prepared to this point early in the day.)
- To serve, pat pears dry, place in dish, and cover with sauce.

A sophisticated finale to an elegant dinner.

▶ 1966 will be remembered as the year when 17 players either held or shared the lead during the tournament. Nicklaus held the lead at the end of 18 holes and shared it at the end of 54. In all, Jack held or shared the lead much more than any other player and therefore it is fitting that he finally became the winner.

1966 Masters®

THE BOMBE

Yield: 8 servings

½ gallon vanilla ice cream,
  softened

¼ cup Amaretto

• Whip softened ice cream until firm but fluffy.
• Slowly beat in Amaretto.
• Pour into lightly greased 8-cup springform pan which has been chilled in freezer. Cover with foil tent and return to freezer immediately.
• Freeze at least 12 hours.
• 1-2 hours before serving, remove from springform pan. Place on serving plate and return to freezer.
• Transfer from freezer to refrigerator 30 minutes before serving.

Sauce:

1 29-ounce can yellow cling
    peaches, drained

¼ cup Amaretto

• Purée peaches in blender.
• Add Amaretto. Blend well.
• Drizzle 1 tablespoon sauce over each serving.

Variation: Line a springform pan with plain ladyfingers that have been sprinkled with Grand Marnier, and substitute Grand Marnier for Amaretto.

A LITTLE TOUCH OF HEAVEN

Yield: 10-12 servings

⅔ cup chopped almonds
6 tablespoons butter, melted
2 cups crushed vanilla wafers
2 teaspoons almond extract

3 pints vanilla ice cream, softened
1 10 to 20-ounce jar apricot
    preserves

• Combine almonds, butter, wafers and almond extract.
• Cover bottom of 8-inch square pan with half the crumb mixture.
• Cover with a layer of ice cream, and then a layer of preserves.
• Add another thin layer of crumbs, ice cream and preserves.
• Top with remaining crumbs.
• Freeze. Remove from freezer 15 minutes before serving. Cut into squares.

OLD ENGLISH CARAMEL APPLES

Dianne Zoeller
wife of Fuzzy Zoeller,
1979 Masters® Champion
Yield: 6 servings

½ cup sugar
½ cup firmly packed light
   brown sugar
1 tablespoon cornstarch
½ cup half and half

½ cup butter or margarine
¼ cup chopped pecans
½ teaspoon vanilla
3 medium apples, cored and
   cubed

- Combine sugars and cornstarch in medium saucepan.
- Gradually stir in half and half.
- Add butter and cook over medium heat, stirring constantly.
- Bring to a boil and boil 1 minute.
- Stir in pecans and vanilla.
- Cool 15 minutes.
- Place cubed apples in individual serving bowls.
- Pour ¼ cup sauce over each serving.

Easy – but so very delicious!

STRAWBERRY COUP

Yield: 8 servings

3 egg whites
¾ cup sugar
½ teaspoon cream of tartar

1 teaspoon vanilla, divided
1 pint whipping cream
3 cups sliced fresh strawberries

- Beat egg whites until stiff.
- Fold in sugar, cream of tartar and ½ teaspoon vanilla.
- Cover cookie sheet with brown paper.
- Drop by tablespoons onto paper.
- Place in 400° oven. Turn heat off.
- Leave meringues in oven 4 hours or overnight. Do not open door.
- When ready to serve, whip cream with remaining ½ teaspoon vanilla.
- Break meringues and mix with whipped cream and strawberries. Especially pretty served in stemmed glasses.

Bright red strawberries floating in luscious whipped cream – lovely.

SUMMER DELIGHT

Mary Ann Baggs
Augusta, Georgia
Yield: 6 servings

1 sponge cake, 8-inches round and 2-inches high	4 cups peeled, sliced fresh peaches
½ cup orange liqueur or Kirsch	4 cups fresh strawberries, thinly sliced
1 cup currant jelly, whipped	Whipped cream to garnish
2 cups whipping cream	
2 tablespoons sugar	

• Slice sponge cake into 4 layers, each ½-inch thick.
• Place 1 layer in bottom of glass serving bowl.
• Sprinkle cake with small amount of liqueur.
• Spread with ¼ cup whipped jelly.
• Whip cream with sugar.
• Arrange a layer of peaches on top of jelly, then a layer of strawberries, and a layer of whipped cream.
• Continue layering with cake, liqueur, jelly, fruit and whipped cream until all ingredients are used, ending with fruit.
• Using a pastry bag, garnish with additional whipped cream.

A fresh summer dessert which must be prepared the day it is to be served.

WINE JELLY

Yield: 6 servings

2 envelopes unflavored gelatin	1½ cups dry sherry
½ cup cold water	1 tablespoon fresh lemon juice
1½ cups boiling water	½ pint whipping cream, whipped, to garnish
1½ cups sugar	

• Soak gelatin in cold water.
• Add boiling water, sugar, sherry and lemon juice. Blend until sugar is dissolved.
• Pour into individual molds or 9-inch square baking dish.
• Refrigerate until set.
• Serve with whipped cream.

An old-fashioned dessert. For a taste of something sweet, but light–
what a delight!

SAVANNAH TRIFLE

Yield: 12-14 servings

6 cups milk	6 almond macaroons
1½ cups sugar	2 cups whipping cream, whipped
2 tablespoons cornstarch	Maraschino cherries and
6 eggs	toasted almonds to garnish
¾ cup cream sherry, divided	
2 5-ounce packages unfilled ladyfingers	

- Scald milk in double boiler.
- Combine sugar, cornstarch and eggs. Beat well.
- Stir a small amount of hot milk into egg mixture. Return egg mixture to remaining hot milk in double boiler and cook, stirring constantly, until custard thickens and coats a metal spoon.
- Cool completely.
- Stir ½ cup sherry into custard.
- Place one half the split ladyfingers in 5-quart serving bowl with 3 crumbled macaroons.
- Sprinkle 2 tablespoons sherry over ladyfingers and let stand 1 minute.
- Pour ½ the custard over ladyfingers.
- Spread ½ the whipped cream over custard layer.
- Repeat layers.
- Garnish top with cherries and toasted almonds.
- Refrigerate.

A favorite Southern recipe.

The golfer (Jack Burke, Jr.) who won the 1956 Masters® is one of the best liked members of his profession. Ever since his first appearance here in 1950 he has been a favorite with his fellow competitors, the spectators and our Club members. A player possessing so much character and such a fine swing just had to win one of the big ones and we are happy the event took place at the Augusta National.

1956 Masters®

FRENCH FRUIT TART

Yield: 8 servings

Tart Pastry:

1 ½ cups all-purpose flour
    Pinch salt
½ cup powdered sugar

½ cup butter, cold
1 egg yolk

- In food processor with steel knife, sift flour, salt and sugar together with quick pulses.
- Add butter in pieces and process to cut into mixture.
- Add egg yolk and process until mixture holds together when pressed between fingers.
- Press dough into 11- or 12-inch false-bottom tart pan.
- Place in freezer 5 minutes before baking.
- Bake at 400° for 15-20 minutes. Cool.

Filling:

3 ounces cream cheese, softened
1 cup whipping cream
¼ cup powdered sugar
½ teaspoon grated lemon peel

1 teaspoon fresh lemon juice
¼ teaspoon almond extract
¼ teaspoon vanilla

- Beat all filling ingredients until smooth.

Glaze:

1 cup apricot preserves or red
    currant jelly, according to color
    of fruit

1 tablespoon water

- Heat preserves or jelly with water in a small saucepan over low heat until dissolved. (1 tablespoon Grand Marnier, or liqueur appropriate for fruit, may be substituted for water when making glaze.)
- Strain if using preserves.

Fresh fruit:
Any combination of strawberries, raspberries, plums, apricots, blueberries, blackberries, kiwi, peaches or oranges.

Assembly:
- Spread Filling on Pastry.
- Decorate top with Fresh Fruit and cover with Glaze.
- Refrigerate until ready to serve.

An elegant ending to a summer meal.

BANANA NUT TORTE

Yield: 1 10-inch cake

1 cup sugar	2 teaspoons vanilla, divided
1 teaspoon baking powder	2-3 ripe bananas
3 egg whites, room temperature	1 cup whipping cream
12 saltines, finely crushed	2 tablespoons powdered sugar
1 ¼ cups chopped walnuts or pecans, divided	

- Sift sugar with baking powder.
- Beat egg whites until soft peaks form.
- Add sugar mixture to egg whites, 2 tablespoons at a time, beating constantly.
- Fold in crackers, ¾ cup nuts and 1 teaspoon vanilla.
- Spread in buttered 10-inch pan.
- Bake at 350° for 20-25 minutes.
- Leave in oven to cool. Remove from pan.
- Slice bananas on top of cake.
- Whip cream, adding powdered sugar and 1 teaspoon vanilla.
- Spread on top, covering bananas completely.
- Sprinkle with ½ cup nuts.
- Refrigerate until ready to serve

KAHLÚA CRÈME CARAMEL

Yield: 6 servings

¾ cup sugar	5 eggs, slightly beaten
2 cups milk	¼ cup Kahlúa
⅓ cup sugar	2 teaspoons vanilla

- Stir sugar in heavy skillet over medium heat until caramelized. Immediately divide among six 8-ounce ramekins, swirling to coat sides slightly.
- In double boiler, simmer milk and sugar until sugar is dissolved.
- Stir together eggs, Kahlúa and vanilla.
- Stir about ½ cup hot milk into egg mixture to warm, then whisk egg mixture into hot milk. (This prevents eggs from cooking.)
- Pour into ramekins.
- Bake at 350° for 30 minutes or until set in center.
- Cool before refrigerating.

This is a delicious and light dessert after a heavy meal.

COEUR à la CRÈME

(Cream Cheese Heart)
Yield: 8 servings

Heart:

1 8-ounce package cream cheese
½ cup powdered sugar
   Pinch salt

1 tablespoon vanilla
1 pint whipping cream

• Beat cream cheese until light and fluffy.
• Slowly add sugar, salt and vanilla.
• Beat whipping cream until it holds its shape.
• Using a whisk, gently combine whipped cream and cream cheese mixture.
• Line a heart-shaped Coeur à la Crème mold with a double thickness of
  damp cheesecloth, extending it 1½-inches beyond rim.
• Fill mold with cheese mixture. Cover carefully with cloth. Refrigerate on
  racks over a jelly-roll pan 6 hours or overnight.
• Carefully unmold onto serving platter. Surround mold with Berry Sauce.
  Garnish with fresh fruit.

Berry Sauce:

¼ cup dry sherry
¾ cup red currant jelly

1½ cups sliced, fresh strawberries
     or raspberries
1   tablespoon fresh lemon juice

• Combine sherry and jelly in saucepan. Cook over low heat until jelly is
  melted. Cool.
• Before serving, toss sliced strawberries or raspberries with lemon juice.
• Add fruit to cooled sherry mixture.
• Serve warm with Cream Cheese Heart.

Makes a beautiful presentation on Valentine's Day and throughout the year.

CHARLOTTE RUSSE

Yield: 6-8 servings

1	envelope unflavored gelatin	¼	cup sherry
¼	cup cold water	2	5-ounce packages unfilled
2	eggs, separated		ladyfingers
1¼	cups milk		Whole maraschino cherries to
½	cup plus 2 tablespoons sugar		garnish
½	pint whipping cream, whipped		

• Combine gelatin and cold water. Let stand 10 minutes.
• Beat egg yolks until frothy.
• Heat milk. Slowly add warm milk to egg yolks, stirring constantly.
• Add sugar. Blend well.
• Cook mixture over medium-low heat, stirring constantly, until custard coats a spoon. (If mixture begins to curdle, remove from heat and beat until smooth.)
• Stir in gelatin mixture. Refrigerate until thickened.
• Beat egg whites until stiff. Fold egg whites into cooled custard.
• Fold in whipped cream.
• Add sherry. Blend well.
• In large serving bowl, layer ladyfingers and custard mixture. (1 10-inch angel food cake sliced into rectangular pieces may be substituted for ladyfingers.)
• Garnish with whole cherries.

This is even better served the next day.

▶ Monday's final round started with Jack Nicklaus 8 strokes back of the leader. He then proceeded to thrill the galleries by demonstrating his great golfing prowess by making birdies on eight holes and ending the tournament tied with Oosterhuis and Jim Jamieson for third place and within 2 strokes of the winner. Top honors of course belong to Tommy Aaron, the winner by 1 stroke. Never had we witnessed better shot-making ability under such intense pressure.

1973 Masters®

RASPBERRY SOUFFLÉ

Yield: 10-12 servings

1 envelope unflavored gelatin	¾ cup sugar
2 tablespoons cold water	1 cup egg whites
1 10½-ounce package frozen raspberries, thawed	(approximately 7-8)
	1 cup whipping cream, whipped

- Prepare waxed paper collar for 1-quart soufflé dish. Brush inside of collar with vegetable oil.
- In medium stainless steel saucepan, soften gelatin in water.
- Purée raspberries and strain.
- Add puréed raspberries and sugar to gelatin. Heat, stirring until gelatin is dissolved.
- Transfer to large bowl. Chill until cool, but not set.
- Beat egg whites until stiff. Fold into raspberry mixture.
- Fold in whipped cream.
- Gently spoon into soufflé dish.
- Refrigerate overnight.
- Pour Raspberry-Framboise Sauce over soufflé.

Raspberry-Framboise Sauce:

1 10½-ounce package frozen raspberries, thawed	2 tablespoons Framboise (raspberry liqueur)
¼ cup sugar	

- Purée raspberries and strain.
- Combine raspberries with sugar and Framboise.

This is a beautiful, delicious, light dessert!

▶ Eleven years after his last Masters® victory and 23 years after his first, Jack Nicklaus once again played the brand of championship golf only he can play. In this most remarkable of Masters®, this most remarkable of Champions once again rose to the top. At age 45, Jack Nicklaus—the man whose time they said had passed—passed them all.

April, 1986

SNOWY EGGS

Yield: 4 servings

2 cups milk
3 eggs, separated
½ cup sugar, divided

⅛ teaspoon salt
1 teaspoon vanilla or ½ teaspoon
   grated lemon rind

- Scald milk in double boiler over simmering water.
- Remove milk from heat. Slowly stir in slightly beaten egg yolks, ¼ cup sugar, and salt.
- Place over water. Stir constantly until mixture begins to thicken.
- Remove from water. Beat mixture as it cools to release steam.
- Add vanilla or lemon rind.
- Pour into a 9x9-inch square baking dish. Chill.
- Beat egg whites until stiff. Gradually add remaining ¼ cup sugar.
- Drop generous tablespoons of meringue onto cooled custard.
- Preheat oven to broil.
- Place custard filled dish in a pan of ice water.
- Put in hot oven. Heat until tips of meringue are browned. (Watch carefully during browning process. Custard must not get warm.)
- Served chilled.

An adaptation of a classic French dessert.

▶ "We love ya, Larry," someone in the gallery called as Larry Mize made his way to the first tee, surrounded by a swarm of fans wearing buttons that read "Mize's Missiles" or "Mize's Misses." The boyish Mize, a native of Augusta, beamed politely. He would be teeing off as the sentimental favorite in his fourth Masters®, and with several of the most talented golfers in the world playing behind him, he welcomed all the support he could get.

This Masters® was already one for Mize to savor. The night before, as the last stragglers were leaving the course, he had lingered near the verandah with his wife, Bonnie, and his year-old son, David, in his arms. What had begun as a boy's fantasy was now tantalizingly close to fulfillment. As a teenager, Mize had worked on the Masters® leaderboards, and his ambition had always been to win here. He'd idolized the great golfers who had scored their triumphs on the Augusta National course that was now quiet and banked in long shadows. Tomorrow, maybe, he would earn the right to be ranked as one of them.

April, 1987

CRANBERRY CHARLOTTE

Yield: 10-12 servings

2¼ cups sugar, divided	1 tablespoon grated lemon rind
2½ cups water, divided	¼ teaspoon salt
1 pound fresh cranberries	18 unfilled lady fingers, split
2 envelopes unflavored gelatin	3 egg whites
1 tablespoon fresh lemon juice	2 cups whipping cream, whipped

• Boil 2 cups sugar with 2 cups water for 5 minutes.
• Add cranberries and cook until skins burst.
• Set aside 1 cup cranberry mixture for garnishing. Purée remaining cranberry mixture in blender or food processor.
• Soften gelatin in remaining ½ cup water in saucepan.
• Add puréed mixture. Heat until gelatin is dissolved, stirring constantly.
• Add lemon juice, rind and salt.
• Chill until mixture begins to set.
• Line sides and bottom of 9-inch springform pan with split ladyfingers.
• Beat egg whites with remaining sugar until stiff.
• Add whipped cream to chilled mixture, then fold in egg whites.
• Spoon into springform pan.
• Chill. Garnish with reserved 1 cup cranberry mixture.

A classic finish to a holiday meal.

▶ Arnold Palmer led the field at the end of each day of play on all four days of the 1960 Tournament. He is the only player to have done so excepting Craig Wood who was an every-day leader in 1941.

Arnold's finish was most dramatic. With two holes to go, he was one stroke down to Ken Venturi who had finished ahead of him. Aided by a 35 foot birdie putt at the seventeenth, Arnold planted his second shot on the home hole within six feet of the pin and holed that one too. He is the sixth two-time winner of the Masters® and we at this club are delighted that this popular and capable player has attained his distinction along with Smith, Nelson, Demaret, Snead and Hogan.

1960 Masters®

COLD LEMON SOUFFLÉ

Martha Fleming
Augusta, Georgia
Yield: 12-16 servings

3	envelopes unflavored gelatin	¾-1	cup freshly squeezed lemon juice
1	cup cold water		
6	eggs, divided		Grated rind of 3-4 lemons
2	cups sugar	3	cups whipping cream
2	teaspoons vanilla		Whipped cream and fresh strawberries to garnish

• Prepare 8-cup soufflé dish with collar of waxed paper. Lightly grease waxed paper.
• Sprinkle gelatin over cold water in saucepan. Melt over low heat.
• Beat egg yolks until frothy. Add sugar and vanilla.
• Combine gelatin mixture with egg yolk mixture. Add lemon juice and lemon rind. Refrigerate.
• Whip cream until it will fold (not until stiff). Refrigerate.
• Beat egg whites until stiff.
• Fold whipped cream into gelatin mixture.
• Fold in egg whites.
• Ladle mixture into soufflé dish. Refrigerate at least 2 hours or overnight.
• When ready to serve, garnish with additional whipped cream and fresh strawberries.

This is outstanding – light, refreshing, and impressive!

▶ Perhaps most important, however, is the record he established this year. At age 46, precisely twice as old as he was when he became the youngest Masters® Champion, Jack Nicklaus became the oldest Masters® Champion.

Twenty years ago, when Jack won his third Masters®, Bob Jones was moved to observe, "He plays a game with which I'm not familiar." But during the last few seasons, Jack himself had lost touch with that game.

"I'm looking for that guy I used to know on the golf course," he said at the beginning of this week.

At the end of the week, his search was over, "I found him," he told his wife, Barbara. "It was me."

April, 1986

STEAMED ORANGE MARMALADE PUDDING

Amelia Cartledge
Augusta, Georgia
Yield: 8-10 servings

1 16-ounce loaf French bread	½ cup sugar
2 cups finely ground suet	2 cups orange marmalade
2 tablespoons grated orange rind	1 teaspoon baking soda
⅔ cup orange juice	3 eggs, slightly beaten

• Trim crusts from bread and discard. Grate or process bread to make 5 cups fine crumbs.
• Combine crumbs with suet. Set aside.
• In saucepan, cook orange rind, orange juice, sugar and marmalade over medium heat 15 minutes.
• Pour liquid over crumb-suet mixture. Blend well.
• Combine baking soda and eggs. Fold into pudding mixture.
• Pour into well greased 2-quart melon mold. Cover tightly with foil.
• Place on rack in steamer. Steam 3½ hours.
• Loosen edges with spatula. Unmold onto platter.
• Serve hot with Golden Sauce.

Golden Sauce:

2 eggs, separated	2 teaspoons vanilla
1 cup sugar, divided	2 tablespoons Grand Marnier,
1 cup whipping cream	optional

• Beat egg yolks. Gradually add ½ cup sugar. Set aside.
• Beat egg whites until foamy. Gradually beat in remaining ½ cup sugar until stiff peaks form.
• Fold whites into yolks.
• Whip cream, adding vanilla and Grand Marnier, if desired.
• Fold into egg mixture.
• Chill.

The most elegant holiday dessert imaginable.

UNCLE ROBERT'S BREAD PUDDING

Yield: 10-12 servings

4 cups milk
2 cups sugar
½ cup butter, melted
3 eggs
2 tablespoons vanilla
1 10-16-ounce loaf stale French
   bread, broken into bite-size
   pieces (6-8 cups)

1 cup raisins
1 cup shredded coconut
1 cup chopped pecans
1 teaspoon cinnamon
½ teaspoon nutmeg

• Beat together milk, sugar, butter, eggs and vanilla.
• Mix in bread, raisins, coconut, pecans, cinnamon and nutmeg.
• Pour into buttered 3-quart baking dish.
• Bake at 350° for 1 hour and 15 minutes or until top is golden brown.
• Serve warm with Rum Sauce.

Rum Sauce:
Yield: 1½ cups
½ cup butter
1½ cups powdered sugar

1 egg yolk
½ cup rum

• In saucepan, heat butter and sugar over medium heat until all butter is
  absorbed. Remove from heat.
• Blend in egg yolk.
• Slowly add rum, stirring constantly. (It will thicken as it cools.)

For added flavor, soak raisins in rum or bourbon.

SWEETIE'S BREAD PUDDING

Yield: 6-8 servings

1 cup light brown sugar
4 slices raisin bread, well buttered
   and cubed

2 cups milk
2 eggs, beaten
1 teaspoon vanilla

• In double boiler, layer sugar, then bread. Do not stir.
• Combine milk, eggs and vanilla. Blend well.
• Pour over bread. Do not stir.
• Cook over simmering water 2-3 hours.
• To serve, ladle sauce from bottom of pan over each serving.

GREENBRIER BREAD PUDDING

The Greenbrier Hotel
White Sulphur Springs,
West Virginia
Yield: 8-10 servings

¼ loaf white bread	1 cup sugar
½ cup butter, melted	Vanilla to taste
6 eggs	1 cup raisins
1 quart milk	

• Cut bread into 1-inch cubes. Toast lightly in hot oven.
• Place bread in baking dish. Drizzle with butter.
• Beat together eggs, milk, sugar and vanilla. Stir in raisins. Pour over bread. Allow to soak for 5 minutes, pushing down with a spatula so that bread will absorb liquid.
• Bake at 350° until custard is firm, approximately 45 minutes.
• Serve with Vanilla Sauce.

Vanilla Sauce:
Yield: 1 quart

2 cups whipping cream	1 tablespoon vanilla
½ cup sugar	¼ teaspoon salt
4 egg yolks	2 scoops vanilla ice cream
1 tablespoon all-purpose flour	

• Heat cream and sugar to boiling in 2-quart saucepan. Remove from heat.
• Beat together egg yolks, flour, vanilla and salt.
• Stir a small amount of hot cream into egg mixture. Mix and return to remaining cream.
• Cook, stirring constantly, until just thickened. Remove from heat.
• Add ice cream. Stir until melted.
• Serve hot or cold.

ECLAIRS

Yield: 24

Pastry:

1 cup water

½ cup butter or margarine

1 cup all-purpose flour

4 eggs, beaten

- Bring water and butter to a full rolling boil.
- Add flour. Stir vigorously over low heat about 1 minute or until mixture forms a ball.
- Remove from heat. Add beaten eggs, one at a time. Continue beating until smooth.
- Drop dough from ¼ cup measure onto ungreased baking sheet.
- Bake at 400° for 35-40 minutes.
- After baking pastry, set aside to cool. (The pastry may be frozen, but should not be filled until just before serving.)
- With serrated knife, cut off tops of pastry.
- Gently remove soft pastry from inside.
- Fill pastry with Filling. Replace tops and drizzle with Icing.

Filling:

1 3½-ounce package instant French Vanilla pudding mix

1¼ cups milk

6 ounces non-dairy whipped topping

- Combine pudding mix with milk. Blend until smooth. Chill until partially set.
- Fold in whipped topping.

Icing:

2 ounces unsweetened chocolate

2 teaspoons butter or margarine

2 cups powdered sugar

4 tablespoons hot water

- Combine chocolate and butter in saucepan. Heat until melted.
- Remove from heat. Blend in powdered sugar. Add hot water.
- Beat until smooth.

Delectable!

PRALINE COOKIE CUPS WITH RASPBERRY SAUCE

Yield: 24-30 cups

Cups:

1 cup all-purpose flour
1 cup finely chopped pecans
¼ cup butter
¼ cup shortening
½ cup light corn syrup

⅔ cup firmly packed light brown sugar
2 oranges to form cups
Vanilla ice cream
Fresh strawberries, sliced

• Combine flour and pecans.
• In heavy saucepan, melt butter and shortening.
• Add syrup and sugar. Bring to a boil.
• Remove from heat. Add flour mixture and blend well.
• Drop by heaping tablespoons onto greased cookie sheet, allowing only 2 cookies for each sheet.
• Bake at 325° for 8-10 minutes.
• Cool 1 minute, then remove with spatula and place over orange to form cup.
• Allow to cool and harden.
• Cups may be made in advance and stored in zip-lock freezer bags. Cups are delicate.
• To serve, fill praline cups with ice cream and strawberries. Top with Raspberry Sauce.

Raspberry Sauce:

2 10-ounce packages frozen raspberries, thawed
1 tablespoon cornstarch

2 tablespoons fresh lemon juice
2 tablespoons Kirsch

• In blender, purée raspberries.
• Press mixture through a sieve into saucepan.
• Combine cornstarch and lemon juice. Add to raspberry mixture.
• Bring to a boil and cook until slightly thickened.
• Add Kirsch.
• Chill before serving. (Sauce may be stored in refrigerator.)

FROZEN CHOCOLATE ELEGANCE

Yield: 10 servings

8 ounces semi-sweet chocolate	½ teaspoon vanilla
½ cup butter	4 extra large eggs, separated
½ cup plus 2 tablespoons powdered sugar, divided	Pinch salt
	Whipped cream to garnish

- Melt chocolate in double boiler. Cool to room temperature.
- Cream butter. Add ½ cup sugar, 2 tablespoons at a time, beating well after each addition.
- Add vanilla.
- Beat egg yolks. Add chocolate.
- Beat egg whites until foamy. Beat in remaining 2 tablespoons sugar and salt until stiff peaks form.
- Fold egg whites into chocolate mixture.
- Pour into buttered 9x5-inch loaf pan. Freeze.
- Unmold and ice with Glaze. Return to freezer.
- When ready to serve, slice into ½-inch slices.
- Garnish with whipped cream. For a special touch, serve with our RASPBERRY SAUCE.

Glaze:

3 ounces semi-sweet chocolate	2 tablespoons coffee
2 tablespoons powdered sugar	2 tablespoons butter

- Combine all ingredients in medium saucepan, stirring until melted.

A chocoholic's delight.

▶ Tying the record for the second nine of Augusta National, Nicklaus roared past his formidable young rivals with a spectacular exhibition of shotmaking, putting, and absolute courage. His six-under-par performance on the incoming nine—seven under on the last ten—brought Jack a record sixth green jacket and the 20th major championship he had sought for so many years.

Nicklaus later called it "probably the finest golf of my career."

April, 1986

ROBIN K'S CHOCOLATE MOUSSE

Yield: 30 servings

18 ounces semi-sweet chocolate
2 cups whipping cream
6 eggs, divided
2 tablespoons powdered sugar

2 tablespoons liqueur (Creme de Cacao or Cointreau), optional
1 tablespoon vanilla
Chocolate leaves to garnish

• Melt chocolate. Cool to room temperature.
• Whip cream until medium-stiff.
• Separate 4 eggs. Set whites aside.
• Combine the 4 egg yolks with remaining 2 eggs.
• Beat until thick and lemon colored.
• Beat whites. Add powdered sugar. Beat until soft peaks form.
• Add chocolate to beaten egg yolks.
• Add cream to chocolate mixture.
• Fold in liqueur, if desired, and vanilla.
• Fold in egg whites. This doubles easily, and freezes beautifully. Take out 1 day before serving and refrigerate.
• Garnish with chocolate leaves. Serve with Pirouette cookies.

Served in a trifle dish, this dessert makes a gorgeous addition to a party table.

WORLD'S BEST CHOCOLATE MOUSSE

Yield: 12 servings

2 5-ounce packages unfilled ladyfingers
1 pound German sweet chocolate
½ cup plus 2 tablespoons water
8 eggs, separated

1 cup sugar
Pinch salt
2 teaspoons vanilla
½ pint whipping cream
Shaved chocolate to garnish

• Butter bottom and sides of 10-inch springform pan. Line pan with ladyfingers, breaking some to seal bottom.
• Melt chocolate with water in double boiler.
• Beat egg whites until stiff and shiny. Set aside.
• Beat egg yolks and sugar until light and creamy. Add salt, vanilla and chocolate mixture.
• Fold in egg whites.
• Pour mixture into pan. Refrigerate 24 hours.
• Before serving, top with whipped cream.
• Garnish with shaved chocolate.

RUM MOUSSE WITH SWISS CHOCOLATE SAUCE

Mary Ann Baggs
Augusta, Georgia
Yield: 8 servings

¾ cup sugar
½ cup water
6 egg yolks
½ cup rum

1 tablespoon orange juice
Grated rind of 1 orange
2 cups whipping cream, whipped

• Boil sugar and water until sugar is dissolved. Boil 5 minutes longer. Cool.
• Place sugar mixture in double boiler over simmering water.
• Add egg yolks and rum. Stir constantly until mixture coats a spoon.
• Remove from heat and beat until cold. (If time is short, beat over a bowl of ice.)
• Beat in orange juice and rind.
• Fold in whipped cream.
• Pour into a rinsed mold and freeze at least 4 hours.
• Unmold and serve with warm Swiss Chocolate Sauce.

Swiss Chocolate Sauce:

2 triangular bars Toblerone
   Chocolate

½ cup whipping cream
1 tablespoon rum

• Melt chocolate in double boiler.
• Beat in cream until sauce is light and creamy.
• Flavor with rum.

▶ My New Year's wish is that I may become the first triple winner of the Masters®. I also wish every lover of the game of golf might have the privilege of either playing or seeing this tournament.

From a BYRON NELSON letter
Written January 1, 1946

CHOCOLATE FRENCH SILK WEDGES

Yield: 12 servings

Macadamia Nut Crust:

1   cup vanilla wafer crumbs, (about 20 wafers) crushed

¾ cup finely chopped macadamia nuts

⅓ cup butter or margarine, melted

• In small bowl, combine crust ingredients. Mix well.
• Press firmly on bottom of 9-inch or 10-inch springform pan.
• Bake at 375° for 8-10 minutes. Cool.

Filling:

1¼ cups sugar

¾ cup butter or margarine, softened

3   eggs

3   ounces unsweetened chocolate, melted and cooled

1½ teaspoons vanilla
Sweetened whipped cream and chocolate shavings to garnish

• In medium bowl, combine sugar and butter. Beat until light and fluffy.
• Add eggs, one at a time, beating at medium speed at least 2 minutes after each addition.
• Blend in chocolate and vanilla. Mix well.
• Pour into crust.
• Refrigerate at least 4 hours before serving.
• When ready to serve, loosen edges of pan and remove carefully.
• Cut into wedges. Garnish with whipped cream and chocolate shavings.

Best ever! Forget dieting and let temptation win!

A 66 on the final round, the lowest closing day score (up to 1957) in the history of the Masters® Tournament, brought Doug Ford the 1957 Championship.

1957 Masters®

CHOCOLATE MOUSSE CAKE

Yield: 12 servings

12 ounces chocolate wafers,
    crushed
½ cup butter, melted
16 ounces semi-sweet chocolate
    chips
2 eggs

4 eggs, separated
1 teaspoon vanilla
4 cups whipping cream, divided
10 tablespoons powdered sugar,
    divided
Chocolate curls to garnish

• Combine wafers and butter.
• Press on bottom and sides of greased springform pan. Chill.
• Melt chocolate chips in double boiler (or microwave).
• Add whole eggs. Mix well.
• Add yolks. Mix well.
• Add vanilla.
• Beat 2 cups cream until soft peaks form.
• Add 6 tablespoons powdered sugar and beat until stiff.
• Beat egg whites until stiff.
• Fold whipped cream and whites into chocolate mixture until well blended.
• Pour into crust. Chill overnight. (May be frozen at this point. The texture of this mousse is actually better when it is slightly frozen.)
• Whip remaining 2 cups cream and 4 tablespoons sugar until stiff.
• Loosen crust from sides of pan with knife.
• Top with sweetened whipped cream.
• Garnish with chocolate curls or chocolate leaves.

An unforgettable chocolate experience.

> In the glow of his 20th major victory, Nicklaus answered the question that was being asked in every corner of the world of golf.
> "I'm not quitting," he said. "Maybe I should say goodbye. Maybe that would be the smart thing to do. But I enjoy competition, I love golf, and I can still play a little, so I plan to keep on competing."
> It was exactly the answer the world of golf wanted.
> April, 1986

HEAVENLY CHEESECAKE

Yield: 1 10-inch cheesecake

Vanilla Wafer Crumb Crust:
2½ cups vanilla wafer crumbs   ½   cup butter, melted

• Stir together crumbs and butter until moist.
• Press mixture on bottom and ¾ of the way up the sides of a 10-inch springform pan.
• Refrigerate while preparing Filling.

Filling:
4   8-ounce packages cream   ⅛   teaspoon salt
     cheese, softened   1   tablespoon fresh lemon juice
1   pint sour cream   1   tablespoon vanilla
1½ cups sugar   1   tablespoon all-purpose flour
4   eggs

• Combine cream cheese and sour cream. Beat until smooth and creamy.
• In separate bowl, combine sugar and eggs. Beat well.
• Combine egg mixture and cream cheese mixture. Blend well.
• Add salt, lemon juice, vanilla and flour. Mix well.
• Pour mixture into crust.
• Bake at 350° for 55-65 minutes. (55 minutes makes a very creamy cake, 60-65 minutes makes cake slightly drier. Both are excellent.)
• Cool in pan at room temperature 3 hours.
• Refrigerate overnight before removing sides of pan.

This cheesecake is delicious plain or topped with seasonal fruit.

▶ A great player finally rendered a very great service to the Masters® Tournament by adding his name to its list of champions.
Ben Hogan had played enough good golf on the Augusta National course to win, with a little luck, several first prizes. Each year that he failed, the number of well-wishers grew until in 1951, one of the largest galleries ever to support an individual player brought Ben in the winner.

1951 Masters®

AVIS'S CHEESECAKE

Yield: 1 9-inch cheesecake

Graham Cracker Crumb Crust:

½ cup graham cracker crumbs   1 tablespoon sugar

- Generously butter a 9-inch springform pan.
- Combine crumbs and sugar. Shake mixture over sides and bottom. Gently shake out excess crumbs and reserve.

Filling:

5	8-ounce packages cream cheese, softened	3	tablespoons all-purpose flour
¼	teaspoon vanilla	¼	teaspoon salt
¾	teaspoon grated lemon peel	1	cup eggs (4-5)
1¾	cups sugar	2	egg yolks
		¼	cup whipping cream

- Beat cream cheese until smooth.
- Add vanilla and lemon peel.
- In separate bowl, combine sugar, flour and salt. Gradually blend into cheese mixture.
- Add eggs, 1 at a time, and egg yolks, beating well after each addition.
- Gently stir in whipping cream.
- Turn mixture into crust.
- Sprinkle with remaining crumbs.
- Bake at 450° for 12 minutes. Reduce heat to 300° and continue baking 55 minutes.
- Cool 1 hour, then remove sides of pan. Cool an additional 2 hours before cutting.

This is a creamy, New York-style cheesecake.

▶ Playing once again the brand of golf that had won him a record five Masters®, Jack Nicklaus won his sixth. Truly this was a golden moment for the man called the Golden Bear.

The fact that this superb athlete and competitor, Jack Nicklaus, reached back and summoned a spectacular victory, his 20th major championship, should be reason for celebration, not simply in Augusta, Georgia, but wherever the game of golf is played.

Hord Hardin, 1986

CHOCOLATE COVERED CHEESECAKE

Yield: 1 9-inch cheesecake

Crust:
1 ½ cups crushed chocolate wafers   ¼ cup butter, melted

• Combine wafer crumbs and butter.
• Line bottom and sides of a 9-inch springform pan with crumb mixture.

Filling:
3   8-ounce packages cream   4   eggs
    cheese, softened   ⅓   cup Kirsch or Kahlúa
1 ½ cups sugar

• Beat cream cheese until light and fluffy.
• Gradually add sugar, mixing well.
• Add eggs, one at a time, blending well after each addition.
• Stir in liqueur.
• Pour mixture into prepared pan.
• Bake at 350° for 1 hour.
• Cool completely at room temperature.

Topping:
4 1-ounce squares semi-sweet   Whipped cream and maraschino
   chocolate   cherries to garnish
½ cup sour cream

• In double boiler, melt chocolate over simmering water. Cool slightly.
• Stir in sour cream.
• Spread mixture on top of cooled cheesecake. Chill thoroughly.
• Before serving, remove sides of pan. Garnish with whipped cream and
  cherries.

If Green (Ken) adapted quickly to the treacherous Augusta greens, it was not through any help from his caddie. Green's 29-year-old sister, Shelley, is his fulltime bagtoter, and although she was by far the most attractive caddie in the Masters® field, in her brother's words, "She has no clue when it comes to golf. On the 13th hole today I asked her whether I should go for it on the second shot. She said 'No,' so I went for it." Green made four on that hole, one of his seven birdies for the day.

April, 1986

CHOCOLATE CHEESECAKE

Yield: 1 10-inch cheesecake

Crust:

2½ cups crushed chocolate   ½-⅔ cup butter, melted
     wafers

• Combine crushed wafers and enough melted butter to moisten crumbs.
• Press mixture on bottom and halfway up sides of a 10-inch springform
  pan.
• Refrigerate.

Cake:

1 12-ounce package chocolate   1 cup sugar
   chips   4 eggs
2 tablespoons strong coffee   2 tablespoons all-purpose flour
3 tablespoons Kahlúa   1 tablespoon vanilla
3 8-ounce packages cream   ½ cup whipping cream
   cheese, softened   Pinch salt

• Combine chocolate chips, coffee and Kahlúa in double boiler. Heat over
  simmering water until chocolate is melted. Set aside to cool.
• Combine cream cheese, sugar, eggs, flour, vanilla, cream and salt. Beat
  until smooth and creamy.
• Add chocolate mixture. Blend well.
• Pour into crust.
• Bake at 350° for 50-60 minutes.
• Let stand 2-3 hours at room temperature.
• Chill overnight.

▶   ...Number eleven takes its name from the white dogwood, Cornus Florida, a small
flowering tree native to the eastern United States. Only sixteen to 24 feet in height at
maturity. The white dogwood blooms in the springtime with an opulence out of pro-
portion to its size.

MARIE NEEL'S KAHLÚA CHEESECAKE

Yield: 1 9-inch cheesecake

Crust:
16 graham crackers, crushed   ½ cup butter, melted

• Combine cracker crumbs and melted butter. Line bottom and sides of 9-inch springform pan with crumb mixture.

Filling:
3   8-ounce packages cream   5   eggs
    cheese, softened   ¼   cup Kahlúa
1   pint sour cream   1½ teaspoons vanilla
1½ cups sugar

• Beat cream cheese until smooth.
• Add sour cream and blend well. Add sugar and blend well.
• Add eggs, one at a time, mixing well after each addition.
• Stir in Kahlúa and vanilla.
• Pour mixture into prepared pan.
• Bake at 325° for 1 hour.
• Turn oven off. With oven door cracked, allow cheesecake to cool in oven 1 hour.
• Refrigerate overnight.

A pinch of cinnamon added to the cracker crumbs enhances the flavor of the crust. A most versatile recipe, as any liqueur may be substituted for the Kahlúa.

▶ ...Zoeller stepped up and flashed his putt into the heart of the cup to become the first man to win the Masters® in sudden death and the only golfer of the modern era to win in his first Masters® appearance. (1979)

PRALINE CHEESECAKE

Yield: 12-16 servings

Crust:

1½ cups graham cracker crumbs   ¼ cup chopped pecans, toasted
¼ cup sugar   ¼ cup butter, melted

- Combine crumbs, sugar and chopped pecans.
- Stir in butter.
- Press mixture on bottom and 1½-inches up sides of a 9 or 10-inch springform pan.
- Bake at 350° for 8-10 minutes or until set.

Filling:

3 8-ounce packages cream   2 tablespoons cake flour
  cheese, softened   1½ teaspoons vanilla
1 cup firmly packed light brown   3 eggs
  sugar   1 cup pecan halves, toasted
1 5-ounce can evaporated milk

- Combine cream cheese, brown sugar, milk, flour and vanilla. Beat until light and fluffy.
- Add eggs, beating just until blended.
- Pour mixture into baked crust. Bake at 350° for 50-55 minutes, or until set.
- Cool in pan 30 minutes, then loosen sides and remove rim from pan.
- Cool completely.
- Arrange pecan halves on top.
- Slice and serve with Praline Sauce.

Praline Sauce:

1 cup dark corn syrup   2 tablespoons light brown sugar
¼ cup cornstarch   1 teaspoon vanilla

- Combine syrup, cornstarch and brown sugar in small saucepan.
- Cook over medium heat until thickened and bubbly, stirring constantly.
- Remove from heat. Stir in vanilla.
- Cool slightly.
- Spoon sauce over each serving.

A memorable dessert.

FREEZER VANILLA ICE CREAM

Yield: 4 quarts

1 pint whipping cream
3 cups sugar
1 12-ounce can evaporated milk

1 tablespoon vanilla
Milk

• Combine cream and sugar. Mix well.
• Add evaporated milk and vanilla. Beat until foamy.
• Add whole milk to "fill" line.
• Freeze as directed.

This is a light, not-too-sweet ice cream. Its icy texture complements a heavy meal.

BUTTERMILK ICE CREAM

Yield: ½ gallon

1 quart buttermilk
1 pint whipping cream
2 cups sugar

1 tablespoon vanilla
2 eggs, beaten, optional

• Combine all ingredients, stirring well.
• Pour into ice cream churn. Freeze as directed.

Delicious.

PINEAPPLE ICE CREAM

Yield: 4 quarts

1 envelope unflavored gelatin
4 tablespoons cold water
1 20-ounce can crushed pineapple,
  drained, reserving juice
1 quart buttermilk

2 cups sugar
2 teaspoons vanilla
2 cups whipping cream
2 egg whites, stiffly beaten

• Soften gelatin in cold water.
• Heat juice from pineapple and stir into softened gelatin mixture.
• Combine gelatin mixture, buttermilk, sugar, pineapple and vanilla. Stir well.
• Add cream, stirring constantly.
• Fold in egg whites.
• Pour into ice cream churn. Freeze as directed.

THREE-OF-A-KIND SHERBET

Yield: 4 quarts

2 cups sugar
3 tablespoons all-purpose flour
3 cups hot water
3 cups cold water
Juice of 3 large oranges

Juice of 3 large lemons
3-4 ripe bananas, mashed
1 15½-ounce can crushed
pineapple in heavy syrup,
drained

- Combine sugar and flour in saucepan. Mix well.
- Add hot water. Bring to a boil. Reduce heat and simmer 4-5 minutes or until clear.
- Stir in cold water.
- Add orange juice, lemon juice, bananas and pineapple. Blend well.
- Pour into ice cream churn. Freeze as directed.

SHERRY ICE CREAM DESSERT

Yield: 12 parfaits

6 ounces coconut macaroons, crushed
½ cup sherry or 4 tablespoons whiskey

½ gallon vanilla ice cream, softened
1 pint whipping cream, whipped

- Combine macaroons and sherry or whiskey.
- Add ice cream. Mix well.
- Spoon mixture into parfait glasses. Freeze.
- When ready to serve, remove from freezer and let stand at room temperature 5-10 minutes. Top with whipped cream.

HOMEMADE PEACH ICE CREAM

Yield: 4 quarts

4 eggs
2½ cups sugar
2 12-ounce cans evaporated milk

6 cups milk
1 tablespoon vanilla
1-2 cups puréed fresh peaches

- Beat eggs until foamy.
- Add remaining ingredients. Blend well. (Prepared mixture can be refrigerated several hours before churning to reduce churning time.)
- Pour mixture into ice cream churn. Freeze as directed.

Georgia peach ice cream and summertime—a great "pairing."

PINEAPPLE SUNDAE

Yield: 6-8 servings

¼ cup firmly packed brown sugar
2 teaspoons cornstarch
1 15¼-ounce can crushed
   pineapple (in its own juice)

¼ cup margarine or butter
¼ teaspoon rum extract
   Vanilla ice cream
   Cherries to garnish

• In saucepan, combine sugar, cornstarch and undrained pineapple.
• Cook, stirring constantly, until thickened and translucent.
• Stir in margarine and rum extract.
• Serve warm over vanilla ice cream.
• Garnish with cherries, if desired.

An "Ace-in-the-Hole" for unexpected company.

TOFFEE SAUCE FOR ICE CREAM

Yield: 2½ cups

1½ cups sugar
1 cup evaporated milk
4 tablespoons butter
4 tablespoons light corn syrup

   Dash salt
6 large Heath bars or Skor bars,
   chopped

• Combine sugar, milk, butter, corn syrup and salt in heavy saucepan.
• Bring to a boil and boil one minute.
• Remove from heat. Stir in candy.
• Serve warm over ice cream.
• Refrigerate unused portion.

A perfect gift when put in glass jars and tied with a decorative ribbon.

PRALINE SUNDAE SAUCE

Yield: 3 cups

1½ cups light brown sugar	1 5-ounce can evaporated milk
⅔ cup light corn syrup	1 teaspoon vanilla
4 tablespoons butter	⅔ cup chopped pecans

- Combine sugar, syrup and butter. Heat to boiling.
- Remove from heat. Cool.
- When cooled to lukewarm, add milk and blend well.
- Stir in vanilla and pecans.
- Store in refrigerator.

Serving Suggestions:
- In tall glass, layer 1 scoop vanilla ice cream and Praline Sauce. Continue layering until glass is full. Top with whipped cream, chopped pecans and a cherry.
- Pecans may be omitted in sauce. Instead, roll a scoop of vanilla ice cream in chopped nuts. Place in champagne glass. Spoon Praline Sauce over. Serve.

Set in a cathedral of lofty pines, the eleventh tee is one of the most secluded and peaceful spots on the Augusta National golf course. The pines—there are a dozen of them—are a hundred years old and a hundred feet tall. They are the majestic entrance to Amen Corner, that trinity of holes where the Masters® has so often been lost...

FROSTED CREAM CHEESE BROWNIES

Yield: 24-30 squares

Brownies:

1   4-ounce package German sweet chocolate

5   tablespoons butter, divided and softened

1   3-ounce package cream cheese, softened

1   cup sugar, divided

3   eggs, divided

½   cup plus 1 tablespoon all-purpose flour, divided

1½ teaspoons vanilla, divided

½   teaspoon baking powder

¼   teaspoon salt

½   cup chopped nuts

¼   teaspoon almond extract

- Combine chocolate and 3 tablespoons butter in small saucepan. Melt over low heat, stirring constantly. Cool.
- Combine remaining butter and cream cheese. Beat until smooth.
- Slowly add ¼ cup sugar, beating well.
- Add 1 egg, 1 tablespoon flour and ½ teaspoon vanilla. Blend well. Set aside.
- Beat 2 eggs until light in color.
- Slowly add remaining sugar, beating until thickened.
- Add baking powder, salt and ½ cup flour. Beat well.
- Add cooled chocolate mixture, nuts, remaining vanilla and almond extract. Mix thoroughly.
- Spread half the chocolate batter into greased 8 or 9-inch square pan.
- Spread cream cheese mixture evenly on top.
- Drop remaining chocolate mixture by tablespoons onto cream cheese. Swirl through cream cheese mixture with knife to give marbled effect.
- Bake at 350° for 35-40 minutes, or until top springs back when lightly pressed in center. Cool, frost and cut into squares.

Frosting:

1   ounce unsweetened chocolate

¼   cup butter

2   cups powdered sugar

½ teaspoon vanilla

¼ teaspoon almond extract

   Milk, as needed

- Melt chocolate and butter over low heat.
- Add sugar. Beat well.
- Add vanilla and almond extract.
- Add milk, as needed, beating until frosting is of spreading consistency.

FRAN'S CREAM CHEESE BROWNIES

Yield: 2½-3 dozen

Brownies:

1 23-ounce box Duncan Hines brownie mix
1 8-ounce package cream cheese, softened
6 tablespoons butter

⅔ cup sugar
2 eggs
3 heaping tablespoons self-rising flour
1 ounce almond extract

• Prepare brownie mix according to "cake-like" directions found on package.
• Spread ⅓-½ the batter on bottom of greased 9x13-inch baking dish.
• Combine remaining ingredients. Blend until smooth.
• Pour cream cheese mixture over brownie mixture.
• Spread remaining brownie mixture on top.
• Using a knife, swirl mixture to make a marbled design.
• Bake at 350° for 30-40 minutes, or until springy, not dry.
• Remove from oven and ice while still hot.
• Cool. Cut into squares.

Icing:

3 tablespoons butter
2 tablespoons cocoa
1½ cups powdered sugar

2 tablespoons milk
1 teaspoon vanilla

• Melt butter over medium-low heat.
• Stir in cocoa. Blend until smooth, then remove from heat.
• Add sugar, milk and vanilla. Blend until smooth. Add more milk if necessary.

The almond extract makes these easy brownies a special treat for Masters®
guests, steeplechase parties or tailgate picnics.

▶ "It is probably the most watched tournament, the tournament that is the most important to the public. To win it helps shape your career and it makes it more rewarding after you look back on winning."
Comment by Tom Watson, 1977, 1981 Masters® Champion

AMARETTO BROWNIES

Yield: 32 brownies

Brownies:

1 23-ounce package Duncan
   Hines brownie mix
¼ cup vegetable oil

3 eggs
1 cup chopped walnuts
6 tablespoons Amaretto

- Prepare brownie mix according to package directions, using ¼ cup oil and 3 eggs, and omitting water. Stir in walnuts.
- Spread on bottom of 9x13-inch greased baking dish.
- Bake at 350° for 25-30 minutes.
- Remove from oven and sprinkle with 6 tablespoons Amaretto.
- Cool completely.
- Spread Filling on brownies. Chill at least 1 hour.
- Spread Topping over Filling. Chill.
- Cut and serve.

Filling:

½ cup butter, softened
2 cups powdered sugar

3 tablespoons Amaretto

- Combine filling ingredients.

Topping:

6 ounces semi-sweet chocolate

4 tablespoons butter

- Melt topping ingredients in medium saucepan.

Chocolate and Amaretto pair together to make this brownie irresistible.

▶ The first time you play in the Masters®, you know it is a great tournament and you're overjoyed by it. The more you play there, the more respect you have for the golf course. The history of the tournament becomes more important to you.
Gary Player, 1961, 1974, 1978 Masters® Champion

CHOCOLATE SHERRY CREAM BARS

Yield: 2½-3 dozen

Brownies:

4 ounces semi-sweet
  chocolate
1 cup butter
4 eggs

2 cups sugar
1 cup all-purpose flour
½ teaspoon salt
1 teaspoon vanilla

- Combine chocolate and butter in double boiler. Melt over medium-high heat. Cool slightly.
- Beat eggs until light.
- Slowly add sugar, flour, salt and vanilla.
- Beat one minute. Blend in chocolate mixture and egg mixture.
- Pour into greased and floured 9x13-inch pan.
- Bake at 350° for 25 minutes. Cool.
- Spread Filling over brownies. Chill.
- Slowly pour Topping over Filling.
- Chill until firm. Cut into squares.

Filling:

½ cup butter, softened
4 cups powdered sugar
¼ cup half and half

¼ cup sherry
1 cup chopped pecans

- Combine butter and sugar. Beat well.
- Slowly add half and half and sherry. Beat until light and fluffy.
- Stir in pecans.

Topping:

1 6-ounce package semi-sweet
  chocolate chips

4 tablespoons water
4 tablespoons butter

- Combine chocolate chips with water and butter in double boiler. Melt over medium-high heat.

A special brownie that is well worth the effort.

> In perhaps the finest hour of his unparalleled career, Jack Nicklaus reached into his past and summoned nine holes of the most electrifying golf the game has ever seen.
> 1986 Masters®

RUTH'S ORANGE CRISPS

Yield: 8 dozen

1 cup butter, softened
1 cup sugar
　Grated rind of 2 oranges

1 16-ounce loaf very thin white bread

• Cream together butter, sugar and orange rind.
• Trim crusts from bread.
• Spread butter mixture on each slice, top side only. Cut into four strips.
• Arrange slices on an 11x15-inch jelly-roll pan.
• Bake at 250° for 40 minutes or until crisp.

These keep well in a cookie tin. A fresh, light cookie.

PRALINE BARS

Yield: 25 bars

½　cup unsalted butter
1　16-ounce box light brown sugar
1　cup all-purpose flour
1　teaspoon baking powder

1½ teaspoons vanilla
1　teaspoon salt
4　eggs
1½ cups chopped pecans

• Cream butter and sugar. Add flour, baking powder, vanilla and salt. Blend well.
• Add eggs, one at a time, mixing well after each addition.
• Stir in pecans.
• Pour into greased 9x13-inch pan.
• Bake at 375° for 20-25 minutes.
• Spread Icing quickly over warm cake.

Icing:
1　cup firmly packed light brown sugar
½ cup whipping cream

¼ cup butter
½ teaspoon vanilla

• In heavy saucepan, combine sugar, cream and butter. Bring to a boil and cook until soft ball stage is reached. (Use candy thermometer, if necessary.) Stir constantly, taking care not to burn.
• Remove from heat. Stir in vanilla.
• Beat until mixture has thickened.

GLAZED SPICE BARS

Yield: 2½ dozen

Bars:

¾   cup vegetable oil
¼   cup honey
1   cup sugar
1   egg
2   cups all-purpose flour

½   teaspoon salt
1   teaspoon baking soda
1   teaspoon cinnamon
1   cup chopped pecans

• Combine all bar ingredients and mix well. Dough will be stiff.
• Spread into ungreased 9x13-inch pan.
• Bake at 350° for 25-30 minutes.
• Remove from oven and spread with Glaze while still hot.

Glaze:

1 cup powdered sugar
1 teaspoon vanilla

1 tablespoon mayonnaise
1 tablespoon water

• Combine glaze ingredients and mix until smooth.
• Spread over hot bars.
• Cool. Cut into 2-inch squares.

Fills the home with a wonderful cinnamon aroma.

MADELEINES

Yield: 2 dozen

¾ cup butter
2 eggs
¾ cup sugar
1   cup all-purpose flour

1   teaspoon grated lemon rind
3   tablespoons vegetable oil
½ teaspoon vanilla or Grand
Marnier

• Grease madeleine pan with shortening.
• Melt butter. Allow to cool.
• In medium mixing bowl, beat eggs.
• Add sugar. Beat until light and fluffy.
• Mix in flour.
• Add lemon rind.
• Add oil, butter and vanilla or Grand Marnier.
• Fill madeleine pan ⅔ full.
• Bake at 425° for 18 minutes.

OLD-TIME ICEBOX COOKIES

Yield: 5 dozen

1	cup butter, softened	3½	cups all-purpose flour
1	cup sugar	½	teaspoon salt
1	cup light brown sugar	½	teaspoon baking soda
2	eggs	½	teaspoon baking powder
1	teaspoon vanilla	1	cup chopped nuts

• Cream butter and sugars.
• Beat in eggs and vanilla.
• Sift together flour, salt, baking soda and baking powder. Add to creamed mixture.
• Fold in nuts.
• Shape into 2 long rolls, 1½-inches in diameter. Wrap in waxed paper. (Dough freezes well.) Refrigerate overnight.
• Thinly slice dough and place on ungreased cookie sheet.
• Bake at 350° for 10 minutes.

*This recipe was published in our league's first cookbook, **Junior League Recipes from Southern Kitchens,** in 1940. The recipe at that time was 60 years old.*

CRUNCHY KRISPIES

Yield: 12 dozen

1	cup sugar	1	teaspoon baking soda
1	cup light brown sugar	1	teaspoon salt
1	cup margarine, softened	1	teaspoon cream of tartar
1	cup vegetable oil	1	cup Rice Krispies
1	egg	1	cup shredded coconut
1	teaspoon vanilla	1	cup oats
3½	cups all-purpose flour	½	cup chopped pecans

• Cream sugars, margarine and oil.
• Beat in egg and vanilla.
• Sift together flour, baking soda, salt and cream of tartar. Slowly add to creamed mixture.
• Fold in Rice Krispies, coconut, oats and pecans.
• Drop from a teaspoon onto ungreased cookie sheet.
• Bake at 350° for 12-15 minutes.

PEANUT BUTTER KISSES

Yield: 4 dozen

½ cup butter or margarine, softened
½ cup creamy peanut butter
½ cup sugar
½ cup firmly packed light brown sugar
1 egg

1 teaspoon vanilla
2 teaspoons milk
1¾ cups all-purpose flour
1 teaspoon baking soda
½ teaspoon salt
1 14-ounce bag chocolate kisses

- Cream butter, peanut butter and sugars.
- Beat in egg, vanilla and milk.
- Sift together flour, baking soda and salt. Slowly add to creamed mixture. Chill.
- Roll dough into 1-inch balls and place on greased cookie sheet.
- Bake at 375° for 12 minutes.
- Remove from oven and immediately top each cookie with a chocolate kiss. Press lightly.
- Allow to cool on rack.

CHOCOLATE MACAROONS

Yield: 24 cookies

1 6-ounce package semi-sweet chocolate chips
2 egg whites
¼ teaspoon salt

½ cup sugar
1 3½-ounce can flaked coconut
1 teaspoon vanilla

- Melt chocolate over low heat.
- Beat egg whites with salt until stiff.
- Add sugar, one tablespoon at a time.
- Fold beaten egg whites into chocolate.
- Fold in coconut and vanilla.
- Drop teaspoons of dough several inches apart onto cookie sheets lined with brown paper bags.
- Bake at 350° for 13 minutes.
- Cool 2 minutes. Remove to wire rack.

GINGER PUFF COOKIES

Yield: 3 dozen

¾ cup shortening
1 cup sugar
1 egg
¼ cup molasses
⅛ teaspoon salt
1 teaspoon cloves

1 teaspoon ginger
1 teaspoon cinnamon
2 cups all-purpose flour
2 teaspoons baking soda
   Sugar

• Cream shortening and sugar.
• Beat in egg and molasses.
• Sift together salt, spices, flour and baking soda. Slowly add to creamed mixture.
• Refrigerate until dough is no longer sticky.
• Roll dough into 1-inch balls. Roll in granulated sugar and place on ungreased cookie sheet.
• Bake at 350° for 12 minutes.

Men love these—a great ginger cookie.

CHRISTMAS COOKIES

Yield: 6-7 dozen

½   cup butter, softened
¾   cup firmly packed light brown sugar
2   eggs, beaten well
1½ cups all-purpose flour
½   teaspoon baking soda
½   teaspoon salt

½-1 teaspoon cinnamon
½-1 teaspoon nutmeg, optional
4   tablespoons bourbon
1   cup golden raisins
6   slices candied pineapple, diced
1   cup candied cherries, diced
4   cups coarsely chopped pecans

• Cream butter and sugar.
• Beat in eggs.
• Combine flour, baking soda, salt, cinnamon and nutmeg, if desired. Add to creamed mixture.
• Add bourbon. Blend well.
• Fold in raisins, pineapple, cherries and pecans. Batter will be stiff.
• Drop dough from a teaspoon onto ungreased cookie sheet.
• Bake at 300° for 20 minutes. Remove to wire rack. Cool completely.

GIANT COOKIES

Yield: 2 dozen

1 cup butter, softened	1½ teaspoons cinnamon
1 cup sugar	½ teaspoon allspice
1 cup firmly packed dark brown sugar	½ teaspoon cloves
	¼ teaspoon ginger
2 eggs	½ teaspoon salt
1 teaspoon vanilla	½ teaspoon baking soda
1½ cups all-purpose flour	3 cups quick oats

- Cream butter and sugars.
- Beat in eggs and vanilla.
- Sift together flour, spices, salt and baking soda. Slowly add to creamed mixture. Mix well.
- Fold in oats. Allow to stand at room temperature 2 hours.
- Drop ¼ cup dough for each cookie onto lightly greased cookie sheet. Flatten with spoon.
- Bake at 375° for 10 minutes. Do not overbake.

A delicious cookie to share with friends.

MOLASSES COOKIES

Yield: 2 dozen

¾ cup butter, softened	½ teaspoon cloves
1 cup sugar	½ teaspoon ginger
¼ cup molasses	1 teaspoon cinnamon
1 egg	½ teaspoon salt
1¾ cups all-purpose flour	½ teaspoon baking soda

- Cover cookie sheet with aluminum foil.
- Cream butter, sugar and molasses:
- Beat in egg.
- Sift together flour, spices, salt and baking soda. Add to creamed mixture.
- Drop tablespoons of dough 3-inches apart onto cookie sheet.
- Bake at 350° for 8-10 minutes.

A wonderful, thin but chewy cookie.

"GOOD FOR YOU" CHOCOLATE CHIP COOKIES

Yield: 3 dozen

⅓ cup butter, softened	½ teaspoon baking soda
⅓ cup shortening	½ teaspoon salt
½ cup light brown sugar	¼ cup wheat germ
½ cup granulated sugar	1 tablespoon unprocessed bran
1 egg	1 6-ounce package semi-sweet
2 teaspoons vanilla	chocolate chips
1¼ cups all-purpose flour	½ cup chopped nuts

• Combine butter, shortening and sugars. Beat until creamy.
• Add egg and vanilla. Blend well.
• Gradually blend in flour, baking soda and salt.
• Stir in wheat germ and bran.
• Fold in chocolate chips and nuts.
• Drop dough from a teaspoon onto cookie sheet.
• Bake at 375° for 10-12 minutes.

CHOCOLATE CHIP LACE WAFERS

Yield: 3 dozen

1 pound unsalted butter, softened	1½ teaspoons salt
3 cups light brown sugar	2 teaspoons baking soda
1 cup sugar	1 12-ounce bag semi-sweet
4 eggs	chocolate chips
2 teaspoons vanilla	2 cups pecans, broken into small
3½ cups all-purpose flour	pieces, optional

• Cream butter and sugars.
• Beat in eggs and vanilla.
• Sift together flour, salt and baking soda. Add to creamed mixture.
• Fold in chocolate chips and nuts, if desired.
• Drop dough from a teaspoon onto greased cookie sheet.
• Bake in top ⅓ of oven at 375° for 8-10 minutes.
• Allow to cool on cookie sheet 1-2 minutes. Remove with spatula. (These cookies should be thin and lacy around the edges with a candy-like texture. If they become too hard to remove from pan, return them to the oven for a minute to soften.)

Patience is the key to perfecting these cookies.

TOFFEE COOKIES

Yield: 4 dozen

½ cup margarine, softened
½ cup shortening
1   cup firmly packed light brown
    sugar
½ cup sugar
2   eggs

2   teaspoons vanilla
2½ cups all-purpose flour
1   teaspoon baking soda
½ teaspoon salt
9   1³⁄₁₆-ounce Heath bars,
    crushed

- Cream margarine, shortening and sugars until light and fluffy.
- Beat in eggs and vanilla.
- Combine flour, soda and salt. Add to creamed mixture.
- Fold in Heath bars.
- Drop dough from a teaspoon onto ungreased cookie sheet.
- Bake at 375° for 10 minutes. Cool slightly on cookie sheet. Remove to wire racks and allow to cool completely.

KATIE'S EASY
PEANUT BUTTER COOKIES

Yield: 2 dozen

1 cup sugar
1 cup creamy peanut butter

1 egg
1 teaspoon vanilla

- Cream all ingredients.
- Roll dough into 1-inch balls and place on ungreased cookie sheet.
- Bake at 350° for 15-17 minutes.
- Allow to cool on wire rack.

Simple enough for the youngest cook.

ELEPHANT EARS

Yield: 28 cookies

1 10-ounce package (6)   Granulated sugar
  Pepperidge Farm puff pastry
  shells, thawed

- On floured board, stack 3 shells. Roll into a rectangle.
- Turn dough over and trim to 7x9-inches.
- Sprinkle heavily with sugar.
- Fold the 7-inch sides inward to meet in the middle. Sprinkle heavily with sugar.
- Fold again with the seam on inside (like a closed book).
- Sprinkle again with sugar, and press firmly.
- Cut 14 ½-inch strips from the unfolded edge of the dough.
- Repeat process with remaining 3 shells.
- Place strips cut-side down on ungreased cookie sheet.
- Bake at 400° for 8-10 minutes, or until lightly browned.
- Turn and bake an additional 3-5 minutes.
- Remove to racks to cool.

Fun to make and fun to eat!

RECEPTION COOKIES

Yield: 5-6 dozen

1   14-ounce bag caramels   1½ cups light brown sugar
⅓   cup milk   ½   cup butter, melted
2   cups Bisquick   1   6-ounce package semi-sweet
2   cups uncooked oats   chocolate chips

- Combine caramels and milk in medium saucepan. Heat until caramels are melted.
- Combine Bisquick, oats and sugar.
- Add butter. Blend well.
- Press half the oat mixture on bottom of 9x13-inch pan.
- Bake at 350° for 10 minutes.
- Sprinkle chocolate chips over crust. Top with caramel mixture.
- Sprinkle remaining oat mixture over caramel layer.
- Bake an additional 15 minutes.
- Cool. Cut into squares or bars.

KOULOURAKIA

Yield: 7 dozen

1½ cups butter	4 teaspoons baking powder
1½ cups sugar	½ teaspoon baking soda
3 eggs	4 tablespoons milk
2 teaspoons vanilla	1 egg, beaten
5 cups sifted all-purpose flour	Sesame seeds, optional

- Cream butter and sugar until fluffy.
- Add eggs and vanilla. Beat well.
- Sift together flour, baking powder and baking soda.
- Add half the dry ingredients. Mix well.
- Add milk alternating with remaining dry ingredients.
- Knead slightly on lightly floured board.
- Pinch off pieces of dough. Roll into pencil-thin strips, about 6-inches long, fold in half and twist into ropes.
- Place 1-inch apart on ungreased cookie sheets.
- Brush with beaten egg and sprinkle with sesame seeds, if desired.
- Bake at 350° for 15 minutes, or until lightly browned.

CARAMEL POPCORN

Yield: 6 quarts

1 16-ounce box light brown sugar	½ teaspoon baking soda
1 cup butter	6 quarts popped corn
½ cup light corn syrup	1-2 cups chopped pecans, almonds or peanuts,
1 teaspoon vanilla	optional

- Combine sugar, butter and syrup and bring to a boil. Boil 5 minutes, stirring occasionally.
- Stir in vanilla and baking soda.
- In large roasting pan, pour mixture over popped corn and nuts, if desired. Mix well.
- Bake at 250° for 1 hour, stirring every 15 minutes.
- Cool.

FUDGE

Yield: 7 dozen

15 ounces milk chocolate, broken into small pieces	1½ teaspoons salt
12 ounces semi-sweet chocolate chips	4½ cups sugar
1 7-ounce jar marshmallow cream	1 12-ounce can evaporated milk
	1 teaspoon vanilla
	1 cup chopped pecans

• Butter a 15½x11½-inch jelly-roll pan. Set aside.
• Combine chocolate pieces, chocolate chips, marshmallow cream and salt in large bowl.
• Combine sugar and milk in saucepan. Bring to a boil over medium-low heat, stirring constantly. Boil exactly 4½ minutes.
• Pour ½ the boiling syrup over chocolate mixture. Mix well. Add remaining syrup. Stir until mixture is well blended and chocolate is melted.
• Add vanilla and pecans.
• Pour into prepared pan. Chill.
• Cut into squares.

MINT PATTIES

Yield: 6 dozen

4 tablespoons butter or margarine, softened	½ teaspoon salt
½ cup light corn syrup	4¾ cups sifted powdered sugar
1 teaspoon peppermint extract	Food coloring

• Combine butter, corn syrup, peppermint extract and salt in large bowl. Mix well.
• Add powdered sugar. Mix with spoon and then with hands until smooth.
• Divide mixture if different colors are desired.
• Knead food coloring into each portion of mixture.
• Shape into 1-inch balls. Place on baking sheets lined with waxed paper. Flatten each ball with tines of fork.
• Let dry several hours.
• Store in airtight tin.

These mints are pretty in pastel colors for a tea or luncheon.
Red, green and white mints add a festive touch to a Christmas table.

TOFFEE

Yield: 2½ pounds

2 cups finely chopped pecans, divided
2 cups butter

1 16-ounce box light brown sugar
6 Hershey bars

- Spread 1 cup pecans on lightly buttered jelly-roll pan.
- Combine butter and sugar in saucepan. Bring to a rolling boil, stirring constantly until mixture reaches hard cracked stage, 300°-310° F.
- Pour over the pecans.
- Lay Hershey bars on top. When melted, spread evenly as icing.
- Sprinkle with remaining pecans.
- Allow to harden. Break into pieces.

Irresistible!

 # MICROWAVE PEANUT BRITTLE

Yield: 36 pieces

½ cup light corn syrup
1 cup sugar
1½ cups peanuts (dry roasted are best)

1½ teaspoons butter
1 teaspoon vanilla
1 teaspoon baking soda

- In 1½-quart baking dish, combine corn syrup and sugar. Blend well.
- Cook in microwave on HIGH 4-5 minutes.
- Stir in nuts. Cook 4 minutes on HIGH.
- Add butter and vanilla. Blend well.
- Cook 1½ minutes on HIGH.
- Add baking soda. Stir until light and foamy.
- Pour onto lightly greased cookie sheet. Spread as thinly as possible.
- Cool completely. Break into pieces.

A great gift for neighbors, teachers, and friends. Ready in 10 minutes.

CHOCOLATE BALLS

Yield: 50 1-inch balls

1   cup margarine
1   cup creamy peanut butter
1½ cups fine graham cracker
    crumbs
1   teaspoon vanilla
1   9-ounce package frozen
    coconut, thawed

1   16-ounce box powdered sugar
1   cup finely chopped pecans
1   12-ounce package chocolate
    chips
½   block paraffin

• Melt margarine. Add peanut butter. Stir until smooth.
• Add cracker crumbs, vanilla, coconut, powdered sugar and pecans.
  Mix well and shape into 1-inch balls.
• Put toothpicks in balls and refrigerate 30 minutes or until set.
• Melt chocolate chips over low heat. Add paraffin.
• Dip balls into chocolate wax mixture and place on waxed paper.

The perfect gift for a chocolate lover.

BOURBON SOAKED CHOCOLATE TRUFFLES

Yield: 30 truffles

6½ ounces semi-sweet chocolate
1½ ounces unsweetened
    chocolate
4   tablespoons bourbon or
    dark rum
2   tablespoons strong coffee
½   cup unsalted butter, softened,
    cut into 1-inch pieces

¾-1 cup finely ground
    gingersnaps
    Finely ground pecans,
    almonds, pistachio nuts,
    hazelnuts, gingersnaps
    or powdered sugar to
    coat truffles

• In double boiler, melt chocolate with bourbon and coffee over simmering
  water. Stir until smooth. (If brewed coffee is not available, use 1 tablespoon
  instant coffee dissolved in 2 tablespoons hot water.)
• Beat in butter one piece at a time.
• Beat in gingersnaps. Chill overnight.
• Form chocolate mixture into 1-inch balls.
• Roll in choice of coating. Refrigerate or freeze.
• Serve in foil candy cups.

TRIPLE CHOCOLATE PEANUT CLUSTERS

Yield: 6-7 dozen

2 pounds white chocolate
1 12-ounce package semi-sweet chocolate chips
1 11½-ounce package milk chocolate chips

1 16-ounce jar unsalted dry roasted peanuts

• Melt white chocolate and chocolate chips in double boiler over simmering water, stirring constantly.
• Cool 5 minutes.
• Stir in peanuts.
• Drop by tablespoons onto waxed paper.
• Cool completely. Wrap in plastic and refrigerate.

PEANUT BUTTER CANDY

Yield: 16-20 squares

¾ cup margarine, softened
1 18-ounce jar extra crunchy peanut butter

1 16-ounce box powdered sugar
1 6-ounce bag semi-sweet chocolate chips, melted

• Combine margarine, peanut butter and sugar. Mix well.
• Spread into 8-inch square pan.
• Spread melted chocolate on top.
• Let stand until set. (May be refrigerated.)

Quick and easy enough for kids to make!

EASY DIP COOKIE ICING

Yield: Icing for 4-6 dozen cookies

9 cups powdered sugar, sifted
¾ cup water
3 tablespoons light corn syrup

1½ teaspoons almond extract
Food coloring, as desired

• Combine sugar, water and corn syrup in saucepan. Mix well.
• Heat on low. Do not allow temperature of fondant to exceed 100°F.
• Remove from heat and stir in almond extract and food coloring, if desired.
• Dip tops of cookies into icing, rotating to coat evenly. Place cookies on wire rack. Allow to stand at least 1 hour.

Icing may be reheated if it cools too much. A beautiful, shiny, smooth icing for cookies! It's delicious, too!

INDEX ✕

NOTES

a-Time Publications
). Box 3232
igusta, Georgia 30904

ease send me_____ copies
   Tea-Time at the Masters®   @ $16.95 each_____
   Postage and handling (within continental U.S.)   @   2.50 each_____
   Postage and handling (outside continental U.S.) @   3.50 each_____
   Georgia residents add sales tax   @   1.02 each_____
ease send me_____ copies
   Second Round, Tea-Time at the Masters®   @ $16.95 each_____
   Postage and handling (within continental U.S.)   @   2.50 each_____
   Postage and handling (outside continental U.S.) @   3.50 each_____
   Georgia residents add sales tax   @   1.02 each_____

   Gift Wrap (optional)   @   1.00 each_____
                           TOTAL ENCLOSED $_____

ıme _____

ıddress _____

ty _____State _____ Zip Code _____

Make checks payable to Tea-Time Publications.
Or call 1-888-JLT-TIME (toll free) or (706) 733-9098 to charge your order.

edit Card # _____ Exp. Date _____

gnature_____

----

a-Time Publications
). Box 3232
igusta, Georgia 30904

ease send me_____ copies
   Tea-Time at the Masters®   @ $16.95 each_____
   Postage and handling (within continental U.S.)   @   2.50 each_____
   Postage and handling (outside continental U.S.) @   3.50 each_____
   Georgia residents add sales tax   @   1.02 each_____
ease send me_____ copies
   Second Round, Tea-Time at the Masters®   @ $16.95 each_____
   Postage and handling (within continental U.S.)   @   2.50 each_____
   Postage and handling (outside continental U.S.) @   3.50 each_____
   Georgia residents add sales tax   @   1.02 each_____

   Gift Wrap (optional)   @   1.00 each_____
                           TOTAL ENCLOSED $_____

ıme _____

ıddress _____

ty _____State _____ Zip Code _____

Make checks payable to Tea-Time Publications.
Or call 1-888-JLT-TIME (toll free) or (706) 733-9098 to charge your order.

edit Card # _____ Exp. Date _____

gnature_____

I would like the following individuals to receive information about **Tea-Time at the M**
and Second Round Tea-Time at the Masters®

Name_____   Name_____
Address_____   Address_____
City_____State_____Zip_____   City_____State_____Zip_____

I would like to see **Tea-Time at the Masters**® and Second Round Tea-Time at the M
in the following stores in my area.

Name_____   Name_____
Address_____   Address_____
City_____State_____Zip_____   City_____State_____Zip_____

I would like the following individuals to receive information about **Tea-Time at the M**
and Second Round Tea-Time at the Masters®

Name_____   Name_____
Address_____   Address_____
City_____State_____Zip_____   City_____State_____Zip_____

I would like to see **Tea-Time at the Masters**® and Second Round Tea-Time at the M
in the following stores in my area.

Name_____   Name_____
Address_____   Address_____
City_____State_____Zip_____   City_____State_____Zip_____